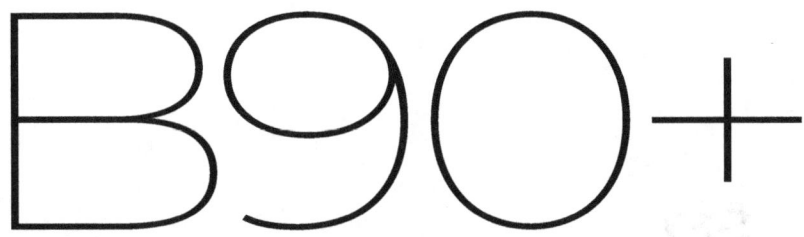

Bible in 90 Days Plus

W.P. CAMPBELL

B90+ Bible in 90 Days Plus

Copyright © 2023 Scripture Awakening, Inc.

ISBN: 978-1-7321668-2-0

Authored by Dr. William P. Campbell. Weekly overview sections authored and compiled by David Smith with excerpts taken from Bible in 90 Days Participant's Guide and Leader's Guide. Edited by Carole Anne Hallyburton and Susie Shields. Cover and interior design by Mark Lucas.

Scripture quotations, unless otherwise indicated, are taken from The ESV® Bible (The Holy Bible, English Standard Version®), copyright © 2001 by Crossway, a publishing ministry of Good News Publishers. Used by permission. All rights reserved.

All rights reserved. No part of this publication may be reproduced, stored in a retrieval system, or transmitted in any form or by any means—electronic, mechanical, photocopy, recording, or any other—except for brief quotations in printed reviews, without the prior permission of the publisher.

Requests for information should be addressed to:

Scripture Awakening
512 N. Grove Street · Ste 202
Hendersonville · North Carolina 28792
Email: info@ScriptureAwakening.com

Printed in the United States of America.

Dedication

To Susie Shields, who gave herself tirelessly to the editing of this book, to the advancement of our ministry, and above all to her Lord, Jesus Christ. Her life inspired me and everyone who knew her.

Table of Contents

Welcome 7
Before You Start 8
Introduction 9
B90/B90+ Integrated Reading Plan 11

Session 1 • Overview 12
Day 1 • The Dark Underside 15
Day 2 • Imperfect Leaders 18
Day 3 • Dreams & Destiny 21
Day 4 • Startling Predictions 24
Day 5 • Your Way Out 27
Day 6 • Introducing God 30
Day 7 • The Golden Cow 33

Session 2 • Overview 36
Day 8 • Consuming Fire 38
Day 9 • Who's in the Details? 41
Day 10 • Any Old Lead Pipe 44
Day 11 • Our Rebellion 47
Day 12 • Bad as Balaam 50
Day 13 • Memory Matters 53
Day 14 • Your Refuge 56

Session 3 • Overview 59
Day 15 • Facing Change 62
Day 16 • Inspiring Courage 65
Day 17 • In Your Weakness 68
Day 18 • Issues of the Heart 71
Day 19 • Giving Birth 73
Day 20 • Enemy of the Best 76
Day 21 • No Quick Fixes 79

Session 4 • Overview 82
Day 22 • Truth or Consequences 85
Day 23 • Finishing Well 88
Day 24 • Summit of Success 91
Day 25 • Footpath of Failure 94
Day 26 • The Greatest Power 97
Day 27 • Touching God's Heart 100
Day 28 • When God Says "Enough" 103

Session 5 • Overview 106
Day 29 • Why All of the Lists? 109
Day 30 • Catch the Context 112

Day 31 • Supernatural Support 115
Day 32 • Humble Yourself 118
Day 33 • Why Church? 121
Day 34 • Rebuild for God 124
Day 35 • On Stage 127

Session 6 • Overview 130
Day 36 • Asking Why 132
Day 37 • Behind the Façade 135
Day 38 • Planted to Grow 138
Day 39 • God's Big Net 141
Day 40 • Dealing with Depression 144
Day 41 • Praise in Hard Times 147
Day 42 • Earnest Worship 150

Session 7 • Overview 153
Day 43 • God's Love Letter 156
Day 44 • God Knows All 159
Day 45 • Wisdom Speaks 162
Day 46 • Gleaning Wisdom 165
Day 47 • The Fulfilled Life 168
Day 48 • Real Love 171
Day 49 • A Vision of God 174

Session 8 • Overview 177
Day 50 • The Naked Truth 179
Day 51 • Supernatural Comfort 182
Day 52 • Reading Backward 185
Day 53 • The Great Motivator 188
Day 54 • Not Too Young 191
Day 55 • A Time to Weep 194
Day 56 • Chaos, Chronos, or Kairos? 197

Session 9 • Overview 200
Day 57 • God's Enduring Word 203
Day 58 • Alas Babylon 206
Day 59 • Growth Through Grief 209
Day 60 • By All Means 212
Day 61 • The Greatest Fall 215
Day 62 • God's Manifest Presence 218
Day 63 • God is in Control 221

Session 10 • Overview 224
Day 64 • Switching the Rules 227
Day 65 • Amazing Love 230
Day 66 • The Day of the Lord 233

Day 67 · Hope on Display 236
Day 68 · Motivation to Get Moving 239
Day 69 · Another Genealogy? 242
Day 70 · The Kingdom Calls 245

Session 11 · Overview 248
Day 71 · Ready for the End 251
Day 72 · Why the Four? 254
Day 73 · The Healer's Heart 257
Day 74 · Radical Compassion 260
Day 75 · Unity in Diversity 263
Day 76 · Kingdom Hospitality 266
Day 77 · Surprise Endings 269

Session 12 · Overview 272
Day 78 · God's Welcome Mat 275
Day 79 · Unstoppable 278
Day 80 · Inseparable 281
Day 81 · The Sinking Ship 284
Day 82 · True Credentials 287
Day 83 · The Jeweled Necklace 290
Day 84 · What Matters in the End 293

Session 13 · Overview 296
Day 85 · Refined by Reality 299
Day 86 · Stay True 302
Day 87 · Treasures Unveiled 305
Day 88 · The Best Ending 308
Day 89 · Continue the Journey 311

Session 14 · Review 314
Day 90 · What's Next? 315

Appendices
1. Facilitator's Guide 317
2. Small Group Discussion Questions 320
3. Patterns in 1 & 2 Kings 327
4. The Prophets in their Place 328
5. The Intertestamental Period 330

About the Author 332

Welcome to B90+

You are about to begin an exciting journey through the Bible, the book that has inspired people, shaped civilizations, and impacted the world. Bible in 90 Days Plus (B90+) will encourage and guide you as you journey through the Bible in just 90 days. B90+ will:

- Provide daily insights and points of application to help you integrate God's Word into your daily life;
- Offer weekly previews of what is coming next which helps keep your sense of direction, inspire your momentum right to the end, and
- Ensure that the **read, study, live** approach (which runs like a stream through every aspect of Scripture Awakening) will support your read through the Bible.

B90+ will challenge you to read every word of Scripture in just three months, approximately 12 pages a day, which takes the average reader about 45 minutes. This concept was first developed by Ted Cooper, an agnostic businessman and accountant, who decided if he was to read the entire Bible it would be most efficient to do so in three months. It changed his life and led him to trust in God. Busy people ever since have been surprised to see how attainable the full reading program really is. And the benefits are inestimable. By reading the entire Bible, cover-to-cover, in 90 days, one is able to remember the early portions of Scripture even as they come to the end, providing greater understanding and appreciation of the entire book.

You can read the Bible on paper or digitally. Or you might listen electronically. With Bible in 90 Days Plus, you can use your own Bible, any version you like. We have found it advantageous to use a Bible specifically formatted for reading. You can buy the Bible in 90 Days Bible at ScriptureAwakening.com.

You can enhance your journey through the Bible by inviting your friends to join you in weekly, face-to-face, small group gatherings. These gatherings, whether in person or online, last about 60–90 minutes. This allows you to reinforce your weekly Scripture reading through discussion of some of your week's questions. A short teaching video is available as well. Guidelines and suggestions can be found in the Facilitator's Guide in the back of this book (page 317).

Discover and learn about more free resources at ScriptureAwakening.com.

Yours in Christ,

W.P. Campbell
Founder & President · Scripture Awakening

Before You Start

Choose your track. You have two reading options. We encourage you to choose the one best for you, your small group, or church, and remain on the same track for your entire journey through the Bible.

Full Reading

Which means reading the entire Bible, cover-to-cover. This is the mainstay for the Bible in 90 Days program. God's Word is transformative; reading every word thoughtfully should be a life-time goal for every believer. Surveys reveal that most people, including non-Christians, would like to fully read what God authored at least once in their lifetime.

The Bible in 90 Days approach is very doable. People routinely read an intriguing novel in just a few days. Why not read God's book in three months? It takes the average person 45–60 minutes a day to do their readings. It can be especially helpful to read from the Bible in 90 Days Bible. Depending on circumstances, some also also found it helpful:

- To receive Bible in 90 Days Plus (B90+) digitally, which is accessible on a phone or other mobile device. B90+ emails serve as daily reminders while reading from the book. Subscribe to Bible in 90 Days Plus emails for free here: **ScriptureAwakening.com/b90+subscribe/**
- To listen to an audio recording. Some find it easier to listen to God's Word during a morning walk or commute. Or they might listen as they read the hard copy, providing pronunciation of difficult words and enhancing comprehension. Free online audio Bibles can be found at BibleGateway.com and many other websites.
- To break the readings into smaller portions: read fifteen minutes before each meal, dividing the daily readings into thirds.

Whole churches around the world have successfully read the entire Bible in 90 Days. You, your small group, or your entire church or ministry network can do it too!

Overview Option

This means reading a one key chapter of the Bible each day. Some individuals or entire churches may find the overview option to be their first choice. The Overview Option uses the exact same Bible in 90 Days Plus commentaries, but guides you to read only one chapter per day.

Those who choose the Overview Option and those who do the Full Reading can easily participate together in weekly small group meetings if they are all using Bible in 90 Days Plus.

B90+

Pastor Testimonies

"I am moved at a level I can't even put into words."

"The only curriculum we've ever offered that actually changes lives!"

"It seemed to bring everything together in a way as never before in my reading and in my study."

Personal Testimonies

"I actually was excited to do each day's reading. If I missed a day, I felt it!"

"I was so blown away by the experience that I offered to facilitate it at my church and have since facilitated several more times…"

"Bible in 90 Days has brought me closer to God and blessed my life. I am on my 3rd time now!"

"This simple God-inspired plan has brought our community together and blessed our church. I am now on my third time through the Bible in 90 Days and it gets better every time!"

Introduction

The Journey Begins: Reading, Revelation, Growth

Before we begin this 90-day journey through the Bible together, it's important to recall how the Bible is organized and what we expect to gain by reading every word, attentively, in 90 days.

Bible Overview

The Bible consists of 66 books written by more than 40 authors, over 1,500+ years, in 3 languages, and on 3 continents. Yet, despite its unique composition, it forms a unified whole tracing the story of redemption from Genesis all the way through to Revelation. Through it, we learn of God's divine plan to reconcile humanity back to Himself and His plan for the ultimate restoration of the entire universe. *Testament* means "covenant" or "agreement," and both portions of the Bible describe God's covenant for our salvation. The Scriptures are divided into two major parts: the Old Testament consisting of 39 books and the New Testament consisting of 27 books.

Old Testament Organization

The Old Testament is arranged by book type: Pentateuch (the Law, known as the 5 books of Moses), History, Poetry, and Prophecy. The historical narrative begins with the Pentateuch and continues with the 12 Historical Books. The 5 Poetical Books address some of life's most challenging issues. Finally, the 17 Prophetical Books, with the 5 major prophets followed by the 12 minor prophets, provide God's divine message through His chosen messengers.

Pentateuch (5)	Poetry (5)	Major Prophets (5)
Genesis	Job	Isaiah
Exodus	Psalms	Jeremiah
Leviticus	Proverbs	Lamentations
Numbers	Ecclesiastes	Ezekiel
Deuteronomy	Song of Solomon	Daniel
History (12)		**Minor Prophets (12)**
Joshua		Hosea
Judges		Joel
Ruth		Amos
1 Samuel		Obadiah
2 Samuel		Jonah
1 Kings		Micah
2 Kings		Nahum
1 Chronicles		Habakkuk
2 Chronicles		Zephaniah
Ezra		Haggai
Nehemiah		Zechariah
Esther		Malachi

New Testament Organization

The New Testament is also arranged by book type: Gospels, History, Pauline Epistles, General (Non-Pauline) Epistles, and Prophecy. The 4 Gospels present the life of Jesus from 4 perspectives. They are followed by the Historical Book of Acts which describes the explosive growth of the Church after the coming of the Holy Spirit. Next are the 13 Pauline Epistles (letters) ordered generally by length, providing instruction, correction, and encouragement to the early Church. The 8 General Epistles, composed by authors other than Paul, provide additional instruction and guidance to believers everywhere. The arrangement concludes with Prophecy, the Book of Revelation, which offers both a warning and hope for the future.

Gospels (4)	Pauline Epistles (13)	General Epistles (8)
Matthew	Romans	Hebrews
Mark	1 Corinthians	James
Luke	2 Corinthians	1 Peter
John	Galatians	2 Peter
	Ephesians	1 John
History (1)	Philippians	2 John
Acts	Colossians	3 John
	1 Thessalonians	Jude
	2 Thessalonians	
	1 Timothy	**Prophecy (1)**
	2 Timothy	Revelation
	Titus	
	Philemon	

We'll follow this organizational format for the two testaments for each of the weekly previews.

Expectation

While B90 and B90+ are reading and not study programs, we still expect to gain a much better understanding of what the Bible is about and what God reveals about Himself through it. We believe and expect that:

> *Consistent daily Bible reading results in increased understanding through the revelation of the Holy Spirit, leading to spiritual rebirth and consistent growth toward maturity.*

That is why it is so important to make a personal commitment to complete all the readings and to seek to join with others for mutual encouragement and accountability.

B90/B90+ Integrated Reading Plan

This chart provides quick reference to your reading options and to which daily commentaries connect to each small group session.*

KEY
B90 = Bible in 90 Days Traditional
B90+(Plus) = This Book
SGS* = Small Group Sessions
*B90 Session 1 is conducted before the daily readings begin.

Day	B90/B90+ Full Reading	B90+ Overview	B90+ Commentary	SGS
1	Gen 1–15	Gen 3	The Dark Underside	
2	Gen 16–28	Gen 22	Imperfect Leaders	
3	Gen 29–40	Gen 37	Dreams & Destiny	Session 2
4	Gen 41–Exo 2	Gen 49	Startling Predictions	
5	Exo 3–15	Exo 12	Your Way Out	
6	Exo 16–29	Exo 19	Introducing God	
7	Exo 30–Lev 4:26	Exo 32	The Golden Cow	
8	Lev 4:27–16:14	Lev 10	Consuming Fire	
9	Lev 16:15–Num 1	Lev 19	Who's in the Details?	
10	Num 2–11	Num 3	Any Old Lead Pipe	Session 3
11	Num 12–23	Num 14	Our Rebellion	
12	Num 24–36	Num 25	Bad as Balaam	
13	Deu 1–11	Deu 4	Memory Matters	
14	Deu 12–28:14	Deu 19	Your Refuge	
15	Deu 28:15–Jos 6	Jos 1	Facing Change	
16	Jos 7–19	Jos 14	Inspiring Courage	
17	Jos 20–Jud 7	Jud 7	In Your Weakness	Session 4
18	Jud 8–19	Jud 16	Issues of the Heart	
19	Jud 20–1 Sam 8	1 Sam 1	Giving Birth	
20	1 Sam 9–20:17	1 Sam 15	Enemy of the Best	
21	1 Sam 20:18–2 Sam 3:21	1 Sam 26	No Quick Fixes	
22	2 Sam 3:22–16:23	2 Sam 11	Truth or Consequences	
23	2 Sam 17–1 Kng 1	2 Sam 24	Finishing Well	
24	1 Kng 2–10	1 Kng 3	The Summit of Success	Session 5
25	1 Kng 11–21	1 Kng 11	The Footpath of Failure	
26	1 Kng 22–2 Kng 9	2 Kng 5	The Greatest Power	
27	2 Kng 10–20	2 Kng 20	Touching God's Heart	
28	2 Kng 21–1 Chr 5	2 Kng 21	When God Says "Enough"	
29	1 Chr 6–17	1 Chr 9	Why All the Lists?	
30	1 Chr 18–2 Chr 1	1 Chr 28	Catch the Context	
31	2 Chr 2–17	2 Chr 16	Supernatural Support	Session 6
32	2 Chr 18–31	2 Chr 26	Humble Yourself	
33	2 Chr 32–Ezr 7	Ezr 7	Why Church?	
34	Ezr 8–Neh 9	Neh 2	Rebuild for God	
35	Neh 10–Est 10	Est 7	On Stage	
36	Job 1–19	Job 1	Asking Why	
37	Job 20–36	Job 23	Behind the Façade	
38	Job 37–Psa 17	Psa 1	Planted to Grow	Session 7
39	Psa 18–37	Psa 19	God's Big Net	
40	Psa 38–60	Psa 42	Dealing with Depression	
41	Psa 61–78	Psa 73	Praise in Hard Times	
42	Psa 79–102	Psa 100	Earnest Worship	
43	Psa 103–119:72	Psa 119	God's Love Letter	Session 8
44	Psa 119:73–146:10	Psa 139	God Knows All	
45	Psa 147–Pro 11	Pro 1	Wisdom Speaks	

Day	B90/B90+ Full Reading	B90+ Overview	B90+ Commentary	SGS
46	Pro 12–22	Pro 12	Gleaning Wisdom	
47	Pro 23–Ecc 5	Ecc 1	The Fulfilled Life	Session 8
48	Ecc 6–Isa 1	Song 8	Real Love	
49	Isa 2–14	Isa 6	A Vision of God	
50	Isa 15–29:10	Isa 20	The Naked Truth	
51	Isa 29:11–41:29	Isa 40	Supernatural Comfort	
52	Isa 42–52	Isa 45	Reading Backward	Session 9
53	Isa 53–65	Isa 53	The Great Motivator	
54	Isa 66–Jer 8	Jer 1	Not Too Young	
55	Jer 9–20	Jer 9	A Time to Weep	
56	Jer 21–31:22	Jer 25	Chaos, Chronos, or Kairos?	
57	Jer 31:23–44:30	Jer 36	God's Enduring Word	
58	Jer 45–51	Jer 51	Alas Babylon	
59	Jer 52–Eze 6	Lam 3	Growth Through Grief	Session 10
60	Eze 7–20	Eze 16	By All Means	
61	Eze 21–31	Eze 28	The Greatest Fall	
62	Eze 32–42	Eze 40	God's Manifest Presence	
63	Eze 43–Dan 5	Dan 4	God is in Control	
64	Dan 6–Hos 7	Dan 9	Switching the Rules	
65	Hos 8–Amo 4	Hos 14	Amazing Love	
66	Amo 5–Mic 7	Amo 9	The Day of the Lord	Session 11
67	Nah 1–Zec 3	Hab 3	Hope on Display	
68	Zec 4–Mal 4	Zec 4	Motivation to Get Moving	
69	Mat 1–12	Mat 1	Another Genealogy	
70	Mat 13–23	Mat 13	The Kingdom Calls	
71	Mat 24–Mark 5	Mat 25	Ready for the End	
72	Mark 6–15:20	Mark 10	Why the Four?	
73	Mark 15:21–Luke 8	Luke 1	The Healer's Heart	Session 12
74	Luke 9–18	Luke 15	Radical Compassion	
75	Luke 19–John 4	John 1	Unity in Diversity	
76	John 5–13	John 13	Kingdom Hospitality	
77	John 14–Acts 4	John 21	Surprise Endings	
78	Acts 5–15	Acts 10	God's Welcome Mat	
79	Acts 16–27	Acts 16	Unstoppable	
80	Acts 28–Rom 14	Rom 8	Inseparable	Session 13
81	Rom 15–1 Cor 14	1 Cor 1	The Sinking Ship	
82	1 Cor 15–Gal 3	2 Cor 11	True Credentials	
83	Gal 4–Col 4	Col 1	The Jeweled Necklace	
84	1 Ths 1–Tit 3	2 Tim 4	What Matters in the End	
85	Phi–Jam 2	Heb 12	Refined by Reality	
86	Jam 3–3 John	2 Pet 2	Stay True	
87	Jude–Rev 17	Rev 1	Treasures Unveiled	Session 14
88	Rev 18–22	Rev 22	The Best Ending	
89	Grace Day	Grace Day	Continue the Journey	
90	Grace Day	Grace Day	What's Next?	

Session 1 • Overview

● PREVIEW Days 1-7
Pentateuch, Part 1: Beginnings, Enslavement, Deliverance

 Now is the time for you (if you're reading alone) or your small group to preview the week's Scripture readings and watch the Essential Snapshot video. Point your mobile device's camera on the QR code to access the video entitled "Session 1: Overview". Or enter this link into your browser: **ScriptureAwakening.com/plus/**.

- For tips on facilitating a small group, see Appendix 1 Facilitator's Guide in the back of this book on page 317.
- Questions marked by an asterisk (✽) in each of the **Respond** sections are to be used for small group discussions.
- Watch the Session 1 video* (individually or with a small group).
    1. What insights from the video would you like to explore further?
    2. Do you agree with the common idea that the Bible is filled with the words of men and women but is not the Word of God? Why or why not?
- Summarize the Preview (below) of what is coming next week, encouraging group members to read it on their own.

*****Facilitators note:** In order to watch the Essential Snapshot video with your group, you will need a large video monitor, if meeting in-person. If hosting a small group remotely, use Zoom (or similar service) to stream the video from your device to share with group participants.

Summary

This week's reading introduces us to the first three books of the Bible, to the Pentateuch (the five books of Moses), and to the Old Testament at large. The narrative chronicles Creation, the Fall of man, the devastating global Flood, and the confusion at the Tower of Babel.

God then selects the family of Abraham through whom He will begin to reestablish His relationship with mankind. But that family must first grow to a nation while remaining uncorrupted by pagan beliefs during a 430 period of bondage and enslavement in Egypt. Moses is called to both deliver and instruct them as they learn what it means to be God's chosen people and His precious possession. Chronologically, the narrative moves from eternity past to around the year 1444 BC. Geographically, the story begins in the cosmos and ends at the foot of Mount Sinai.

Genesis Overview

The adventure begins. God creates the universe and all things in it, providing an idyllic home for Adam and Eve. When the serpent tempts them to turn their back on God, they plunge the world into sin by their disobedience and sever their relationship with God. The rest of the Bible is about God's solution to that problem. His intention for a relationship with humans is apparent throughout the Scriptures through the descriptions of His faithfulness and covenants with His chosen ones, even in the face of their unfaithfulness.

The first 11 chapters of the book focus on 4 key events: Creation, the Fall, the Flood, and Babel (nations). Mankind's continued rebellion against God and the resulting loss of knowledge about Him dominate the story. Chapters 12 to the end of the book shift to 4 key individuals: Abraham, Isaac, Jacob, and Joseph. God's promise to Abraham of land, seed, and blessings foreshadow the rich and eternal relationship God intends to establish between Himself and all who believe through the ages.

Exodus Overview

Four hundred years pass after the death of Joseph at the end of Genesis. The family of Abraham has lost the privileges and protections they enjoyed long ago when Joseph was second in command over Egypt. They have become slaves. God delivers them from their bondage, showing the world that they are His chosen ones.

Israel's miraculous deliverance from Egypt fosters the birth of a young nation which, like a young infant, must be trained and instructed by God. The Law given on Sinai becomes the foundation for a solemn agreement (covenant) between God and His people. The construction of the Tabernacle provides a physical place where God can manifest His divine presence among them.

Leviticus Overview (Introduction)

This book of rules provides direction to the Levitical priests about the rituals needed for the children of Israel to live in holiness before the LORD. Modern readers may marvel at the seeming harshness of some directives; yet Leviticus also includes God's earliest command to "love your neighbor as yourself." The legal and ceremonial stipulations provided to them would help them to show such love while maintaining civil and practical standards essential to their survival during their wilderness wanderings.

The book of Leviticus may be considered one of the greatest statements about the grace of God found in the Old Testament. The Tabernacle and its adjoining sacrificial system point toward the anticipated sacrifice of Christ for our sins. And the Law shows us our need for a Savior. Further details concerning the Law will be highlighted in our readings next week.

Things to Look for This Week

A number of key Biblical themes are introduced. Many of these focus on the effects of sin (rebellion against God's moral authority) which severed the relationship between God and mankind, obscured knowledge about Him, and marred the beauty and perfection of His creation. As you read, consider:

1. How would the relationship between God and mankind be restored? Could the relationship be restored? How will broken, sinful man live in the presence of a holy God?

2. God's continued revelation of His divine nature and character began through the communication of His personal name (Exodus 3) and His character attributes (Exodus 34) which are essential to our understanding of who He really is.

3. God's promise of blessing to Abraham initiates a process of restoration of the original state of nature in the Garden of Eden. Watch for revelations from God concerning how He will accomplish this restoration.

Day 1 · **The Dark Underside**

My wife recently warned me about a new electric teapot she had purchased. It looked just like the one we place daily on our gas stove, but it could only be used on an electric base on an adjacent counter. The obvious difference between the two teapots was the dark plastic underside on the electric version.

One morning I got up before dawn to do some writing. Keeping the lights dim and not being fully awake, I placed the kettle with the dark underside on a gas burner. A minute later I smelled burning plastic and looked over to see the base of the tea kettle engulfed in flames. I grabbed the smoldering pot by the handle and stuck it under the kitchen faucet. That was the easy part. It was much more difficult to clear the smell of burning plastic out of our house and to explain my blunder to my wife. I had overlooked the dark underside.

Fortunately, my wife forgave me, and our son gave us a new and very different-looking electric tea kettle for Christmas. The gift reminded me of the opening chapters of Genesis, the first book of the Bible, where the dark underside of humanity is revealed, and God steps in to provide a better option.

Coaching Tip

Pray before you read. Ask the Lord to give you insights to inspire your day and to impact your life.

Read

You have two reading options: read the full selection of Scripture or a single overview chapter each day.

- Full Reading: Genesis 1–15
- Overview Chapter: Genesis 3

Reflect

The opening chapters of Genesis show our need for God's grace. The dark underside of humanity is made plain to us very early in the Creation story, along with foreshadowed warnings of the consequences we face when we attempt to live our lives without God.

This "book of beginnings," Genesis, opens with a separation of light and darkness. God's light prevails and God declares the Creation to be good. In chapter two, humans are created as free moral agents. They are given the option of following the way of God—the way of light—or of turning from God and walking in darkness. Adam and Eve decide to give the dark side a try. With their fall into sin, havoc comes into the world. God steps in and by grace provides an alternative. He sacrifices an animal to cover Adam and Eve's nakedness, a picture and foreshadowing of the ultimate sacrifice that would eventually be provided by God when He would send His Son, Jesus Christ, to become a sacrifice for our sins.

This same theme—the human choice between light and darkness—dominates the first 15 chapters of Genesis. In chapter 4, Cain kills Abel. God provides Adam and Eve a third son named Seth as a replacement for the son they lost. Launching the godly line through which the Messiah will eventually come, Seth reminds us that God loves us enough to provide a way to be reconciled with Him even when we fall miserably short. The chapter continues by warning humanity about the destructive influence and depressing results of trying to live for ourselves rather than for God. Through Cain's lineage, from the 7 generations beginning with Adam and ending with Lamech, we see the tragic consequences of sin: hate, revenge, and death.

In Chapter 5: the fruits of righteousness are seen in the 9 generations listed, from Adam to Noah, who brings the world a promise of rest. Lives in this line become freer and fuller, with reminders of the blessings that will come to those who love and obey God.

In Genesis 6, God expresses His grief about humanity's dark underside. Things became so bad that, "every inclination of the thoughts of the human heart was only evil all the time" (Genesis 6:5 NIV). God guides Noah to build the Ark, another foreshadowing of the salvation God would later offer through Christ, the one Door to eternal life. Only Noah and his family board the boat to be part of a new beginning. The earth is covered in water in chapter 7, and the water recedes in chapter 8. Chapter 9 reveals the covenant with Noah—a promise of a new start with all of humanity—along with God's assurance that He won't again bring a worldwide flood. We will later see in the destruction of Sodom and Gomorrah by fire, however, a hint of God's plan to eventually remake heaven and earth through an inferno that burns away the dark underside forever. Chapter 10 provides a table of the nations and in Chapter 11, evil begins to dominate once more. This time, God divides people by languages. Much as firewalls are created by firefighters to prevent a forest fire from spreading, God uses division through languages to slow the spread of evil.

In chapters 12 to 15, we are introduced to the first of the patriarchs, Abraham. He is called by God to travel to the land God will show him, where God's covenant with him is reconfirmed and strengthened.

Respond

1. What most troubles you as you read about the fall of humanity? What encourages you in this reading?

....

....

....

2. List things you would like to discuss with others. If you are not in a group that allows for such discussion, consider gathering some friends—online or in person—to meet each week. Check out the Facilitator's Guide in the back of this book to get you started. Keep a list of your questions to fold into the discussion.

....

....

....

✱ 3. There are numerous stories and symbols in Genesis showing the sinful nature of humanity and God's gracious plan of redemption. Describe one that especially impacts you and explain why.

....

....

....

Pray

Thank you, Lord, that Jesus came to place His righteousness over us, that we might be Your children and live in Your light. Forgive my sins, known and unknown, and transform me into Your image. And deepen Your work in me as I learn and grow through this Bible-reading journey. Amen.

Impact

Everyone struggles with their dark underside. People need to be regularly reminded about God's bright upside: He loves us and offers us His grace. Take a few minutes to write a note or share a word of encouragement to someone who needs it.

Close

Congratulations! You've just completed Day 1 of Bible in 90 Days Plus . . . and taken your first step on an amazing 90-day adventure through the Bible! Wait 'til you see what's coming tomorrow!

B90+

Coaching Tip

For this 90-day reading of the Bible, it is important to keep a good pace and not be distracted. Imagine trying to set a hiking record by veering off the trail every few minutes. As you read, it may help to take note of topics and themes you want to pursue later, but don't veer off course. Keep on reading!

Day 2 · **Imperfect Leaders**

We want perfect leaders. We expect those who guide us—whether president or priest, principal or parent—to do everything right. We have replaced the appropriate desire for excellence with demands for perfection. Once a leader falters in today's media-driven society, that person's flaws and failures are placed in the public spotlight. The critique and condemnation of our public officials has become a national pastime, almost a new sport. The problem is, we all lose in the end. As the old adage says, "As goes the leader so go the people."

Why this insistence for perfecting those at the top? One might think it was derived from the Bible, the book that provided the moral backbone for our culture. In truth, the pages of Scripture show us another way. The Bible is a thousand year-long narrative of imperfect leaders trying to find their way. Even the three great patriarchs of Israel had their flaws. We can learn key insights from their lives to gain a more realistic perspective on leadership today.

Read

You have two reading options: read the full selection of Scripture or a single overview chapter each day.

- Full Reading: Genesis 16–28
- Overview Chapter: Genesis 22

Reflect

When we read Genesis 16-28, it becomes clear that even God's respected servants are far from perfect. Abram conspires with his wife, Sarai, to treat their Egyptian maid, Hagar, harshly; they later drive her out of their home. Abram's nephew, Lot, offers his two innocent daughters as a shield to protect his guests from a gang of wicked men. On two different occasions, Abraham lies about his wife, Sarah, claiming her to be his sister to save his own skin at the peril of her safety. Perhaps learning from his father's example, Isaac does the same thing with his wife, Rebekah. Isaac and Rebekah play favorites between their two sons who eventually struggle for prominence. With Rebekah's encouragement, Jacob steals his brother's blessing.

For each of these stories we might attempt to come up with a defense of the leader's actions based on circumstances. Yet does not the cumulative effect of three generations of patriarchs remind us that even the great founders and early leaders of God's people were far from perfect? We learn from Abraham, Isaac, and Jacob that the key to a leader's success is not absolute perfection but a willingness to learn and to grow from one's mistakes. The people in the Bible who become instruments of God to lead others are those who walk humbly, trusting God, and being open to correction. Abraham, for example, was considered righteous by God because he was willing to obey God—even to the point of sacrificing his own son. Isaac, the sacrificial gift, was spared, and became a prototype of the sacrifice God our Father would offer us through the sacrifice of Jesus Christ on the Cross.

Despite his mistakes, Abraham is recognized by Jews and Christians alike as the father of our faith (Romans 4:16). So it was with Isaac, who did not accomplish any spectacular feats yet received the promises first given to Abraham. Jacob was less than stellar in his life's journey; nevertheless, God renamed him Israel, which means "an overcomer with God" or "a prince with God" (Genesis 32:28). This tendency in the Bible to show people as they are, warts and all, is a subtle yet powerful evidence that the Bible is inspired by God. When we humans write our own stories, we tend to make ourselves look great and gloss over our mistakes.

Let us remember that to some extent we are all leaders. Leadership may be defined simply as influence; we each influence others for good or for bad. Let us then humble ourselves and be willing to receive correction. In this way, we can pursue excellence but not demand the impossible of ourselves: ongoing and absolute perfection. And then maybe, just maybe, we can remind the world around us that God is in the habit of giving us imperfect leaders.

Respond

✱ 1. What insights can you draw from 1 Timothy 2:1-6 about our responsibility to pray for those who influence our lives as leaders?

....

....

....

....

2. What is likely to occur if an entire society becomes so negative about leaders that they refuse to respect them altogether?

....

....

....

....

3. Prayerfully consider any changes you will make in your own way of thinking, talking, and acting toward leaders. Write down specific commitments you will make in this regard.

....

....

....

....

Pray

Lord, help me to pray more often for those in leadership. Forgive me for the times I have latched onto the cultural tendency to criticize and condemn leaders rather than seeking to discern and to pray for correction and improvement. Help me to see that, because I am a leader to someone, I need to humbly focus first and foremost on striving for excellence in my own life before I criticize others. Amen.

Impact

Leadership is influence. You can influence others through these daily Bible in 90 Days Plus posts. How? By sharing them with others. Or by forming a group of friends and facilitating discussion about your read through the Bible.

Close

Congratulations on completing Day 2 of Bible in 90 Days Plus. Even though this is a long journey, it's *so* worth it! We'll be waiting for you tomorrow as we take our next steps through Genesis.

Day 3 · **Dreams & Destiny**

You have a destiny, determined by God before the world began. Your challenge is to discover it. The discovery may come to you through careful search and inquiry, reading Scripture and seeking wise counsel; or it may come to you suddenly through a dream, as happened to people in the Bible. For most of us, the understanding of one's destiny unfolds gradually and perhaps imperceptibly as we walk the course of our lives. As a rule, they are not made obvious to us until we enter God's presence. The Almighty is leading us through life—sometimes through dark valleys—until one day we step on the high vista where our vision will become perfectly clear. Then we will know that nothing in our lives, not even the difficult and rugged portions of the journey, was a mistake; God has been working all things for good.

Wonderfully, such confidence can be ours today if we will take a few minutes to read and reflect on the lives of the patriarchs of the faith: Abraham, Isaac, and Jacob.

Read

You have two reading options: read the full selection of Scripture or a single overview chapter each day.

- Full Reading: Genesis 29–40
- Overview Chapter: Genesis 37

Reflect

Jacob was fleeing a brother who sought to take his life. Walking the long and treacherous path toward Haran, Jacob became too tired to press on and lay down to sleep with a rock as his pillow. God spoke to him in the night through a dream that would be remembered and retold for generations to come. His dream revealed his destiny and its part in God's larger plan for the nation of Israel. Jacob's son, Joseph, would likewise have a dream that spoke into the future. After telling his family about the dream, Joseph was ripped from the comforts of his childhood home to accomplish God's greater plan. His path was more difficult than Jacob's, and the fulfillment of his dream was more pronounced. He was raised up by God to second-in-command over Egypt. Both men's stories remind us that God is continually unfolding His purpose in people's lives.

It is easy, when pondering the lives of Jacob and Joseph, to recognize their significance in the plan of God. The more difficult task is to recognize how each of us—along with every person recorded in the pages of Scripture—is equally important in God's divine scheme. It is easy to forget that there would be no Jacob if not for Rebekah who gave him birth. Joseph could

Coaching Tip

Try reading out loud when needed. Hearing the words as you read them can aid comprehension, and it will help you to stay awake and be attentive. You might even read aloud with a friend or with your spouse.

not have risen to power in Egypt had not Judah earlier spared his life by convincing his brothers to sell young Joseph into slavery. Neither Rebekah nor Judah could have known at the time how their ordinary decisions and actions were being used as part of God's larger purpose. Yet the promise was as much for them as it was for more prominent characters in God's divine drama: "And we know that in all things God works for the good of those who love him, who have been called according to his purpose" (Romans 8:28, NIV). This glorious truth was being worked out through Israel's patriarchs hundreds of years before Paul stated it in his letter to the believers in Rome. He was stating a timeless reality: God is always working out His purposes; ours is to believe that we play an important part on God's overall plan even when we cannot see or understand it.

You may think of your life as a disjointed series of bad choices and failures. Look again. Use the stories of Jacob and Joseph as your lens. Realize that God's plan is still being realized, even through you and me. We may catch glimpses of it in a dream or simply believe that God is at work in our daily circumstances—using even our missteps. Then one day—when we see Him face-to-face—it will all make sense. God is working everything for good.

Respond

1. Do you believe God has a destiny for your life? Can you support your answer with specific Scriptures?

....

....

....

....

....

2. Have you ever had a dream that you felt was from God? Describe.

....

....

....

....

....

✱ 3. Ponder the lives of Jacob and Joseph alongside the words in Romans 8:28. Can you see how God is also working all things for good in your life as well? Explain.

....

....

....

....

....

Pray

Gracious God, I surrender all to You. Use the dark and difficult parts of my life to accomplish Your purpose and to shape my destiny. I choose to believe the promise that You work all things for good for those who love You. Please help me love You more. Amen.

Impact

Many people have dreams that cannot be fulfilled without the help of others. Think, for example of those behind bars as Joseph was. Scripture Awakening is bringing encouragement and hope to prisoners through God's Word. Pray about impacting their lives.

Close

Way to go . . . Day 3 of Bible in 90 Days Plus is in the can! B90+ is a 90-day journey through God's Word. Tomorrow: some very "Startling Predictions" are coming!

Coaching Tip

Be consistent. It is helpful to find a quiet, non-distracting place and time to do your reading each day.

Day 4 · **Startling Predictions**

When we read the Old Testament stories, we come face-to-face with the God who knows the future. And we have two choices. One is to assume that prophetic statements and/or their fulfillments were fabricated—written into the Biblical text after-the-fact. In other words, we can embrace the philosophy that says there is no God, or if there is one, He is weak and does not know or control the future. A serious and holistic study of the Biblical text reveals a different story. And if one looks carefully at prophecy as set against history, there seems to be no way around the verifiable futuristic element found throughout Scripture. God knows the future. And He makes it happen. Yet we have the freedom and responsibility to live for God. This is a conundrum that only makes sense when we acknowledge that God's ways are higher than ours. We are called to live well in the present, trusting in God and obeying Him, in order to make for a better tomorrow. To get your mind around how it is that we—people locked in a time-bound world—should interact with a God who knows the past, present, and future, join us in our read through the Bible; you will see how it works itself out even in the latter part of Genesis.

Read

You have two reading options: read the full selection of Scripture or a single overview chapter each day.

- Full Reading: Genesis 41 – Exodus 2
- Overview Chapter: Genesis 49

Reflect

In Genesis 41, the great Pharaoh over Egypt has a dream that speaks into the future. We are not left to wonder who gave him the dream for only God's servant, Joseph, is given the ability to interpret it. Only the God who inspired the dream would have the ability to declare its meaning.

The dream is essentially a prophecy describing the famine coming on the earth. We see the prophecy fulfilled in the rest of our narrative as Joseph is placed over the administration of Egypt. His brothers come to him, and he acknowledges that it is God who "sent me before you to preserve your life" (Genesis 45:5). Jacob, now known as Israel, moves his family to Egypt and settles in Goshen, a good place for flocks and herds and for the people of Israel to grow into a great nation (Genesis 46:32-34). Jacob speaks over Joseph's sons, prophetically stating which one will dominate the other (Genesis 48:19). And as a last act to demonstrate God's sovereign knowledge of the future, Jacob pronounces blessings over each of his sons (Genesis 49). The predictive elements in many of his words find fulfillment in the way each son becomes a nation that later inhabits territories in and around the region of Palestine.

The most vividly prophetic statements concern Judah, who gives birth to the tribe from which will come the Messiah. Judah is described as a "lion's cub" (Genesis 49:9). The image of the lion would become the symbol of Judah; hence the Biblical reference to Christ as the "Lion of the tribe of Judah" (Revelation 5:5). As king of the forest, a lion represents the sovereignty that is rightly ascribed to God incarnate.

This Christ is predestined to reign. Hence Israel's prophecy:

> *The scepter shall not depart from Judah, nor the ruler's staff from between his feet, until tribute comes to him; and to him shall be the obedience of the peoples.* (Genesis 49:10)

This is the first of many prophecies that God has given through the ages predicting Christ's eternal reign. Many of the prophets, however, also describe a humble, suffering Messiah. The two clashing images are reconciled when we understand that Christ was destined to come first as a sacrificial lamb and then to come a second time to reign as the lion. The God who came to us first, in the flesh, to die for us will come again in glory that we might live with Him.

Respond

1. On a scale of 1–10, how convinced are you that there is a God who knows the future? Explain why.

....

....

....

....

2. Jacob was renamed Israel, the name of a nation that is with us still today. What do you know, if anything, about history that makes the existence of Israel unique, if not miraculous?

....

....

....

✱ 3. How does the belief that God knows the future give you greater confidence to live for the Lord today?

....

....

....

....

Pray

Lord, thank you that You know the future. It is enough for me to live a day at a time. Knowing who knows the future enables me to trust You, even when things seem terribly out of control. Teach me to trust You more fully, even as I read through Your Word and learn more about how You have worked in the world. Amen.

Impact

It is difficult for people to ponder the future when they are struggling just to get through the next day. For many people it is true that "a little help goes a long way." Pray for an opportunity to be a support and to serve someone in need today.

Close

All right! Day 4 down and done! Did you know that Bible in 90 Days has been used by over a quarter million people worldwide? You've now joined the journey with them!

Day 5 · **Your Way Out**

Perhaps, you are stuck in a difficult situation and are looking for a way out. It might be a relationship that pushes you down, a job that keeps you down, or a trying circumstance that won't let up. You are not alone; there is Someone who will see you through. The name Exodus means "a way out." Embedded in this book's pages are insights to help us face life's trials and challenges. It also shows us a way out. In Exodus, that way is a person—Moses—who leads the Israelites out of Egypt and toward the Promised Land. Moses prefigures Someone humbler and mightier, One who is ready to help us today.

Read

You have two reading options: read the full selection of Scripture or a single overview chapter each day.

- Full Reading: Exodus 3–15
- Overview Chapter: Exodus 12

Reflect

In Exodus 3, Moses is startled to see a bush that is blazing with fire and yet not consumed. He is about to learn how a person can be filled with God's blazing and glorious presence without being consumed. Such a transformation will be necessary for Moses to become God's instrument to show the Israelites a way out of their difficulties. They have become slaves in Egypt and are desperately looking for a way out; in Exodus, God answers their cry.

God appointed Moses to show them the way. Moses in turn promised the Israelites that one day God would raise up a prophet like him, to lead God's people more fully out of their bondage (Deuteronomy 18:15). Other prophets reinforced this sense of expectation which culminated when Jesus came on the scene and pronounced Himself to be "the way" (John 14:6). Indeed, He came to set us free from sin and its consequences. He is with us—even now—to help us in our trials, eventually to lead us out of the difficulties of this world and into a place of perfect rest, our land of promise.

Aware of these promises, Paul gave this advice about the tests and temptations that overwhelm us today:

> *No temptation has overtaken you except what is common to mankind. And God is faithful; he will not let you be tempted beyond what you can bear. But when you are tempted, he will also provide a way out so that you can endure it.* (1 Corinthians 10:13 NIV)

The word for temptation used here, *peirasmos*, can mean "trial, temptation, or test." In Hebrews, we are reminded that Jesus ". . . in every respect

B90+

Coaching Tip

Find a friend who is doing the reading as well; check in with each other daily to encourage each other to keep up. If you're in a Bible in 90 Days group, it will likely be someone from the group.

has been tempted as we are, yet without sin" (Hebrews 4:15). When tempted and tested by Satan in the desert, for example, Jesus faced three major temptations, being obedient almost to the point of death. Still, He did not disobey His Father. Thus, when we face our own temptations and trials, He is fully able to help us. The author of Hebrews concludes, "Let us then with confidence draw near to the throne of grace, that we may receive mercy and find grace to help in time of need" (Hebrews 4:16).

Our focus should not be simply on how to get "out" of our trials and temptations; it should also be on how to get closer to God. That is, God likes to turn our "way out" of difficulty into a "way into" His presence. He uses our challenges and trials to help us grow closer to Him. Our situation is much like the Israelites who looked for a way out of Egypt. God did not offer them a simple solution or a quick fix; He did something much better. He stood with them and took care of them along the way, that they might truly own Him as their God. It took but a single night for God to deliver the Israelites out of Egypt, but it took 40 years to get Egypt out of the Israelites. Similarly, day by day, step-by-step, He guides us and changes us in life's challenges.

Respond

1. What trial, test, or temptation are you facing today?

....

....

....

....

✶ 2. Does the Bible encourage us to expect immediate solutions and quick fixes when we are dealing with difficulties? Support your answer with Scripture if you can.

....

....

....

....

3. Looking back, were there challenging times in your life about which you can say, "I would never have chosen to go through that experience. But now, on the other side of it, I wouldn't want to change it?" Explain.

....

....

....

....

Pray

Lord, please forgive me for the times I have tried to make my own way. Teach me to hear Your voice and to follow You, for You are truly the Way to the Father. You came to give me life and to guide my life. I surrender all to You. Amen.

Impact

Think of someone who is facing a time of trial and hardship right now. Ask yourself, "If I were in their situation, how would I want others to respond?" Then prayerfully ask God how you can step in and be part of that response to the one in need.

Close

Hey—you're now five days into Bible in 90 Days Plus. If B90+ has encouraged you, why not share it with your family or friends? Tell them B90+ is designed to help them get into God's Word daily. They can subscribe at ScriptureAwakening.com.

Day 6 · **Introducing God**

After God delivered the Jews from slavery in Egypt, He led them into the privacy of the desert where He introduced Himself. Much of what they learned about God is described in the book of Exodus. Revelations of God's person and purpose continued throughout the ages, culminating with the most personal revelation of God the Father through Jesus Christ. Yet today, it seems that vast numbers of people have forgotten who God is. We have redefined God. When we read the Old Testament, we may even think of God as distant. Skeptics declare the Jehovah of Israel to be mean, vindictive, and obsessed with laws. Yet even a cursory look at the narrative in Exodus reveals a different picture. There we find a God who needs to be rediscovered today; a God who loves us deeply and who has pursued us patiently, longing for us to know Him in truth.

Read

You have two reading options: read the full selection of Scripture or a single overview chapter each day.

- Full Reading: Exodus 16–29
- Overview Chapter: Exodus 19

Reflect

In the book of Exodus, God introduces Himself to the nation of Israel as One who loves them and desires to be in relationship with them. In this regard, God really has not changed. God's means of dealing with humanity has been altered through time, however, as His people have grown in their understanding. This is how relationships work. Our part is to see and understand who God really is, that we might trust Him and learn to love Him. This is the primary message of the Old Testament God. The Great Commandment, the call to love God with our whole being, is derived from Exodus and other Old Testament Scriptures. We can see this, for example, by noting how God revealed Himself in Exodus on four levels:

First, the **practical** side of God. He cares for us and will meet our practical, physical needs when we trust Him. Exodus 16 to 18 shows how He provided both food and water for the wandering camp of Israelites. He also provided insight and wisdom for Moses through Jethro, enabling Moses to successfully lead the nation of Israel.

Second, the **moral** side of God. God wants us to live righteously for our own sake and for the sake of others. In Exodus 19-20, for example, God gives Israel the Ten Commandments. When we study these commands, we find the first four commandments guide our relationship with God, and the final six bring instruction for our relationships with each other. These moral guidelines have become timeless standards for ethical conduct in much of the

Coaching Tip

If you are having problems finding time to sit down and read each day, consider listening to an audio version of the text as you are resting, washing dishes, driving, or doing any activity that allows you to listen. BibleGateway.com and other Bible internet sites provide this option.

world. They help us to live our lives fully and to enjoy the freedoms we need in order to flourish.

Third, we see the **civil** side of God. In Exodus 21-24, the Almighty builds on the moral guidelines of the Ten Commandments to provide specific laws and principles to help His people bring justice and righteousness into their community. These civil laws applied to nomadic Israelites as they wandered the desert. Agrarian and urban societies would need their own additional standards for living and working together to ensure that fairness, equity, and goodness would prevail. The timeless, moral aspects of God, as seen in the Ten Commandments, provide a basis for the creation of such laws, though the laws may themselves change and adapt to each new location and situation.

Finally, we are shown the **relational** side of God, demonstrating that God's desire was, and always will be, to dwell with His people. He gave instructions in Exodus 25-29 for the construction of the Tabernacle, the place where His people would meet with Him. Special garments were provided for the priests, and sacrifices were instituted, all symbolizing God's grace and our need to humble ourselves as we come into His presence.

Thus we see, in each of these four aspects of God's interactions with Israel, that God has always been motivated by love in His dealings with humanity.

Respond

1. When you think of the God of the Old Testament as compared to the God of the New Testament, what are the main differences? Do they seem almost like two different Gods to you?

....

....

....

....

....

2. What is the main reason for the Law (Galatians 3:24)? Does this help explain how God's dealings with humanity have changed even though He Himself has not? Explain.

....

....

✱ 3. What distortions may occur in our perspective of God if we read only the Old Testament? What if we read only the New Testament? Why are both parts of the Bible important?

Pray

God, help me to know You fully, not in part. Show me how it is that You never change, yet You deal with humanity and each person according to our need and based on your desire for us to know You. Help me to love You more and in this reading through the Bible to be able to explain You better to my family and friends. Amen.

Impact

Sometimes we are enabled to see God in His fullness through the insights of others. Hearing different perceptions and perspectives about God and the Bible can open our eyes to new aspects of God's person. Find a friend with whom you can discuss what you are learning in your daily reading.

Close

Reading through the Old Testament may seem laborious. But remember: A read through the Old Testament can help you understand the New Testament. The Old Testament is the foundation, the New Testament its completion. By reading both, you are being introduced to God in His fullness.

Day 7 · **The Golden Cow**

I made the mistake of test driving a particular sports car. And it began driving me—I kept thinking about it even though I knew it wasn't the right car for my wife and me at this stage in our lives. Perhaps you know the feeling. We all tend to love the things of the world. When our love for such things diminishes our love for God, however, we may be looking at an idol. We may make an idol out of a particular home, a step up the corporate ladder, a change in our physical appearance, or even the hope to be accepted by someone else. None of these things in and of themselves are bad or wrong to pursue; however, if anything begins to eclipse our intimacy with God or our love for Him, that thing has become an idol. A good way to learn to identify and deal with our idols is to read the story of the golden calf in the book of Exodus. It is a stunning display of the ease with which we humans forget our very reason for existence: to know God and to enjoy Him forever. We are His treasured possession.

Coaching Tip

Identify your distractions. Once you become aware of the things that cause your mind to drift from your daily readings, ask God for steps you can take to make your special time together more focused and fulfilling.

Read

You have two reading options: read the full selection of Scripture or a single overview chapter each day.

- Full Reading: Exodus 30 – Leviticus 4:26
- Overview Chapter: Exodus 32

Reflect

It is difficult for us to understand how, in the book of Exodus, the Israelites could have turned away from God to worship a golden calf. After all, God brought them miraculously out of Egypt and through the Red Sea with great signs and wonders. God provided them with bread from heaven and water from a rock as they wandered the desert wilderness. Why would they suddenly replace the living God with a lifeless image of a calf of their own making?

Studying the text, we learn that the Israelites did not think they were replacing God. They thought of the golden calf as an image to help them follow God. This little twist in logic may be a key to identifying and understanding idolatry in our own lives. It often begins when we redefine who God is and what God wants, and then live accordingly.

Idolatry is often subtle, creeping into our hearts by degrees and gradually taking over. For the Israelites, it probably began when they longed for the comforts of their homes back in Egypt where food was placed on the table rather than found on the desert floor. How quickly the sting of the Egyptian whip was forgotten as their stomachs ached for lamb chops and goat's milk. This longing for what used to be was likely compounded by the "mixed multitude" that accompanied God's people when they left Egypt (Exodus

12:38). A contingent in their camp included Egyptians had who grown up worshipping, among other gods, the Apis Bull, a sign of strength and leadership. The people were now devoid of such leadership because Moses had gone up the mountain for 40 days to receive the Law of God. Without Moses, the people longed for a god that was visible, tangible, and convenient. Approaching Aaron, they demanded,

> *Up, make us gods who shall go before us. As for this Moses, the man who brought us up out of the land of Egypt, we do not know what has become of him.* (Exodus 32:1b)

Aaron told them to remove their gold earrings from which he fashioned a golden calf and declared, "These are your gods, O Israel, who brought you up out of the land of Egypt" (Exodus 32:4b)! The next morning, "the people sat down to eat and drink and rose up to play" (Exodus 32:6c). While Moses was on the mountain receiving the Ten Commandments, the people down below were profaning the first two. They demonstrated a universal reality: when we exchange the God of the Bible for a mere image of God, it will soon impact the way we live.

The Israelites repented and were given a second chance. Moses climbed Sinai again and for a period of 40 days received a second edition of God's Law. Afterward, the people renewed their covenant with God, the planned Tabernacle was constructed, and they began a journey with God that has been unparalleled in history: a million plus people growing closer to God in the wilderness as their needs are miraculously met from heaven.

What about us? Does not this story call us to humble ourselves, to let go of our idols, and to get right with God? Our idols may be asset accounts, cars, codependent relationships, food addictions, grudges, or anything we hold onto rather than a growing trust and love for God.

Respond

1. Make a list of some of the things we tend to idolize in modern society.

....

....

....

....

2. What were the consequences of the Israelites' idolatry (Exodus 32:11-35)?

....

✱ 3. From your daily reading and the commentary, what were the benefits the people of God experienced when they put aside their idols and made God first in their lives?

Pray

Lord, please search me and show me each day those things that can easily become idols in my life. Help me to love You so fully that everything and every person will dim in comparison. Thank you that You love me perfectly, even with my imperfections. Amen.

Impact

Idolatry is insidious. It shows up in our culture in dozens of ways. Take a few minutes to look at the free podcasts offered by Scripture Awakening to help us stay true to God in a world of compromise. Find a topic that "scratches where you itch" and consider listening to it on your own or with your small group. Go to: ScriptureAwakening.com/podcasts.

Close

Congratulations! You've completed your first week of Bible in 90 Days Plus! Feels good, huh? So here's the thing: pace yourself, you have another 83 days to go. Just keep taking it one day at a time!

Session 2 • Overview

● REVIEW Days 1-7

Pentateuch, Part 1: Beginnings, Enslavement, Deliverance

 Now is the time for your small group meeting to review the week's Scripture readings, cover the discussion questions, and watch the Essential Snapshot video together (or by yourself if reading alone). Point your mobile device's camera on the QR code to access the video entitled "Session 2: Beginnings". Or enter this link into your browser: **ScriptureAwakening.com/plus/**

- For tips on facilitating a small group, see **Appendix 1 Facilitator's Guide** in the back of this book on page 317.
- Discuss the questions marked by an asterisk (✱) from the **Respond** sections in Days 1-7, perhaps adding others if time permits.
- Watch the Session 2 video* (individually or with a small group).
  1. What insights from the video would you like to explore further?
  2. The creation account and modern theories about the world's beginnings appear to many to be in conflict to some and to harmonize for others. Why is it important to focus on the who and why rather than the what and when of creation as we ponder the beginnings of the universe and humanity?
- Summarize the Preview (below) of what is coming next week, encouraging group members to read it on their own.

*Facilitators note: In order to watch the Essential Snapshot video with your group, you will need a large video monitor, if meeting in-person. If hosting a small group remotely, use Zoom (or similar service) to stream the video from your device to share with group participants.

● PREVIEW Days 8-14

Pentateuch, Part 2: Holiness, Wandering, Renewal

Weekly Reading: Leviticus 4:26 to Deuteronomy 28:14

Summary

Having received the Law at the base of Mount Sinai, the Israelites are ready to begin their journey to the Promised Land. Their journey soon turns into a 40-year tragedy as they lose faith, rebel, and refuse to go into the land. After the succeeding generation is finally poised to take possession of their inheritance, Moses must prepare them to succeed where their parents had failed but under Joshua's leadership.

Leviticus Overview (Conclusion)

Continuing from last week, this book outlines the specific things that a sinful people must do to live in the presence of a holy God.

Numbers Overview

At the beginning of this book, the Israelites number 603,550; at the end, they number 601,730. What occurs in between is a lesson in the dangers of failing to submit to God and His plans.

After getting organized, the Israelites travel to Kadesh Barnea. From there they send spies into the Promised Land. The spies return with a discouraging report leading to general rebellion. As a result, God requires the people to wander aimlessly in the desert for 38 more years until all who are 20 years of age and older perish. Thus does the next generation resume the journey with a greater respect for God's plans and promises. After fighting and defeating several local kings, they ultimately arrive on the plains of Moab, on the east side of the Jordan River.

Deuteronomy Overview (Introduction)

The Israelites approach the Promised Land, and Moses instructs them in the Law through a series of three sermons. Many elements of the previous four books are revisited, including the Ten Commandments.

Looking backward, Moses reminds them of what God has already accomplished for them. Looking at the present, he teaches what God now requires of them. Finally, looking forward, he outlines the blessings that are contingent on their continued obedience and the curses that will fall on them if they turn from God.

The conclusion of Moses' ministry to the Israelites will be covered next week.

Things to Look for This Week

As you read, consider:

1. How the Law's standards for cleanliness and purity reveal, both physically and symbolically, what is required to live in the presence of a holy God.
2. The refusal of the Israelites to go into the land revealed their complete lack of faith in the Lord. Despite seeing many miraculous demonstrations of God's power, protection, and provision, they remained rebellious, stubborn, stiff-necked, and faithless.
3. Deuteronomy is not just a retelling of the Law to the generation that survived the wilderness wanderings but also an opportunity for corporate renewal through recommitment to the Covenant.

Coaching Tip

God's Word is like a mirror, given to help us see more clearly who we are that we might allow God to change us (James 1:22-25). As you read each day, ask God specifically to help you to learn, to obey, and to be changed.

Day 8 · **Consuming Fire**

As a child, I once played with a magnifying glass in the bright morning sun, capturing rays of sunlight and concentrating them on little dried leaves near my house. I was thrilled to be able to burn black holes in the leaves and create smoke. When I came home from school later that day, I saw fire trucks parked in front of my house. Panic coursed through my body. I kept my head low as I entered the house and quickly learned that my smoldering leaves had ignited a larger pile of dried grass clippings and almost took down the house. I had underestimated the power of fire.

Fire is used in the Bible to represent God's holiness. God's ways are much greater than ours, even as the sun is greater than the earth in size and firepower. If we draw too close to the sun without protective covering, we can be consumed. In the same way, coming into God's presence without the protection He prescribes can be dangerous. Safety guidelines are provided for us in the book of Leviticus.

Read

You have two reading options: read the full selection of Scripture or a single overview chapter each day.

- Full Reading: Leviticus 4:27–16:14
- Overview Chapter: Leviticus 10

Reflect

The Book of Leviticus is about the Levites, the tribe that became priests for Israel. The priests' role was to help people draw near to God. Priests foreshadowed Christ. They were needed because God is "set apart" from us which is what the word holy means. We often think of holiness as a behavior routine guided by a list of do's and don'ts. Holiness, however, is actually the essence of God's Personhood from which such moral guidelines arise.

Holiness has two primary aspects: **process** and **perfection**. We humans are in the process of becoming like God who alone is perfect. Because we, in our mortal flesh, cannot be perfectly holy, the perfectly holy God sent His Son as a sacrifice to atone for, or cover, our shortcomings and sins. He bridged the gap; our part is to believe it and live into it. And Leviticus helps us understand how to do that. We become holy by drawing near to God according to His prescription and allowing His Spirit to change us from within. We thus become "set apart" for God's purposes in the world.

Leviticus opens with a description of five types of Old Testament sacrifices. Taken together, they show us that once we choose *holiness*, we learn to live in *wholeness*. The *burnt* offering shows us that wholeness begins when we realize that God has paid the price to make us holy; our part is to believe. No amount of effort on our part will bring us to perfection.

The *grain* offering is essentially a celebration in faith of what God has done through the burnt offering, providing our salvation. The *peace* offering points to the results of our faith in God's finished work: peace with God and each other. The *sin* offering reminds us to confess our shortcomings and sins each day to God. And the *guilt* offering shows how God is making us holy, changing our lives from the inside out. We must not cling to things of the world or to habits that dishonor God; if we do, we will experience guilt as a sign that we need to repent.

The consequences of entering God's presence without God's prescribed standards was made obvious to the camp of Israel even as the sacrificial system was getting underway. In Leviticus 10, Aaron's two oldest sons, Nadab and Abihu, offered "strange fire," that is, unauthorized or foreign fire. The text doesn't say exactly what Nadab and Abihu did wrong, but it is clear that they disregarded God's instructions. God wanted to make it clear to everyone that His call to holiness is serious business and prescribed for our own protection. Aaron's sons were consumed by fire in order that the people might fear God. Better two die than have the whole house of Israel be consumed. A parallel occurs later in the New Testament when the Church is just getting underway. Ananias and Sapphira lied about an offering. They died on the spot (Acts 5:1-11).

These passages are a wake-up call to those who claim to be Christians but who think God doesn't care about how we live. He does care about how we live because He cares about us. Holiness leads to wholeness. The Israelites, when following God's prescriptions, avoided diseases and lived life in its fullness (Leviticus 11-16). Likewise, our lives will be made whole as we put God first and obey His Word as well as His Spirit's promptings.

Respond

1. How do you define holiness?

....

....

....

....

✱ 2. Why do you think holiness is important?

....

3. What is the means by which we may become more whole—more like our Lord Jesus?

Pray

Lord, please forgive me for times I have not taken Your call to holiness seriously. Help me to take that call seriously on a daily basis, as I read Your Word and pray. Amen.

Impact

Part of being human is to realize that we all struggle and that none of us is perfect. Being a child of God is to realize that God is with us in our struggles and that none of us is alone. Think of a family member, friend, or a church member who is facing a difficult struggle today and reach out to that person, letting them know you care.

Close

You may not think of yourself as holy. But the word "holy" in the Bible simple means "to be set apart." By reading God's Word every day, you are being set apart for God's purposes.

Day 9 · **Who's in the Details?**

As a young man, I loved motorcycles. One that I owned needed a new gear for its kick-start mechanism. Over several days, I tore down the engine, replaced the stripped gear, and piece-by-piece put the engine back together. When the moment came to try it out, I put my full weight into the kick-start but heard the grinding of gears rather than the anticipated roar of the engine. Frustrated, I tore the engine down again, only to discover that I had installed the newly-purchased gear . . . backwards! As the saying goes: "The devil is in the details."

Did you know this idiom began in the 1800s, likely arising from the expression, "God is in the details"? Indeed, the devil cannot do anything that God does not allow. Scripture teaches that God is involved in every detail of our lives, right down to knowing the number of hairs on our heads and the intentions of our hearts. But what about the minutia of Old Testament rules and regulations as found in the book of Leviticus? In a significant way, they are relevant for our lives today. Let's take a look.

Read

You have two reading options: read the full selection of Scripture or a single overview chapter each day.

- Full Reading: Leviticus 16:15 – Numbers 1
- Overview Chapter: Leviticus 19

Reflect

We read in 2 Timothy 3:16 (NIV) that "all Scripture is God-breathed and is useful for teaching, rebuking, correcting and training in righteousness, so that the servant of God may be thoroughly equipped for every good work." "Who," we might ask, "actually benefits from the mountain of laws and restrictions written in the book of Leviticus?"

As we first concern ourselves with the *size* of the Levitical code, we must remember that it was given as a guideline to help more than a million nomads survive what became a forty-year desert journey. We might actually be surprised that this early collection of national laws was so brief when we compare it to modern standards. There are between 15,000 and 20,000 federal laws governing the United States of America. If one were to add into this large number the legal statutes for every state, city, and county, it could take a person a lifetime to read and understand them all. In Leviticus, however, there are approximately 80 prohibitions. And when we consider them in the context of the entire Torah—the first five books of the Old Testament—the Jewish people traditionally recognized a total of 613 positive and negative commandments . . . not a large number of laws for an entire nation!

Coaching Tip

When, in your 90-day read, you may come to sections of Scripture that leave you deeply confused, make a note in this book and keep on reading. If you are involved in a weekly discussion group, ask for members' insights on such passages. You will soon notice that by reading the entire Bible, many questions are answered along the way.

If we can accept the *size* of the Levitical code, what do we say about its degree of *specificity*? Doesn't the specific focus on so much detail make Leviticus difficult to read? Let us remember, however, that if the laws established for the Israelites were not practical and specific, they would have done the people little good. In the words of Alexander Hamilton, "It will be of little avail to the people . . . if the laws be so voluminous that they cannot be read, or so incoherent that they cannot be understood . . ." ("The Federalist No. 62," February 1788).

Beyond their *size* and *specificity*, we may still be troubled by the *scope* of Levitical laws. The long and seemingly endless passages describing how to isolate people with diseases, for example, does not read like a science fiction thriller. When we realize, however, that this is one of the earliest instances of quarantine in history, a practice that wasn't fully understood until the advent of modern medicine, we suddenly appreciate that we are looking at breakthrough insights for ancient Israel's time. Likewise, the Levitical dietary restrictions may seem archaic to us; but when we realize that such restrictions protected the Israelites from parasites and diseases that cultures of the world have only slowly come to understand, they become rather amazing. Guidelines on sexuality in Leviticus may seem problematic until we realize how such guidelines protected God's people from sexually-transmitted diseases and from the breakdown of family relationships; then they become profound.

The punishments prescribed for certain behaviors may seem extreme to us, but when we compare them to the penal codes of surrounding nations, such as the Code of Hammurabi, it becomes apparent that the Law God gave to Moses was superior in many ways. It did not favor the privileged, rich, or elite in society. Being just, God's Law was built on the premise that all people are equal; it provided protection for the poor, the orphan, the widow, and the alien. Hammurabi's code was written to preserve a nation; God's Law was given to establish a relationship between God and humans, with provisions that demonstrated God's mercy and the sanctity of human life.

Leviticus contains many of the guidelines God provided to help His people live together and honor Him as they wandered toward the Promised Land. It is packed with symbolism and imagery pointing toward the salvation offered to all humanity through Jesus Christ. If we glean nothing else from this book, we must surely come to understand that our holy God cares about the details of our lives; indeed, *He* is *in* the details.

Respond

1. Do you believe any of the Levitical guidelines are still relevant for our day? If so, how can we know which ones are relevant?

2. God cares about our lives, even down to the smallest details. Make a list of details in your life that you would do well to surrender more fully to God.

✱ 3. Do you sometimes find it difficult to believe that God will guide you in ALL of your ways and will give you wisdom whenever you ask? Why or why not? Read Proverbs 3:5-6 and James 1:7. Claim God's promises.

Pray

Lord, help me to be more aware of Your presence and to depend on Your guidance for even the smallest details of my life. Amen.

Impact

It can be comforting to know that God cares about the smallest details of our lives. He also cares about the smallest details in the lives of our friends. Think of someone who is struggling to overcome an insecurity, an addiction, a fear, an anxiety, or a specific difficulty in their lives. Pray for God's peace for them and for God to help them grow through the challenges.

Close

As you continue reading through the Bible, try to read every word attentively. You may not know how to pronounce certain names or understand some of God's ways, but details here and there may become significant, even life-changing. God is in the details.

Day 10 · **Any Old Lead Pipe**

A friend, who has long been used mightily by God, once revealed to me his secret for service: "God can use any old lead pipe that is open on both ends." His words reminded me that God can use anyone who honestly desires to please Him and who is open to His will—even me. What matters most is not my *ability* but my *availability*. This became clearer when I read about a special group of people in the Old Testament called the Levites. From them, we can learn much about the principle of the old lead pipe.

Read

You have two reading options: read the full selection of Scripture or a single overview chapter each day.

- Full Reading: Numbers 2–11
- Overview Chapter: Numbers 3

Reflect

In the book of Leviticus, we learned about Levitical laws and codes. In Numbers, we have the opportunity to learn more about the Levites themselves. The Levites were the priests of Israel. Priesthood status was originally given to the firstborn son from each of Israel's tribes. The Levites alone retained this privileged position when they refused to join the rest of Israel in the worship of the golden cow (Exodus 32:26). Under the New Covenant—through Jesus Christ—we also have the privilege of serving God as priests (see 1 Peter 2:9; Revelation 1:6). The function of a priest is to create a bridge between God and God's people.

The story of the Levites, as found in the book of Numbers, provides three insights that can help us become channels of God's purposes in the world:

1. The first thing we learn is that those who wish to be used by God must be dedicated to God. At the heart of our reading, we find the Levites offering themselves to God. God said that ". . . they are wholly given to me from among the people of Israel" (Numbers 8:16). This standard applies to every follower of God. Paul writes, "I appeal to you therefore, brothers, by the mercies of God, to present your bodies as a living sacrifice, holy and acceptable to God, which is your spiritual worship" (Romans 12:1). This offering of ourselves includes everything, from our marriages (Numbers 5), to our commitments (Numbers 6), to the decision to worship God from our hearts (Numbers 7).

2. As pipelines of God's purpose, we must be positioned properly if we are to be used fully by God. This truth becomes obvious in Numbers 1 with the census, an accounting that demonstrates God's regard for each tribe, family, and person in the camp. In Numbers 2, the point is accen-

Coaching Tip

When you come to portions of Scripture that you would like to study more deeply, highlight them, record them in a notebook, or in the open sections of this book. You can return to them all after your 90-day read with new and special interest.

tuated as each of the tribes receives a special banner and location in the camp. The following two chapters highlight this reality yet further as duties are specifically assigned to the families of the Levites. Levi had three sons, who with their descendants played a special role in the administration of the Tabernacle to orchestrate worship by the people of God. So, it is for each of us. We each have a special assignment, given by God, that no one else can fulfill.

3. Our essential connections, then, are not only to God but also to God's people. The Levites gave their time and talents to serve God's people day and night. Had they refused to use their gifts, the Tabernacle could not have functioned as God intended, and the people would have had a difficult time following God (see chapters 9-10). Likewise, when we fail to offer our spiritual gifts for the service of God's people, everyone misses out (Romans 12:9-13).

You may think of yourself as no more significant than an old lead pipe. I agree. That is my status as well. Our significance and impact before God and in our spheres of influence come through a dynamic connection between God and God's people.

Respond

1. In Romans 12:1-2, we are called to offer ourselves to God. Who misses out when we fail to follow through on this command?

✱ 2. Romans 12:3-8, reminds us that we each have specific spiritual gifts given to us by God. What do you perceive your spiritual gifts to be? Are you content with your gifts, or do you find yourself trying to be like someone else?

3. In Romans 12:9-13, Paul exhorts us to get active, using our spiritual gifts to serve others. Describe a time when this command worked itself out well in your life. Pray for it to happen again, today and each day forward.

....

....

....

Pray

Lord, help me to see and understand that You can use me as a channel of Your purpose in the world if I will surrender my all to You and seek to use the gifts of service You have given me. Guide me to live according to Your design and purpose for my life, that others might be connected to You, somehow, through my obedience. Amen.

Impact

How have the daily readings and commentaries impacted your life? Find someone to share with about how God is changing your life through reading His Word.

Close

In 1999, Ted Cooper attempted to read the Bible in three months and over time launched a movement that would impact countless lives for years to come. It was God's Word that made the impact. You too, even if you think of yourself as just an old lead pipe, can point people to the Word and become a channel of great blessing to many!

Day 11 · **Our Rebellion**

As a young child, I was forced to take piano lessons. I wasn't happy about plunking the keys. I preferred to add to my rock collection. So, I took out my rock hammer and chipped all the ivories. The memory of my exploratory, rebellious actions lived on when my wife and I inherited that chip-keyed piano, trained our kids on it, and had to live with chipped keys until we could afford to buy a keyboard of our own. In the same way, the Old Testament book of Numbers is given to us as a perpetual reminder of what happens when people rebel against God. We can learn from Numbers what rebellion looks and feels like, and how and why to avoid it.

Read

You have two reading options: read the full selection of Scripture or a single overview chapter each day.

- Full Reading: Numbers 12–23
- Overview Chapter: Numbers 14

Reflect

As we read Numbers, we find ourselves center stage in the drama of Israel's rebellion against God. It begins in Numbers 12 when Moses' own siblings, Aaron and Miriam, challenge his authority. As a consequence of that rebellion, Miriam is struck with leprosy. Next, the 12 spies come onstage in Numbers 13. Ten of them return from their tour of Canaan to report all the reasons why the people should not take the land, despite God's promise to be with them and to give them success. In response, the people rebel. As a result, the Israelites are subject to 40 years of additional desert wanderings (Numbers 14). Just two chapters later, the sons of Korah, of the tribe of Levi, instigate yet another rebellion when they again challenge the authority of Moses and Aaron. The earth opens up and swallows not only Korah's sons but all that belongs to them.

A few chapters later in Numbers 20, Moses himself—now infected by the impatience and demands of the people—acts out in anger and forfeits his opportunity to personally enter the Promised Land. With God's chastening for rebellion reaching all the way to the top, one might expect the Israelites to finally get the point: *Trust God, even when you don't understand the details of His plans.* Nevertheless, they offer a chorus of complaint against God and Moses about the monotony of their daily menu (Numbers 21:5). In response, God sends them biting serpents with a fiery sting that kills many Israelites. They are spared further destruction when, according to God's command, Moses creates a bronze serpent and positions it high on a pole. God then promises, " . . . everyone who is bitten, when he sees it, shall live" (Numbers 21:8b). Pointing to this incident fifteen hundred years later, Jesus

Coaching Tip

When your reading of Scripture is interrupted, believe that God can use even the interruptions to accomplish His purpose. Ask Him for wisdom and the ability to keep up with your reading even as you deal with the challenges and occasional changes in your schedule.

promises us that despite our rebellious tendencies, we too will live if we look to Him (John 3:14).

Numbers teaches us that rebellion against God results in punishment by God. We can understand why when we look for rebellion's source. It all began with an insurrection against God by Satan himself (Isaiah 14:12-15). What the devil attempted at the beginning of time he will instigate again at the end of time, empowering "the man of lawlessness"—the Antichrist—to launch a worldwide system that will repress the faithful (2 Thessalonians 2:1-12). Being influenced by this dark power, most people's hearts will grow cold (Matthew 24:12).

We are wise, therefore, to search our hearts and to eradicate all rebellion. We must humble ourselves before God (James 4:10; 1 Peter 5:6; Matthew 23:12). Whatever life brings, we should thank God for all good things and trust Him to grow us through our difficulties. He really loves us and is helping us to find our own way to the Promised Land (Hebrews 12:6).

Respond

1. Does it surprise you that the leaders and people of Israel rebelled so often and so boldly against God? Explain.

✱ 2. How does Paul link these Old Testament stories with ours (see 1 Corinthians 10:1-11)? How does he tell us to deal with any rebellion or complaining thoughts that have filled our hearts (1 Corinthians 10:12-33)?

3. Prayerfully consider and record below any attitudes or actions in your life that are tainted by a rebellious spirit. Ask God for the grace and humility needed to get your heart right in each area.

....

....

....

....

Pray

Lord, You know my human tendency to rebel against You. Please forgive my sins and help me to know and trust You more each day, that I might know Your endless love and walk in Your wisdom. Amen.

Impact

The opposite of rebellion against God is obedience and worship to God. Bless God's heart today by worshipping Him as you go about your activities. Seek to find ways all day to honor Him in your thoughts, words, and actions.

Close

The nature of the world is to be in rebellion against God. The nature of the Word is to get people right with God. By reading the Bible in 90 Days, you are part of a movement that has impacted people in all 50 states in America and in 21 countries spanning 5 continents. Pray for God to help many turn back to Him!

Coaching Tip

Balaam might have avoided his blunders had he been held accountable by true followers of God. Close fellowship can, in fact, benefit each of us. If you have not yet found a few good friends to connect with you online or in person at least once a week around your read of the Bible, think about the benefits of doing so and seek it out.

Day 12 · **Bad as Balaam**

Balaam looked good on the outside, but his heart was not surrendered to God. As a prophet with mixed motives, he had the ability to talk with God. Unfortunately, he had little will to follow God. This blending of faith in one's head and rebellion in one's heart is spiritually lethal. It's a set-up for the deception of God's people in a big way. Satan is a master at disguising himself as a messenger of light; so are his servants—even those who serve darkness unwittingly. Let us heed the warnings drawn from Balaam's story that we might not repeat them.

Read

You have two reading options: read the full selection of Scripture or a single overview chapter each day.

- Full Reading: Numbers 24–36
- Overview Chapter: Numbers 25

Reflect

The last few chapters of yesterday's reading introduced us to Balaam even as we pondered the dangers of rebellion. Balaam launched rebellion in a private but powerful manner. His style was subtle, sly, and insidious. His was the worst kind of bad—the kind that is covered up by a façade that misleads many. His name became a byword for people who seem to be honoring God but are actually working against God (Revelation 2:14).

It all began when Balak, king of Moab, sought to find a way to defeat the encroaching Israelites. Believing that Balaam had some kind of magical powers, he sent for the diviner, asking him to put a curse on the Israelites (Numbers 22:1-8). Balaam and God had a conversation in which God refused to allow Balaam to curse the Israelites; thus began a struggle in Balaam's soul. On the surface, we read about the prophet's blessings over Israel. Between Numbers 24 and 25, however, Israel fell into heinous sin. Balaam was the cause; hence his notoriety for spiritual compromise. He died an untimely death as a further consequence of his actions (Joshua 13:22).

The hidden secrets of Balaam's story are unveiled when we turn to the New Testament. Peter and Jude both wrote about Balaam's love of money rising above his love of God (2 Peters 2:15; Jude 11). And John explains where Balaam's love of money led him. Desiring the king's gold, Balaam encouraged Balak "to put a stumbling block before the sons of Israel, so that they might eat food sacrificed to idols and practice sexual immorality" (Revelation 2:14c). Sly Balaam knew that if the Moabites held a feast to honor their gods and could entice the Hebrews to participate in the associated idolatrous worship and sexual immorality, God would be obligated to keep His Word and chasten them. The king followed Balaam's advice and once the

Israelites fell into transgression, God afflicted them with a plague (Numbers 25:1-3; 31:16).

What can we learn from this story? Perhaps the words of Jesus summarize it best: "No one can serve two masters, for either he will hate the one and love the other, or he will be devoted to the one and despise the other. You cannot serve God and money" (Matthew 6:24). How easily we, like Balaam, can slip into the dangerous realm of compromise where we declare our love for God while making idols of material things. The real test is this: Do you wish to please God above all else, even above your own comforts and desires? If not—if we long for the things of the world more than we love God—we may eventually become as bad as Balaam. And there is nothing good about that.

Respond

1. Why is a person who seems to be good on the outside but who is evil within potentially more dangerous than a person who is bold and brazen about his or her evil intentions?

2. The Israelites fell through sexual immorality. In what ways is this problem becoming paramount in the Western world, even among God's people? What is the outcome of such compromise?

✱ 3. The Israelites also ate food sacrificed to idols. A modern parallel would be the pursuit of enjoyments at the expense of God's declared will. Give examples of the ways we do this in our society today or ways in which you struggle with this personally. Pray for God's help and strength to remain faithful.

....

....

....

Pray

Lord, we can see the dangerous tendencies in our hearts to walk the pathway of Balaam. As You used a donkey to stop him in his tracks, please rebuke us as well. And help us to change, to truly repent, and to put You first and foremost forever. Amen.

Impact

Balaam might have found correction and help for his spiritual deficiencies had he been trained in the ways of God. So it is with many people today. When it comes to Biblical truth, ours is a culture of compromise. This Bible in 90 Days Plus program is designed to help people know God and His Word. Share your readings with friends from time to time, inviting them to join you on the journey.

Close

We should never be as bad as Balaam. To this end, let's pray for the Lord to instruct and correct us each day through our readings in His Word and through repentance as God guides us.

Day 13 · **Memory Matters**

In 1770, fourteen-year-old Wolfgang Amadeus Mozart visited the Sistine Chapel with his parents. He listened attentively to a performance of Gregorio Allegri's *Miserere*, a musical piece written during the 1630s for the exclusive use of the Sistine Chapel's annual Holy Week Tenebrae services. *Miserere* carried an aura of mystery because it had been kept out of circulation for more than a century. Only three copies of the work existed, and the Pope threatened excommunication to anyone who shared them. After hearing *Miserere* once, young Mozart was able to transcribe the complex cantata's melody lines entirely from memory. A few months later, the genius composer was called back to Rome by Pope Clement XIV, who granted him honors for his unusual talents. Even if our memories are not as keen as Mozart's, it is of utmost importance that we use them well. Insights for doing so are found in the book of Deuteronomy.

Read

You have two reading options: read the full selection of Scripture or a single overview chapter each day.

- Full Reading: Deuteronomy 1–11
- Overview Chapter: Deuteronomy 4

Reflect

Deuteronomy was Moses' address to the people of God before they made their grand entrance into the Promised Land. The book is packed with Moses' heart-felt advice to help his flock remember God's ways in order that they might survive and hopefully thrive in the years ahead. The entire book of Deuteronomy is laced with more than a hundred reminders of its purpose with words such as "remember" and "do not forget," along with warnings such as "be careful" and "be diligent." Standing on the territory of Moab, near the point where the Jordan flows into the Dead Sea (Deuteronomy 1:5), Moses wove into his Deuteronomic sermon two devices to help the people engage their memories to the fullest:

1. **Repetition.** The title *Deuteronomy*, from the Greek version of the Old Testament, means "second law." Indeed, Deuteronomy is a second telling of the core truths the people of God would need to remember in the Promised Land. Repetition, a well-known mnemonic device, could help them do so. When Jesus lived on earth, one account of His life was not sufficient; hence, four Gospels. In the same way, Moses used repetition in Deuteronomy to emphasize key elements of the Israelite's 40-year desert journey, described in Leviticus and Numbers, as things the new generation must never forget.

Coaching Tip

Keep a journal or notepad with you as you read through the Bible, and note important truths that you have forgotten or don't want to forget. That notebook may become for you a treasure chest of insights to inspire further study for years to come.

2. Ceremony. If we hope to remember things most essential and pass them on to generations to come, we should memorialize such truths. To this end, God gave the Israelites three key festival seasons described in earlier books and summarized in Deuteronomy 16: Passover, Pentecost, and Booths.

The first—was to take place in spring and memorialized Israel's exodus from Egypt. The corollary for us is our release from the bondage of our sins through Jesus Christ. We remember and reflect on this release through the celebration of the Lord's Supper, or communion, along with the calendar season of Lent which includes Easter.

The second ceremony of the Jews, held in summer, was Pentecost. It focused on the second biggest event in the Old Testament, the giving of the Law. The modern corollary is found in the Day of Pentecost when the Church was born.

If Passover focused on the sacrifice of the Son and Pentecost on the power of the Spirit, the third ceremony points to the love of the Father, our provider. Occurring in the fall, the feast of "Booths"—or "Tabernacles"—was a time to give thanks to God for His provision, mercy, and grace. A modern corollary might be the season of Thanksgiving.

As we read Deuteronomy, we note how repetition and ceremony helped the people of God remember important events that they might weave them into the fabric of their lives. In our day, we would do well to follow in their steps. Memory matters.

Respond

1. How is your memory? What tricks or techniques help you to recall and live by the things God says are most important?

2. As you read Deuteronomy, are you dragged down, or challenged and refreshed, by Moses' heartfelt retelling of the history and teachings found in Leviticus and Numbers? Why?

✱ 3. What is one core truth from your reading in Deuteronomy that you hope never to forget?

Pray

Lord, how is it that I often forget You—the most important Person in my life? I can run through the course of an average day and hardly notice Your presence. The Bible is the most important book in my life; yet, I can go days without meditating on and memorizing Your promises and principles. As I continue to read through the Bible, help me to remember key truths and to enjoy Your presence. Amen.

Impact

God wants us to remember not only His precepts but His people. We offer the Bible in 90 Days Plus program to help the truths of Scripture reach all kinds of people, including those who are easily overlooked: people in nursing homes, hospitals, the military, and the poor in many parts of the world. Pray that we can reach people who might otherwise be forgotten.

Close

You're well into your journey through God's Word. Keep it up! Because Bible in 90 Days gets us through the entire Bible in just three months, it enables us to connect key historical persons, events, and themes from Genesis to Revelation.

Coaching Tip

When our hearts are not right with God, our ability to understand and apply our readings will be hampered. Take time before you read every day to pray, asking God to help you come to the Scripture with a pure heart.

Day 14 · **Your Refuge**

Having been pulled over for a speeding ticket, I showed up in court to contest the charge. I wasn't going all that fast, and I didn't need points on my license. I sat and waited as person after person appeared before the judge, some facing criminal charges. Some appeared not to have been given the opportunities in life that had been mine. Their stories spoke of hardship, and their clothes suggested lives on the edge of poverty. With no doing or inherent value of my own, I had been born into a family and lifestyle that, in contrast with many in the courtroom, opened a world of opportunities to me. I listened for hours to people trying to argue their way out of fines they could not afford until my heart melted and I really didn't care about my fine. Then the judge called my name and declared that my charges were dropped. At that point, I felt I had been shown undeserved favor. We have all received such favor, through God's grace. We can see this truth all the way back in Deuteronomy.

Read

You have two reading options: read the full selection of Scripture or a single overview chapter each day.

- Full Reading: Deuteronomy 12–28:14
- Overview Chapter: Deuteronomy 19

Reflect

The concept of cities of refuge is introduced in Exodus 21:12-13, explained more fully in Numbers 35:9-34, specified in Deuteronomy 4:41-43, and summarized in Deuteronomy 19:1-13. Six cities were allocated to the Levites, designated to provide asylum for perpetrators of unintentional manslaughter. Underlying this concept are important truths about justice and mercy that are timeless and relevant for each of us, both in society and before God.

Justice and Mercy in Society

Despite common misconceptions held by many who don't read the Bible carefully, the laws given by God to govern Israel were tempered by grace and mercy. The law of retaliation—"An eye for an eye, a tooth for a tooth" (Exodus 21:23-25)—provided a means to curb criminal activity as the Israelites wandered the desert. It was also meant to ensure the punishment meted out for a crime was not worse than the crime itself. Later, when God's people settled into Canaan, they would establish a communal system of civil jurisdiction with trials and ruling judges.

The merciful side of God was highlighted by cities of refuge. These cities provided protection for the person who committed manslaughter, the unintentional taking of another's life. If, for example, two friends were chopping wood and the axe head came off the handle as one friend wielded the axe, killing the other, an extra layer of protection was needed (Deuteronomy 19:5-6). Based on the law of retaliation, an avenger from the deceased's family would be expected to pursue the killer to take his life. With the establishment of cities of refuge, however, the accused could flee within a day's journey and remain safe in that city until the resident Levites held court. If it was decided that the perpetrator did not commit murder, he could remain safely in the city until the death of the High Priest, at which time he was to go free.

Justice and Mercy Before God

Cities of refuge are one of many ways we see, in the days of the Old Testament, how the Israelites stood out from surrounding nations because of the mercy extended by their God. The elaborate sacrificial system, for example, was given to prepare the world for the mercy that would be extended to all who come to God through the sacrifice of Jesus Christ, our *refuge* (Hebrews 6:18).

Respond

✱ 1. How should we respond to the grace and mercy of God shown to us through the sacrifice of Christ (Hebrews 10:19-23)?

2. What does 1 John 1:8-10 say about the need for us to bring our sins to God through confession? Do you really believe God has forgiven all of your sins? If there are some you feel He cannot forgive, what do you think is blocking such forgiveness?

3. Why is it important that we likewise forgive others (Matthew 18:21-35)? Ask God to search your heart and help you to fully forgive those who have wronged you.

....

....

....

....

Pray

Lord, help me to so appreciate Your mercy and kindness, extended toward me every day, that I do the same toward everyone in my life. Amen.

Impact

Prayerfully consider the broken relationships in your life. Are there any people who need to hear that you forgive them? Remember how freely the Lord has forgiven you at such a great cost . . . then obey Him by forgiving others just as you have been forgiven.

Close

God gives us His Word that we might know Him. It teaches us, above all, that Christ is our refuge. We can rest securely under the shelter of His grace. This is the primary message of the Bible, beginning to end.

Session 3 • Overview

● REVIEW Days 8-14
Pentateuch, Part 2: Holiness, Wandering, Renewal

Now is the time for your small group meeting to review the week's Scripture readings, cover the discussion questions, and watch the Essential Snapshot video together (or by yourself if reading alone). Point your mobile device's camera on the QR code to access the video entitled "Session 3: Patterns". Or enter this link into your browser: **ScriptureAwakening.com/plus/**

- For tips on facilitating a small group, see **Appendix 1 Facilitator's Guide** in the back of this book on page 317.
- Discuss the questions marked by an asterisk (✱) from the **Respond** sections in Days 8-14, perhaps adding others if time permits.
- Watch the Session 3 video* (individually or with a small group).
    1. What insights from the video would you like to explore further?
    2. In your own words, what is "typology" as found in the Old Testament? Why is it important?
- Summarize the Preview (below) of what is coming next week, encouraging group members to read it on their own.

*Facilitators note: In order to watch the Essential Snapshot video with your group, you will need a large video monitor, if meeting in-person. If hosting a small group remotely, use Zoom (or similar service) to stream the video from your device to share with group participants.

● PREVIEW Days 15-21
History, Part 1: Conquest, Cycles, Transition

Weekly Reading: Deuteronomy 28:15 to 2 Samuel 3:21

Summary

Under Joshua's leadership, the Israelites finally enter, conquer, and settle the Promised Land. Disobedience, however, leads to 300-plus years of repeated oppression by their enemies and intermittent deliverance through God's appointed judges (deliverers). Wanting to be like the nations around them, the people demand a king and soon find themselves ruled by a paranoid madman, King Saul. His successor, David, finally takes the throne and strives to unite the people as one.

Books You'll Encounter This Week

Deuteronomy Overview (Conclusion)

The new generation of Israelites recommit to the Covenant. Moses gets to view the Promised Land from Mount Nebo but dies before his people enter it.

Joshua Overview

Joshua, Moses' former assistant, becomes leader of the nation of Israel. The book celebrates the many victories that God brings to the Israelites under Joshua's leadership.

Faithful obedience to the Law and trust in the Lord lead to the successful conquest of the land in three military campaigns. The Israelites complete the division and settlement of the land by tribal areas and reaffirm their commitment to the Lord in a national assembly. It is not long, however, before their ongoing disobedience sets them up for dismal failure.

Judges Overview

This book clearly delineates the impact of leaders who follow God from those who do not. In a cyclic pattern of sin, external oppression, repentance, and deliverance, the Israelites experience again and again what happens when "everyone did what was right in his own eyes" (Judges 21:25b).

Some of the favorite Biblical personalities from children's Sunday school are found here: Deborah, Gideon, and Samson. At the conclusion of the book, as the nation descends into idolatry and gross immorality, new leadership is clearly needed.

Ruth Overview

Set during the period of the Judges, Ruth's story of faithfulness is remarkable in its own right. Ruth is from Moab, a nation considered an enemy of Israel. Yet, she is central to the story as one who remains faithful to Israel's God even as the Israelites fall into sin and idolatry.

Boaz's actions as kinsman-redeemer restore Naomi's estate and status and bring a new family and prosperity to Ruth. From that family will come both King David and Christ. Boaz's redemptive role foreshadows the redemption Christ would eventually bring to the world.

1 Samuel Overview

Samuel is not only a priest, prophet, and judge, but also a kingmaker. The people demand a king and, at God's behest, Samuel anoints Saul to be the first king of Israel. God later directs Samuel to anoint Saul's successor, David, beginning a series of conflicts between Saul and David.

Saul's desire to please himself and his subjects rather than God, leads to his growing paranoia and bouts of madness, eventually leading to his ignominious death at the hands of the Philistines on Mount Gilboa.

2 Samuel Overview (Introduction)

David becomes king over Israel and Judah, thus uniting the kingdom. Even though David is "a man after [God's] own heart" (1 Samuel 13:14), he commits grievous sins for which he experiences dire consequences. Nevertheless, his faith in God remains constant.

More details about David's reign will be covered next week.

Things to Look for This Week

As you read, consider:

1. How faithfulness to the Lord leads to blessing and prosperity while disobedience and rebellion leads to discipline and suffering.

2. That personal character and conduct are more important to God then ethnicity and pedigree.

3. The critical transition from Israel's regional leadership under the judges to its national leadership under the kings. Note how the axiom, "as the leader goes, so goes the nation" holds true in these books.

Coaching Tip

As you read Scripture, when the Spirit of God touches you with conviction and insight, take a moment to commit your thoughts to the Lord. His wisdom will enable you to face the challenges of the day.

Day 15 · **Facing Change**

One of the most significant transitions in the Bible occurs when Moses places the leadership of the nation of Israel into Joshua's hands. Moses—who stands as a human symbol of the Law—is unable to enter the land because of a seemingly small infraction he committed when, in anger, he struck the rock at Meribah twice (Numbers 20:1-13). Although Moses acted in human frustration, this is a reminder to us that those who live by the Law must be perfect. Joshua, on the other hand, stands as a picture of the grace God offers to us despite our failures. Joshua foreshadows our Lord, Who alone can bring us into the Promised Land. The name Joshua, when brought into the Greek is "Jesus." Both names, *Joshua* and *Jesus*, mean, "The Lord Saves." Our Lord, then, saves and blesses us even as we face change.

Read

You have two reading options: read the full selection of Scripture or a single overview chapter each day.

- Full Reading: Deuteronomy 28:15 – Joshua 6
- Overview Chapter: Joshua 1

Reflect

Change is often unsettling; yet without it, no aspect of life moves forward. Change is necessary for relationships to grow, for cars to move, and for circumstances to improve. Change is likewise unsettling in that it can involve relationships that unravel, cars that break down, or circumstances that disintegrate before our eyes. Much of our time and energy is thus spent navigating change and attempting to move it in the right direction. There comes a time, however, when we realize that we must trust God in every transition and altered circumstance of our lives. In other words, we must believe His promise to use change for our good and for His glory.

Moses had to deal with change at temporal and eternal levels. After he gave the bulk of his life to leading the nation of Israel, he needed to release the reigns of leadership to Joshua. And he was required by God to climb Mount Nebo where he experienced the greatest change of all—an entrance into glory through the gateway of death.

Following Moses' death, Joshua and the people of Israel had their own transitions to face. After a full generation had been replaced in desert wanderings, they were about to begin life for the first time as a truly independent nation; however, they would have to fight for it and learn to trust God under a whole new set of circumstances. Signifying Israel's dedication to God, every man was circumcised near the entrance to the Promised Land (Joshua 5). It was time to lay down the past and press forward into a new and glorious future.

Joshua received keen insights about change: "This Book of the Law shall not depart from your mouth, but you shall meditate on it day and night, so that you may be careful to do according to all that is written in it. For then you will make your way prosperous, and then you will have good success. Have I not commanded you? Be strong and courageous. Do not be frightened, and do not be dismayed, for the LORD your God is with you wherever you go" (Joshua 1:8-9). So too, as we continue to read through the Word, let us be confident that God will grant us insight to successfully navigate every change we face.

Respond

1. Record some of the changes you are dealing with today. Do they bring you fear and anxiety, or does God's peace prevail in your heart?

✱ 2. According to Joshua 1:8-9, what is the key to being courageous, even in the face of change?

3. What additional step should we take to overcome our anxieties (see Philippians 4:4-9)? Commit yourself to taking time each day to bring your concerns to the Lord.

Pray

Unchanging God, I commit myself to trusting You to guide me through all of life's transitions. Grant me daily insight as I read Your Word that I might trust You more. Amen.

Impact

Think of people in your life who are facing significant change: a health crisis, a broken marriage, the loss of employment, etc. Pray for them to find courage from God and love from their neighbors to not only get through but to grow through their time of change. Consider how you might be an answer to that prayer.

Close

Whatever changes may be in front of you, your friends or your church, keep focused on your Bible reading and the unchanging God who will bless you. Read this testimony from an enthusiastic reader and promoter:

"Want to grow deeper in your faith? Want the Kingdom of God to flourish in your community through your church? Want to see your church grow, give, and serve more? Start with the Bible in 90 Days—you will be blessed!"

— Pastor Ruffin Stepp

Day 16 · **Inspiring Courage**

Joshua received the command to "[be] strong and courageous," first from Moses (Deuteronomy 31:6-7, 23), and then directly from God (Joshua 1:7-9). He soon shared this admonition with the Israelites (Joshua 10:25). The same exhortation applies to us. We may not be conquering *lands* as Joshua was, but we *are* commissioned by God to conquer false ideas that lead people away from God. And the book of Joshua shows us the way to live out that commission.

Read

You have two reading options: read the full selection of Scripture or a single overview chapter each day.

- Full Reading: Joshua 7–19
- Overview Chapter: Joshua 14

Reflect

As we follow the story of Joshua and the people of God into the Promised Land, we can discern three channels through which they were filled with divine courage: God's *plan*, God's *power*, and God's *promises*.

1. Joshua and the people found courage because they embraced God's *plan* for the future. God had determined hundreds of years prior that the people of God would occupy the territory of Canaan. The previous generation didn't take this plan seriously, and now—40 years later—a new generation was ready to enter. Their obedience would be tested as they conquered God's allotted territory. At Ai, they learned the difference between overconfidence and divinely-inspired courage (Joshua 7-8). And when the Gibeonites tricked them, they experienced how overconfidence becomes a diversion away from God's purposes (Joshua 9:14). With these lessons in hand, Joshua and the people followed God's *plan* with great courage and experienced good success.

   God has given us a *plan* as well. Jesus has commanded us not to conquer a nation with swords but to conquer hearts with truth and love, bringing the Gospel to all nations (Matthew 28:18-20). When we forget this Great Commission and lose sight of God's *plan*, we find little reason to be courageous.

2. The Israelites learned not only to embrace God's *plan* for the future, but to trust God's *power* for the present. As they entered the land, God assisted them supernaturally. Angels, insects, pestilence, and acts of nature were all instruments God used to enable His people to conquer a coalition of armies in the south (Joshua 10) and a second coalition of armies in the north (Joshua 11).

B90+

Coaching Tip

When you come across verses that you hope to remember for the future, consider underlining them in your Bible and/or writing them down on small cards so that you can later carry them with you for reflection and meditation.

As Christians, we likewise are promised supernatural power to assist us as we seek to fulfill God's plan. The book of Acts, a short history of the early Church, is replete with stories of the courage of the saints and of the power of God to help them fulfill God's purpose for them on earth (Acts 1:8).

3. God's people lived according to God's *plan* and through God's *power* based on God's *promises*. Again and again, God had promised to be with them and help them conquer the land. As He had enabled them to overcome their enemies in Egypt, He would surely grant them victories in Canaan. Caleb stands out as a prime example of the courage that can be ours when we claim God's promises. Having been faithful during his excursion as a spy and the subsequent 45 years of desert wanderings and conquest, Caleb was ready to go. In Joshua 14, he asked for the privilege of fighting some of the toughest people in the land, the Anakim—descendants of the Nephilim. These giants were a primary reason the Israelites had refused to enter Canaan the first time around (Deuteronomy 9:2, Numbers 13:33).

Following the examples of Joshua and Caleb today, we too can embrace God's *plan*, live in God's *power*, and rest on God's *promises*. As we do so, God's courage will fill our heart and inspire our steps.

Respond

1. If you can, describe a time when you found supernatural courage and inspiration to do God's will, perhaps even to your own surprise.

....

....

....

....

✱ 2. What are the upsides of being courageous? When you are courageous for the Lord, are there any downsides?

....

....

....

....

3. Make a list of areas in which you wish you were more courageous, and with Joshua's story in mind, pray for a fresh infilling of Heaven-sent courage.

....

....

....

....

Pray

Lord, help me to be so set on pleasing You that I forgo the natural tendency to please myself. Let me be so set on bringing You glory that I care less and less about my own. So inspire me with Your commands and concerns as I read Your Word daily that divine courage fills my soul. Amen.

Impact

Did you know that the word *encourage* comes from the Old French compound word *en* ("to make", or "put in") and *courage* ("heart"). The idea was to put strength in the heart. Think of someone who is facing a daunting and difficult task and encourage them with your words, prayers, and actions.

Close

It took courage for you to begin this journey. The Scripture Awakening team and others are praying that the Lord will impart a daily dose of His strength in your heart. May He help you through to the end of the readings, despite any obstacles you may face. If you ever feel like quitting, look up and ask God to renew your courage.

Coaching Tip

When you want to give up on your reading, remember God's promise to help you in times of weakness (2 Corinthians 12:10). Turn to Him and ask for grace, stamina, time, and the ability to keep on track until the end.

Day 17 · **In Your Weakness**

The Israelites fared well under Joshua's leadership; however, they began to drift from obedience to God after Joshua's death. The book of Judges carries us through seven major life cycles of the Israelites. Each cycle begins with the people's foolish idea that they don't need God's approval but are free do "what is right in their own eyes." As a result of such arrogance, God allows nearby enemies to oppress Israel until the nation humbles itself, admits a need for God's help, and cries out to Him in prayer and repentance. God then sends a deliverer—known as a judge—to deliver the Israelites from the woes that result from their disobedience. Through the story of one of these judges, we will find key ingredients to help us avoid the cycles of compromise and live in God's strength.

Read

You have two reading options: read the full selection of Scripture or a single overview chapter each day.

- Full Reading: Joshua 20 – Judges 7
- Overview Chapter: Judges 7

Reflect

The 12 judges portrayed in the book of Judges bring forth a united message: the fact that mankind must realize God's strength while simultaneously accepting and acknowledging mankind's weakness. This theme not only serves as the storyline of the book of Judges, but is the reality behind nearly every great success and failure throughout the Bible. The Psalmist rightly says, "My flesh and my heart may fail, but God is the strength of my heart" (Psalm 73:26); Isaiah understood correctly that God "gives power to the faint, and to him who has no might he increases strength" (Isaiah 40:29); Paul heard quietly from the Holy Spirit that God's "grace is sufficient for you, for [God's] power is made perfect in weakness" (2 Corinthians 12:9); and the Apostle concluded, "I can do all things through Him who strengthens me" (Philippians 4:13).

The message of God's strength through our weakness is especially apparent in the story of Gideon, Israel's fourth judge. When God calls Gideon to assemble an army and deliver the Israelites from Midian, the young man musters 32,000 men. The Lord then tells him, "The people with you are too many for me to give the Midianites into their hand, lest Israel boast over me, saying, 'My own hand has saved me'" (Judges 7:2). The Lord has the army cut down to 10,000 and eventually to 300 men—a mere fraction of a percent of the size of the Midianite army they are to confront; yet with God's help they prevail.

What task are you facing that seems way beyond your capabilities? Pray, asking God for clarity as to whether you are acting in His will. If you sense you are, pray for abilities sufficient to the task. As you depend on God's strength in your weakness, you'll find that He will not let you down.

Respond

1. What do you consider some of your greatest strengths? Do they sometimes become weaknesses for you? Explain.

2. What are some of your greatest weaknesses? How might they become channels of God's great strength in your life?

✱ 3. Have you experienced a time when you really knew you were weak, cried out to God, and saw God move in a powerful manner? If so, describe it.

Pray

Lord, help me to realize how truly weak I am without You. And enable me to live through Your strength always. Amen.

Impact

God is calling forth a Gideon's army in our day. Many, however, may never hear the call if they do not learn to spend quality time in Scripture each day. Think of people you know, even from the distant past or from distant places, and share Bible in 90 Days Plus with them.

Close

May you continue to find genuine strength day-after-day as you go through Bible in 90 Days Plus. Tomorrow we will be looking into "Issues of the Heart." Ask the Lord to help you prepare your heart for tomorrow's study and for each day that follows.

Day 18 · **Issues of the Heart**

Many of us, from our youth, learned the intriguing story of Samson. Having been commissioned from before his birth to live the life a Nazarite, Samson was required never to cut his hair. When he gave in to the ceaseless questions of Delilah, however, he lost both his hair *and* his strength. His disobedience allowed the Philistines to capture and torture him. As we will see, his Nazaritic vow was an Old Testament foreshadowing of Christ's call on our lives to guard our hearts today. King Solomon said it clearly, "Keep your heart with all vigilance, for from it flow the springs of life" (Proverbs 4:23).

Read

You have two reading options: read the full selection of Scripture or a single overview chapter each day.

- Full Reading: Judges 8–19
- Overview Chapter: Judges 16

Reflect

There is a certain level of mystique and mystery surrounding the story of Samson, as well as the history of the Nazaritic vow described in Numbers 6. The word *Nazarite* is from the root word *Nazire* which means "to be set apart," "consecrated," or "separated." This vow was a means by which God allowed a person to choose voluntary and temporary separation from the world as an expression of the person's full dedication to God. For Samson, however, the vow would be neither voluntary nor temporary; he was to be a Nazarite from birth for the entirety of his life.

Numbers 6 lays down three requirements of the Nazarite:

- To abstain from alcohol or anything made from grapes (Numbers 6:3-4),
- To refrain from cutting one's hair (v. 5), and
- To avoid contact with corpses or graves (vs. 6-7)

Some scholars argue that Samson violated the first and third parts of his vow well before he cut his hair and experienced his ultimate demise. Of this we cannot be sure. What we do know, however, is that God's intention was to use Samson as a judge for Israel, delivering them from the yoke of the Philistines (Judges 13:5; 14:4). God likewise intends to use you and me for His glory (Ephesians 1:3-12). We lose our strength and ability to do so, however, when we allow compromise to seep into our hearts.

Above all else, the Nazaritic vow was a symbol of total dedication to God. Like Samson, John the Baptist was apparently called to live as a Nazarite from birth (Luke 1:13-15). His strength was neither physical nor political. His dynamic ministry was grounded in the resolve of his heart to please God. Through this resolve, he called for people to repent of sin and to get right with God. Jesus commended John for his obedience (Matthew 11:11). This

Coaching Tip

As God speaks to us through Scripture, we must discern the difference between conviction and condemnation. Conviction turns us to God for more grace. Condemnation pushes us away from God and leads us down the pathway of guilt, shame, and despair. God doesn't condemn us. Instead, He allows the Holy Spirit's conviction to lead us to the cross for Christ's forgiveness and for the grace to become more like Him.

important question remains: are you and I fully surrendered to God from the heart, that we too might be used of God, now and in the future?

Respond

✱ 1. What is the primary message we should draw from Samson's life? Why?

2. Why might God remove His blessing and strength from us if we willingly compromise His will?

3. What is the Good News for us as we resolve to please and to obey God (see 1 John 2:15-17)?

Pray

Lord, search me, know my heart, and reveal any areas of compromise in my life. Grant me the grace to live fully and completely for You, now and always. Amen.

Impact

Are there areas in your life where you are sensing the Holy Spirit's conviction? Then take this moment to pray, turning that conviction into godly action.

Close

As we spend time in the Word, our hearts become sensitive to God's purposes for our lives. Here is a testimony from one reader: *"I have . . . read the Bible several times throughout my life. But never like this. I had read the words, but I actually was excited to do each day's reading. If I missed a day, I felt it!"* — Christine DeMattie

Day 19 · **Giving Birth**

The story of two incredible women are included in this reading, Ruth and Hannah. They each share a common faith and a unique story of birth. Ruth gave birth to a son who became the grandfather of David. In this lesson we will focus on Hannah and her special son.

Women have a capacity to give birth. We men can watch and wonder—and, perhaps be thankful we are not required to do the same. There is, however, a type of birthing—a travail of the soul—that is not meant to be gender-specific. I am talking about the birthing of God's will through prayer. In a recent meeting, I was moved to watch a woman wrestle and groan before God as she prayed. It seemed to me that she was giving birth to God's great initiatives through her labors. Indeed, such deep travail of the soul has been used again and again to conceive new life in the world for God's glory. Hannah's story provides us one example.

Coaching Tip

When you come across a truth or story in Scripture that moves you, take a moment to turn it into a specific and bold prayer to God.

Read

You have two reading options: read the full selection of Scripture or a single overview chapter each day.

- Full Reading: Judges 20 – 1 Samuel 8
- Overview Chapter: 1 Samuel 1

Reflect

We read in 1 Samuel 1 about the great angst carried in the heart of a woman named Hannah; she desperately wanted to have children. As she cried out to God in prayer, she made a vow to God, "O LORD of hosts, if you will indeed look on the affliction of your servant and remember me and not forget your servant, but will give to your servant a son, then I will give him to the LORD all the days of his life, and no razor shall touch his head" (1 Samuel 1:11). She was in essence saying that her son would be a Nazarite, fully committed to God all of his days. As Hannah poured out of her soul to God, the priest thought she was intoxicated and reprimanded her. When she explained her situation and told him about her vow, however, he gave her a blessing with the promise of God's answer. She soon gave birth to a boy, whom she named Samuel, meaning "asked of the Lord."

Samuel grew up to become one of the great prophets in the Bible. He served as a bridge between Israel's judges and her kings. For his life and influence, we are indebted to Hannah and to God. Hannah was not the only barren woman who against great odds would bring a mighty man of God into the world. We might also think of the mothers of Isaac, Samson, and John the Baptist. Perhaps, like Hannah, these godly women conceived their sons with great labor pains in prayer.

Indeed, prevailing prayer is an essential aspect to the advancement of God's work; for through intercession, human souls join with God's Spirit in the conception, gestation, and eventual birthing of God's purpose on earth, a process that is nothing short of miraculous. In the words of the Apostle Paul,

> . . . *we do not know what to pray for as we ought, but the Spirit himself intercedes for us with groanings too deep for words.* (Romans 8:26b)

Is there a burden on your heart, placed there by God, waiting to be carried to the throne? Your burden might center around a child or friend who needs the life-transforming touch of God. Your call to prayer might focus on a church, a business, a school, or even an entire nation. God gives us His anointing for intercession so that we can partner with Him in His Kingdom's advance.

Respond

1. What burden has God put on your heart?

....
....
....
....

✱ 2. Have some of your heart's desires remained unfulfilled? Should you then give up (see Luke 18:1-8)? Explain.

....
....
....
....

3. What does James 5:16-18 say about the importance of fervent prayer? Ask God to help you lift the burdens He lays on your heart with a Heaven-sent travail.

....

....

....

....

Pray

Lord, teach me to pray. May Your Holy Spirit come along side me as You place Your burdens in my heart that I might pray according to Your will. Use me as You will to give birth to Your purpose in the world. Amen.

Impact

Scripture Awakening is seeking to support student interns and is being supported by retired volunteers using their gifts in speaking, writing, coaching, and social media to impact others with the power of God's Word. But neither the interns and volunteers nor those being reached will be moved without prayer. As God guides you, please pray for great impact on many lives through these efforts by the young and old.

Close

Today we talked about issues of the heart. Tomorrow we will look at how even good things can interfere with God's chosen *best* for our lives.

Coaching Tip

Our daily readings are a key part of seeking God and fulfilling His Great Commandment. Pray as you read for the ability to know and trust God more than ever.

Day 20 · **Enemy of the Best**

You may have heard the expression, "the good is the enemy of the best." But have you really thought about what this means for your life? It is not merely a cliché drawn from human experience. It is a Biblical truth highlighted in the life of King Saul. As you read and reflect on his life, examine your heart carefully to discern whether or not good things have distracted you from God's best.

Read

You have two reading options: read the full selection of Scripture or a single overview chapter each day.

- Full Reading: 1 Samuel 9–20:17
- Overview Chapter: 1 Samuel 15

Reflect

God's desire was that the Israelites trust Him to guide them rather than to be ruled by a human king. The Israelites, however, demanded to be like the nations surrounding them, each of which had a king of its own. The people got their way. But what they considered to be something good replaced God's best for them: they thwarted the divine prerogative for a perfect theocracy with a flawed monarchy.

At first, Saul seemed to be a decent pick for a king. His heart was divided, though and eventually caused the loss of his rulership to David—a man who truly sought God with his whole heart. The evidence of Saul's compromised heart appeared throughout his reign as he often made foolish decisions. This propensity was highlighted, for example, when the prophet Samuel instructed Saul to completely destroy the Amalekites. God had put the Amalekites under a ban for their previous attempt to destroy Israel (Exodus 17:14; Deuteronomy 25:17-18). Through Samuel, God instructed Saul that neither the Amalekites nor their possessions were to be retained (1 Samuel 15:3).

True to form, Saul defeated the Amalekites but kept their king as well as the best of their livestock. When Samuel confronted him for his compromise, Saul justified himself by saying he had preserved the livestock to be used as an offering to God (1 Samuel 15:15); thus came Samuel's stinging rebuke,

> *Has the Lord as great delight in burnt offerings and sacrifices, as in obeying the voice of the Lord? Behold, to obey is better than sacrifice, and to listen than the fat of rams. For rebellion is as the sin of divination, and presumption is as iniquity and idolatry. Because you have rejected the word of the Lord, He has also rejected you from being king* (1 Samuel 15:22-23).

Saul had allowed what he considered to be good things for Israel to replace what God knew was best for Israel. How easily any of us might do the same. Consider, for example, God's declared priority for us in the Great Commandment. We are to love God with our whole hearts (Matthew 22:36-40). Nevertheless, we can become so busy doing things for God that we forget to simply love God. While Martha prepared food for Jesus, Mary sat at His feet being fed by His teaching. Jesus declared that Mary chose the better portion (Luke 10:42b). When we—like Martha—allow good works to get in the way of loving God more each day, those works can become a stumbling block and a snare to our spirituality.

The world offers thousands of good things that can draw us away from God's best. Religious options, too numerous to count, fill the earth as alternatives for true knowledge of God through Jesus Christ. Philosophical ideas, wrapped in partial truths, divert the masses from knowing the One who is the Truth. The pursuit of riches and personal enjoyments—often good in and of themselves—can distract people from God, who is our Best.

Respond

1. Consider all of the good things God has given you. List the top three, based on what first comes to mind, and take time to thank God for them.

....

....

....

....

2. Boldly ask God to reveal to you any good things that have become an enemy of the best and record them below.

....

....

....

....

✱ 3. What do you think Samuel meant by, ". . . to obey is better than sacrifice" (1 Samuel 15:22)? How might you apply that to your life today?

....

Pray

Lord, search my heart and life and reveal any good things that are getting in the way of Your best. Give me the grace to repent and to surrender my all to You. Draw me close and guide me to know You more and to love You more each day. Amen.

Impact

Your relationships, experiences, talents, and spiritual gifts all come together to make a unique *you*. You have the ability to help others in a manner that nobody else can. Commit to being your best and take a bold step to serve others in the way you know best.

Close

One of the *best* things you can do for yourself is remain in God's Book. That's why we produced Bible in 90 Days Plus, to make the Word of God more accessible in our fast-paced world. Don't let the many good things in your day crowd out the best!

Day 21 · **No Quick Fixes**

There are no shortcuts to character development. This truth will show up again and again as you travel through the Bible and note the growth its characters develop over time. You will also find daily opportunity to glean insights, to gain ground for your own spiritual growth. Nothing could be more important, but few things take more time. To this end, we now turn our attention to the life of David. When this young shepherd boy was anointed king, he likely had no idea of all that he would need to go through to be fit for the task to which God had called him.

Read

You have two reading options: read the full selection of Scripture or a single overview chapter each day.

- Full Reading: 1 Samuel 20:18 – 2 Samuel 3:21
- Overview Chapter: 1 Samuel 26

Reflect

Motivated by jealousy and rage for the man with whom God would replace him as king, Saul mustered his troops to attack and kill David. Notice, though, that it was David who was twice given the opportunity—but opted out—to kill King Saul (1 Samuel 24, 26). Why was David so gracious? Given the circumstances, wouldn't David have been justified in taking Saul's life? David had done nothing wrong; he had served Saul faithfully time and again. Furthermore, God had confirmed on many fronts that David was to become the next king. Why should he not simply speed the process along by killing Saul?

David refused to become an opportunist who jumped at every chance to advance himself rather than trust in God. A little history will help us to understand David's viewpoint. Remember that God was intensely reluctant to grant Israel a king in the first place; nevertheless, at the people's insistence, God gave in but warned them of the negative consequences that would follow. He then instructed Samuel to anoint Saul as their first king (1 Samuel 9). David, thus, rightly recognized Saul as God's anointed king until God chose to remove Saul from the throne (1 Samuel 24:6; 26:9-11). Before long, King Saul failed to obey God and Samuel informed the king that his reign would soon end because God had chosen a new king who would honor Him from his heart (1 Samuel 13:14; 15:26). Later, Samuel anointed David to become that next king but did not tell him when the transition would occur. David knew that he would need to wait for Saul's rule to come to an end.

The Bible tells us that God has the ability not only to move the heart of a king (Proverbs 21:1) but to remove and replace a king (Psalm 75:7; Daniel

Coaching Tip

One of the important reasons to keep focused and disciplined as you read every day is that this experience can help you develop the practice, as needed, of a daily time with God. Begin thinking now about how your life may be changed and your character may grow if, even after this 90-day read, you continue to spend about an hour a day in God's presence through prayer and Bible reading.

2:21). David simply waited for God to fulfill His promises. Indeed, at the right time, God would remove Saul (1 Samuel 28:17-19; 31); but until then, David needed to grow and mature. Just a teenager when first anointed by Samuel, David was likely between age 18 and 20 when he killed Goliath. He served Saul for four years, wandered in the desert for four years, and lived in the country of the Philistines an additional year and four months. Finally, at the age of thirty, he was ready to serve as king over Judah. Thirty, in Israelite culture, was the age a person was considered mature enough to enter public service.

What some may have considered wasted time was actually David's training time. He was placed in God's school to be refined and strengthened for his role as shepherd-king over Israel. David's example reminds us that character doesn't grow overnight. Just as a seed that is dug up prematurely cannot germinate, so a life that is removed from earthly challenges cannot reach its full potential. We may be looking for quick fixes and easy outs, but God loves us with a perfect love and knows what training we need to fulfill our best potential for His glory.

Respond

1. Do you usually look for the easiest path in life, or do you tend to see life's challenges as God's instruments for your growth? Explain.

✱ 2. Read Hebrews 5:8. Why do you think that Christ, the sinless God-man, needed difficulties for His personal growth to maturity?

3. Was there a time when you tried to take a shortcut in life that in the end took more time than would have been required had you done the right thing in the first place? Explain.

....

....

....

....

Pray

Lord, forgive me for so often looking for an easy way out of life's challenges rather than seeking You in prayer for the best way forward, even if it takes time. Use every trial in my life for Your glory, and help me to be faithful, always trusting You from my heart.

Impact

We live in a society driven by a "quick fix" mentality. Scripture Awakening aims to grow people deep and strong in their faith through reading, studying, and learning to live the Scriptures: the real fix. To this end, we are developing programs continuously even as you enjoy them this year. We cannot keep ahead of the curve, however, without the prayer support of those who believe with us in the power of Scripture.

Close

Our hope is to inspire and challenge you to read ALL of God's Word for yourself. There is no quick or easy way to do so, but as with so many of the most important aspects of life, it is eternally worthwhile. Hang in there!

Session 4 • Overview

● REVIEW Days 15-21
History, Part 1: Conquest, Cycles, Transition

 Now is the time for your small group meeting to review the week's Scripture readings, cover the discussion questions, and watch the Essential Snapshot video together (or by yourself if reading alone). Point your mobile device's camera on the QR code to access the video entitled "Session 4: Morality Unmasked". Or enter this link into your browser: **ScriptureAwakening.com/plus/**

- Discuss the questions marked by an asterisk (✱) from the **Respond** sections in Days 15-21, perhaps adding others if time permits.
- Watch the Session 4 video* (individually or with a small group).
  1. What insights from the video would you like to explore further?
  2. Do you think the general human sense of right and wrong is evidence of a higher moral being (God)? Why or why not?
- Summarize the Preview (below) of what is coming next week, encouraging group members to read it on their own.

*Facilitators note: In order to watch the Essential Snapshot video with your group, you will need a large video monitor, if meeting in-person. If hosting a small group remotely, use Zoom (or similar service) to stream the video from your device to share with group participants.

● PREVIEW Days 22-28
History, Part 2: Division, Decline, Destruction

Weekly Reading: 2 Samuel 3:22 to 1 Chronicles 5:26

Summary

The unified kingdom reaches its zenith under David and Solomon. Internal stresses, however, fracture the kingdom along tribal lines. Despite repeated prophetic warnings, both the Northern and Southern Kingdoms continue their disobedience to the Covenant, leading to decline and ultimately their complete destruction by Assyria and Babylon.

Books You'll Encounter This Week

2 Samuel Overview (Conclusion)

David's reign begins well as he reunites the kingdom. His military victories strengthen and expand the nation. Tragically, his grave sins open the door for conflict within his family and give way to civil war within the kingdom.

1 Kings Overview

The book opens with the reign of Solomon—the era of Israel's peak prosperity, influence, and worldwide recognition. During the first half of his reign, he completes the construction of a magnificent temple and an elegant palace.

Despite the blessings of wealth and wisdom from God, Solomon is corrupted by the world and the errant faiths of his wives and concubines. At his death, the kingdom becomes divided into the northern (Israel) and the southern (Judah) kingdoms.

2 Kings Overview

Focusing on the kings of the divided kingdom, 2 Kings describes their repeated disobedience to the Covenant, the resultant decline of the nation, and the eventual exile of the people.

In the north, all of Israel's 20 kings fail to follow the Lord. Even Elijah's and Elisha's prophetic ministries cannot halt the decline or prevent the nation's demise and captivity by the Assyrians.

Likewise, in the southern kingdom of Judah, only 8 of the 19 kings and 1 queen follow the Lord. Judah suffers a similar fate at the hands of the Babylonians 136 years after Israel's defeat. Ultimately, Jerusalem and its Temple lie in ruins while her people languish in exile.

1 Chronicles Overview (Introduction)

This book covers much of the same ground as 2 Samuel but from a different perspective. Written after Judah returns from exile, its tenor is meant to encourage the returnees by highlighting the more positive aspects of the era of the kings.

1 Chronicles begins with a detailed genealogy going all the way back to Adam, reminding the people that they are part of God's eternal plan as recorded in Scripture's wondrous story of redemption. The reign of David will be covered next week in a similarly glorious manner.

Things to Look for This Week

As you read, consider:

1. King David responds properly to Nathan's rebuke with confession and repentance. In contrast, many subsequent kings, when confronted by other prophets, harden their hearts.

2. How the "sin of Jeroboam" (1 Kings 12:25-33; 13:33-34) (the establishment of a counterfeit religious system) causes him and all his successors to do "evil in the sight of the LORD" (1 Kings 15:34).

3. The divided kingdoms should have trusted in the Lord and walked in His ways. Instead, each placed their confidence in military might, political alliances, and economic influence. The result was disastrous.

Supplemental Material

As you read this week and as time permits, fill in the table on *Patterns in 1 and 2 Kings* found in Appendix 3 on page 327.

Day 22 · **Truth or Consequences**

Have you ever thought about just how fragile the international economy and infrastructure really are? We are connected to a global economy, and one international catastrophe could bring us to our knees overnight. Ironically, "on our knees" is exactly where we should be spending time each day. When we ignore God's truth, we may face serious consequences. This fact becomes obvious when we look at some of King David's bad decisions and the consequences that followed them.

Read

You have two reading options: read the full selection of Scripture or a single overview chapter each day.

- Full Reading: 2 Samuel 3:22–16
- Overview Chapter: 2 Samuel 11

Reflect

Everything was going well for David: the kingdom was united, major enemies had been defeated, and his armies were once again off to battle. In 2 Samuel 11—with no apparent concern about consequences—David committed adultery with Bathsheba. He then tried to cover up his sin by ensuring that Bathsheba's husband, Uriah, would die in battle. Confronted later by Nathan the prophet, David repented. His confession is written for us in Psalm 51. It is sincere and from the heart; nevertheless, there were consequences. Nathan told the king that the sword would not be taken from his own household; violence would arise from within, and David's wives would be violated publicly. The next several chapters unravel this prediction in painful detail.

When everything is going well, we—like David—are prone to lower the guard over our hearts. We must be careful, for the heart is the place where the most important battles in life are silently won or lost. Unfortunately, many people today seem to assume that God's standards are no longer applicable. In Western culture, for example, Biblical expectations for sexual behavior are often ignored; we see the consequences of this through the erosion of marital bonds and the disintegration of the family unit. As the family collapses, we all lose economically, socially, and spiritually. We become like the Israelites in the days of the Judges when "all the people did whatever seemed right in their own eyes" (Judges 17:6; 21:25 NLT).

David turned back to God and cried out for mercy. Had he not repented, he may have lost his kingdom forever. Accepting the punishments foretold by Nathan, David sought to live out the remainder of his days for the Lord. Eventually, David's son, Absalom, forced David to flee Jerusalem and took the throne. Weeping on the Mount of Olives, David became a symbol of

Coaching Tip

It is important, as you continue your reading, to be honest with yourself and others. Are you reading just to complete the project, or are you reading in order to know, love, and honor your Lord? Ask God to help you make the latter your goal.

Christ, who later wept there also. David wept for his own transgressions; Christ wept for ours. Jesus bore the consequences for our sins on the cross so that grace and forgiveness could be offered to David and to everyone who believes. Still, sin always leaves consequences in its turbulent wake. That it did so in David's life reminds us to live in a way that honors God.

Respond

✱ 1. Do you think God was too harsh on David for his sin with Bathsheba and against Uriah? See 2 Samuel 12:10-12. Explain.

....

....

....

....

2. Would it be a good thing if there were no consequences for our actions? Why or why not?

....

....

....

....

3. Ask God to show you if there are any aspects of His truth that you need to face more squarely. Record your thoughts. Bring these concerns to the foot of the cross, turn away from them, and claim the Lord's forgiveness.

....

....

....

....

Pray

Lord, make me aware of the hurt caused to myself and others when I violate Your will for my life. Help me to be more honest with myself going forward, knowing my actions do have consequences. Temper that awareness with my amazement that You, the sinless One, love me still. Amen.

Impact

Like David, we each have our own weaknesses. If we are wise, we will invite others to help us perceive our personal blind spots in order that we might avoid mistakes we could later regret. If you don't have someone who can offer such insight for your life, then pray and ask God to provide such a person.

Close

Even though King David was a flawed man, God still described him as "a man after his own heart" (1 Samuel 13:14). Despite his flaws, David finished well, and that is exactly what you will discover in tomorrow's lesson. See you then!

Coaching Tip

James tells us that the Word is like a mirror, given to help us see ourselves accurately (James 1:23-25). As you read, ask God to enable you to see yourself as He sees you, that He might bring change where you need it.

Day 23 · Finishing Well

When you think of David's life, does it stand before you as one of honor or one of shame? Clearly his legacy is one of honor. His Psalms have been enjoyed by Christians for two thousand years as some of the most beautiful religious poems ever written; they draw us closer to God. His shepherd's heart and heroic exploits have been the fodder for Sunday school lessons and inspirational sermons. Even his mistakes are retold for our benefit as lessons for life. David's reputation has remained almost stellar despite his mistakes. Why is that? It is because he was a man after God's own heart (1 Samuel 13:14; Acts 13:22). By looking at his life, we can examine our own, gaining insights for both living and finishing well.

Read

You have two reading options: read the full selection of Scripture or a single overview chapter each day.

- Full Reading: 2 Samuel 17 – 1 Kings 1
- Overview Chapter: 2 Samuel 24

Reflect

David, whose early years were framed by the idyllic life of a shepherd, became a man of violence and warfare in his later years. Through it all, the man called to become a shepherd-king over Israel made his share of mistakes. As a monarch over many, each mistake impacted thousands. Near the end of his 40 year reign when he disobeyed God's instructions by taking a census of the people, for example, God sent a devastating plague (2 Samuel 24). As we think today about the lives lost in that plague, we will also ponder how David's good reputation remained intact.

The Census. When David had once again united the northern and southern kingdoms, it was natural for him to want to know how many able warriors were under his charge. A parallel incident occurred centuries earlier when Moses, after delivering the people out of Egypt, was naturally curious about the number of people who remained. Moses had been trained by the Egyptians, who had a love for statistical analysis. God gave Moses the stipulation that if a census was to be taken, each person numbered must give the sum of ½ shekel to the Temple—the equivalent of about five dollars in our day. This small amount served not as our modern idea of a tax but rather as a reminder that each person was equal in the sight of God and that God was to remain first priority in their lives. It was a sign of God's atonement, or covering, for their sin; a way in which each person numbered could say, "Lord, I am Yours." The census thus became an act of worship. God warned Moses that if a census was taken without this symbolic reminder of God's atonement, He would send a plague as punishment (Exodus 30:11-16).

The Confession. David initiated his census and shortly afterward his conscience began to bother him. He knew he had done wrong in trying to discern how many warriors he had (2 Samuel 24:10). In reality, he had none: the nation was God's. He was called as a shepherd to serve God's people not as an overlord to own them. Once again, as with his previous sins, David humbled himself and repented.

None of us will go through this life without making mistakes. If we humble ourselves as David did, repenting for and turning away from our sins, however, we can stand before God as His forgiven and beloved children. David developed a heart for God in his youth and continued to receive correction from God throughout his life; his heart remained true to the Lord until he breathed his last. He left a legacy that we would do well to honor and follow. A heart set on knowing and pleasing God is the key to finishing well.

Respond

1. Thinking about your life thus far, do you feel that you've given God your best? Why or why not?

✱ 2. Make a short list of several things that you most want to be remembered for. What will matter in the end—when you meet God face-to-face?

3. Ask yourself, "If this were my last day on earth, how would I use it to prepare for eternity?" Record your thoughts, then commit to living each day as though it were your last (Matthew 24:44).

....

....

....

Pray

Lord, show me any areas of sinful compromise in my life and help me to live each day faithfully, as though it could be my last. Amen.

Impact

You influence others every day. Is that influence for better or for worse? You can make a positive impact on others by taking a few minutes to share with others, either in person or on social media, how either Scripture or this study is impacting you life.

Close

Congrats! Day 23 is done. Tomorrow we'll look at David's son Solomon, and what kind of "successor" he was to his father's throne.

Day 24 · **The Summit of Success**

Israel had reached her zenith. It had been 480 years since Moses led the people out of Egypt. Now—finally—the nation was settled peacefully in the Land of Promise. King Solomon's reign brought Israel into a golden era with achievements in the nation's economy, politics, art, architecture, literature, wisdom, learning, and probably every measure of societal flourishing a people could hope for. To what can we credit such developments? And how might we follow Solomon's example to ensure good success in our lives?

Read

You have two reading options: read the full selection of Scripture or a single overview chapter each day.

- Full Reading: 1 Kings 2–10
- Overview Chapter: 1 Kings 3

Reflect

When we read and reflect on King Solomon's life, we discover at least three keys he used to open the door to a good, successful life. Each key is accessible to us:

1. King Solomon honored the godly legacy of those who lived before him. He embraced the history and practices of his father David as well as his spiritual ancestors including Joshua, Moses, and those all the way back to Abraham. They shared a common love for the Word, which, if obeyed, brought promise of good success (Joshua 1:7-9). In the same manner, we can imitate the lives of David and those who went before him, along with godly ancestors in our more immediate lineage, to enjoy our own success. As we do so, blessings can be carried forward to our children and grandchildren.

It is informative to note studies that have been done about the legacy of the godly. Take, for example, the prominent pastor and theologian of the eighteenth century, Jonathan Edwards. When looking forward through 5 generations, his legacy includes: a U.S. Vice-President, a dean of a law school, a dean of a medical school, 3 U.S. Senators, 3 governors, 3 mayors, 13 college presidents, 30 judges, 60 doctors, 65 professors, 75 military officers, 80 public office holders, 100 lawyers, 100 clergymen, and 285 college graduates.

In contrast, we may note the legacy of Max Jukes who lived in New York at about the same period as Edwards but who was idle, irreverent, and an alcoholic. Those who came from his family line included 7 murderers, 60 thieves, 190 prostitutes, 150 other convicts, 310 paupers, and 440 who were physically wrecked by addiction to alcohol. Of the 1,200 descendants that

Coaching Tip

As you read, remember that what matters most is not how much you know the Bible, but how well you obey it.

were studied, 300 died prematurely.[1] We cannot choose our past, but we can find within it examples of godliness and embrace their heritage to create a legacy for those who will follow us.

2. King Solomon sought to serve rather than to be served. In 1 Kings 3, when God appeared in a dream and offered to give him anything he chose, Solomon asked for wisdom to serve God and God's people well. In response, God gave him not only wisdom but riches, honor, and good success with it. The king's humility foreshadowed our Lord's who "came not to be served but to serve" (Matthew 20:28). Those who attempt to climb the mountain of opportunity are less likely to fall if they keep their heads low and their eyes on the path.

3. Solomon sought the presence of God. He gave himself tirelessly to the building of the Temple, after which he carefully brought the Ark of God's presence into it. In response, God appeared in glory as in days of old (1 Kings 8:10-11), bringing a blessing over the king and the nation. We too can cultivate the presence of God through active engagement in a good church, which is God's Temple today (Ephesians 2:20-22, 1 Peter 2:5), and by establishing altars of family and personal devotion.

Respond

✱ 1. How do you measure success?

2. Think of times in your life when you experienced success. What were the key ingredients?

---

[1] https://www.jacksonsun.com/story/life/faith/2014/10/10/legacy-leaving-family/17054141/. While the tracing of ancestors so far back is not an exact science, this and other sources confirm the principle of the influence of our lives on our progeny.

3. Reflect on the three keys to Solomon's success as suggested above, and record practical things you can do to posture yourself for good success from a Biblical point of view.

....

....

....

....

Pray

Lord, forgive me for focusing more on my agenda than on Yours. Show me what You consider success to be in the things that really matter. Help me to follow in the steps of Christ, who was faithful to the end. Amen.

Impact

Think of a time when someone's words of encouragement really helped you to press on and to achieve more for God. Now think of someone who really could use encouragement and reach out to that person. You may never see the results of your kind word or deed but pray and believe that God will use it in that person's life, somehow.

Close

Today, success . . . tomorrow, failure. Solomon, like his father David, had it all. But as we shall see on Day 25, it all came crashing down because of wrong desires and poor decisions.

Coaching Tip

You are more than ¼ of the way through the Bible. Sometimes we may struggle to maintain daily time with God due to physical or spiritual obstacles. Consider asking family or friends to pray that you stay on track to complete this journey.

Day 25 · **The Footpath of Failure**

Although known for his great wisdom, Solomon dealt with his share of failures in his later years. As a result of his poor choices, the kingdom of Israel became divided and suffered a period of decline and eventually collapsed. How did this happen? His idolatry occurred one step at a time as the king walked down the footpath of failure. The Bible provides an account of his grievous mistakes that we might avoid them in our own lives.

Read

You have two reading options: read the full selection of Scripture or a single overview chapter each day.

- Full Reading: 1 Kings 11–21
- Overview Chapter: 1 Kings 11

Reflect

The summary of Solomon's errors is given for our reflection: "Solomon . . . did not wholly follow the Lord, as David his father had done" (1 Kings 11:6). He seemed to forget about the advice he himself had given to his people early in his reign, "Let your heart therefore be wholly true to the Lord our God, walking in his statutes and keeping his commandments . . ." (1 Kings 8:61). Solomon took wives for himself from foreign countries to build political alliances. Over time, these women turned his heart away from God. Seeking to keep them happy, he established altars for worship to their gods (1 Kings 11:1-8). It all resulted from making one bad choice after another until Solomon led the entire nation into spiritual degradation. Future leaders followed in Solomon's wayward path and led Israel into an eventual exile.

Leadership Failures. Following Solomon's death, the united kingdom of Israel became divided, with 10 of the tribes coalescing in northern Israel. Israel was led by a succession of 19 kings until it fell to the Assyrians in 722 BC. Not one of Israel's kings followed God. In the southern kingdom of Judah, however, 8 kings were considered mostly good (Asa, Jehoshaphat, Joash, Amaziah, Azariah, Jotham, Hezekiah, Josiah), and a ninth—Manasseh—repented near the end of his life. Overall, Judah was influenced by a lineup of 20 rulers, most of them dishonoring to God, until it was laid waste by the Babylonians in 586 BC.

The Downward Descent. The kings of both Israel and Judah carried behind them the long history of godly leaders including Abraham, Isaac, Jacob, Joseph, Moses, Joshua, Samuel, and David. How could people with such a rich lineage—that had been supplemented by the stunning history of God's miraculous acts—so easily put aside their heritage? For Solomon and the 39 kings who followed him, it was as simple as turning away from

God. The book of Kings is the story of 40 leaders whose lives provide a warning for us today. As the first to fall, Solomon set a pattern for all who followed. Forgetting all that God had done for him, he began to live by his own wisdom. Not remembering how much he once depended on God's help, he began trusting in his own strength. Unaware that God was watching his every action, he disregarded God's standards. We could wish such a foolish turning away from God would never happen again.

Respond

1. Do you find it hard to believe that someone as wise as Solomon could fail so miserably in the end? Why or why not?

✱ 2. What steps could Solomon have taken to guard his heart and stay right with God?

3. Examine your own life. In what ways are you most prone to step away from God's declared will? What steps will you take to avoid the footpath of failure?

Pray

Almighty God, thank you for giving us—through the stories of 40 Hebraic kings—40 reasons to walk the pathway of humble obedience. Help me to walk that pathway every day; discipline me quickly if I begin to veer so that I might remain true to You until the end. Amen.

Impact

The vast majority of people who find salvation in Christ do so before the age of 13. Take a few minutes to pray for the ministry of Scripture Awakening to impact children's lives through family gatherings around God's Word and prayer.

Close

The downward spiral of faltering kings may be depressing, yet God is faithful by raising up more powerful prophets for His people and nation, as we'll see tomorrow. Stay tuned.

Day 26 · **The Greatest Power**

Elijah and Elisha are two of the greatest prophets of the Old Testament. Their lives and ministries were marked by dramatic prophecies, powerful encounters, and miracles. When Elijah was swept into Heaven by a fiery chariot, Elisha received a double portion of Elijah's anointing. One might think it cannot get any better than that, but it can—even for you and me. Each of us, whether leader or learner, rich or poor, young or old, has access to the power of *obedience*. Today, as we study the lives of these two prophets, we will see why obedience is the greatest power of all.

Read

You have two reading options: read the full selection of Scripture or a single overview chapter each day.

- Full Reading: 1 Kings 22 – 2 Kings 9
- Overview Chapter: 2 Kings 5

Reflect

God has demonstrated His great power and authority on earth in special measure at important times in the unfolding drama of redemptive history. The deliverance of Israel from Egypt came with great signs and wonders; the preservation of God's people in the desert was only possible through the miraculous provision of God; and the Israelites followed Joshua into Canaan and defeated their enemies through the outstretched hand of God's strength. Once they settled in the Promised Land, they fell into sin, and God's supernatural manifestations of power became a warning to them rather than to the nations they had conquered. In other words, those who obeyed God benefited from God's great power, and those who disobeyed God experienced punishment.

What could be more important than the power to obey God? This question and the truth behind it are highlighted by the story of Naaman, the captain of the army of the king of Syria (2 Kings 5). Naaman was a leper. Coming to Elisha for help, he was told to bathe himself in the Jordan River seven times. At first, Naaman's pride caused him to resist the instruction. He then humbled himself and obeyed. Immediately, his skin was fully restored. He gratefully sought to give a gift to Elijah in appreciation for his recovery. Elijah appropriately refused to accept a personal reward for God's miraculous act. However, Elijah's servant, Gehazi, having observed his refusal, secretly approached Naaman and received the gift of money and clothing for himself.

The problem Gehazi faced is the problem we all face when we disobey God: there are no secrets before the all-seeing Ruler of the Universe. Gehazi and his descendants were stricken with the very leprosy that had been removed

Coaching Tip

Sometimes we come to passages and stories in the Bible that seem puzzling or confusing. Take note of such passages. Clarity might come to you through group discussion, through your ongoing readings, or upon completion of your read through the Bible and engagement in further study.

from the foreign leader. Obedience is the fulcrum by which God's power works for or against us, whether immediately or over the course of time.

By the standards we know in Western culture, the punishment on Elisha's servant may seem severe. But the story of Naaman and Gehazi was a visual warning of Israel's plight. God's people must either decide to clean up their act, repent, and turn from their sins or face the mighty judgment of God. A fate far worse than leprosy was about to come upon them if they didn't heed the message of God's prophets. God's powerful hand would be turned against them instead of yielding the support they had received for most of their long history.

Many Christians today long for fresh, powerful encounters and miracles; they hope for the days of Elijah and Elisha. But do we really understand those days and their implications for our lives? If so, we will ask God for the power to obey Him. Whether or not we see signs and wonders as occurred through the hands of Elijah and Elisha will be of secondary concern. Yes, God does miracles even today. But the power to choose obedience is the miracle we need above all, the most essential power in the world.

Respond

1. If a prophet like Elijah or Elisha appeared today, do you think the whole nation would fall on its knees and get right with God? Why or why not?

✱ 2. What sins did Gehazi commit in 2 Kings 5? What can we learn from his mistakes?

3. Pray for God's grace to take the message of Elijah and Elisha to heart personally and to help others do the same. In some ways, does Gehazi's sinful behavior foreshadow the sins God's people committed leading to their exile? Explain.

....

....

....

....

....

Pray

Lord, when You came to earth demonstrating miracles, signs, and wonders, only a remnant believed and followed You. So it is today. Help me to be in that remnant. And show me how to reach out in love, calling others to follow You with hearts of humility and obedience. Amen.

Impact

The Scripture Awakening team is always working on new projects to expand the impact of God's Word in people's lives around the world. Their ability to do so depends on the prayers of others. As God moves your heart, pray for someone else to come to know God and to grow in their faith.

Close

Wow—Elijah and Elisha were just amazing! And we hope you're discovering just how truly amazing God's Word is in your life through Bible in 90 Days Plus. Tomorrow we'll read another incredible story about Isaiah and Hezekiah that you won't want to miss.

Coaching Tip

Certain key stories in the Bible are repeated and restated in other parts of the Bible to give us a fuller picture of what occurred. If you have time after today's reading, compare it with the account in Isaiah 38.

Day 27 · **Touching God's Heart**

Hezekiah was one of the godly kings in Judah's line of rulers. He eradicated idol worship and sought to please God. He loved God and knew how to touch the heart of God. By studying Hezekiah's life, we can learn to do the same.

Read

You have two reading options: read the full selection of Scripture or a single overview chapter each day.

- Full Reading: 2 Kings 10–20
- Overview Chapter: 2 Kings 20

Reflect

Hezekiah, the thirteenth king of Judah, was one of the few kings in the nation who sought to please God. The meaning of his name, "God strengthens," describes the experience of his life. He often cried out to God for help and prevailed even when the entire world seemed to be against him. God moved with great and miraculous power to answer the king's prayers because Hezekiah knew how to touch God's heart. He did so through bold, passionate prayers, backed by the deliberate living of a godly life.

Hezekiah boldly eradicated idolatry from Israel; he even destroyed the high places used for idol worship. We read in 2 Kings 20, nevertheless, that Hezekiah became mortally ill (a parallel account is found in Isaiah 38). Isaiah the prophet told him,

> *Thus says the LORD, "Set your house in order, for you shall die; you shall not recover." (2 Kings 20:1c)*

Isaiah dismissed himself from Hezekiah's presence, and the king wept bitterly, reminding the Lord that he had served Him with a whole heart. Before Isaiah had passed through the middle court of the palace, the Lord told the prophet to turn around and let Hezekiah know that He had heard Hezekiah's prayer: God would heal Hezekiah and extend his life by 15 years. God also promised that Jerusalem, which at the time was surrounded and under siege by Assyria, would be miraculously delivered. Considering the greatness of the Assyrian army and the record of their former exploits, this deliverance was even more phenomenal than was the healing of the king. As if all of this was not enough, Hezekiah was given a sign that he would be healed; the shadow on his sun dial would move backward 10 degrees.

The supporting archaeological and extra-Biblical documentation of Hezekiah's reign, of the invasion by Assyria, of their failure to overtake Jerusalem, and dozens of other key elements in the Biblical text all point us to amazing answers to Hezekiah's prayers. We have every reason to believe that these things actually happened. And they may also cause us to ask whether such powerful answers to prayer could happen again in our day. The answer may be found in a hundred promises of Scripture and in our lives when we learn how to touch the heart of God.

Respond

1. Have you ever experienced a time when your heart-felt prayers seemed to move the heart of God? Explain.

✱ 2. As you read the story of Hezekiah, what encourages or challenges your faith?

3. Pray now for a heart like Hezekiah's, one that can touch the heart of God. Record any insights God may have given you as you prayed for such a heart.

Pray

Gracious God, help me to live as wholeheartedly for You as Hezekiah did—able to move You and bless You. Use me to help many turn back to You as well. Amen.

Impact

Like Hezekiah, you may have passions or burdens God has laid on your heart. Pray for God's guidance about how you can act upon them today.

Close

Have you ever lost your patience and felt like you've had enough? Did you know that even God has felt the same way and declared, "Enough!" Day 28's lesson will be an eye-opener for sure.

Day 28 · **When God Says "Enough"**

There comes a time when a people engage in heinous activity for so long, continually refusing God's warnings about resultant judgment, that God says, "Enough." Such was the case for Judah before she was destroyed by invading armies. After the reign of wicked King Manasseh, God told Jeremiah, "Though Moses and Samuel stood before me, yet my heart would not turn toward this people" (Jeremiah 15:1). God likewise told Ezekiel, ". . . when a land sins against me by acting faithlessly, and I stretch out my hand against it . . . even if these three men, Noah, Daniel, and Job, were in it, they would deliver but their own lives by their righteousness, declares the LORD God" (Ezekiel 14:13-14).

Read

You have two reading options: read the full selection of Scripture or a single overview chapter each day.

- Full Reading: 2 Kings 21 – 1 Chronicles 5
- Overview Chapter: 2 Kings 21

Reflect

We have noted that during Hezekiah's reign, God postponed His judgment on Judah and Jerusalem. But Hezekiah's son and successor, Manasseh, brought more wickedness upon the nation than anyone before him. Reigning longer than any of Judah's previous kings, Manasseh promoted idolatry throughout his kingdom, built pagan temples, and even sacrificed one of his sons in the fire to Moloch. Having endured several hundred years of rebelliousness in the hearts of His people, God said, "Enough"!

The prophets warned that because of Manasseh's wickedness, God would "wipe Jerusalem as one wipes a dish, wiping it and turning it upside down" (2 Kings 21:13b). Manasseh's son Amon reigned a mere two years before he was murdered, and his son Josiah began to reign at eight years of age. Josiah repaired the Temple, discovered the book of the Law, and—based on God's Word, led a religious reformation throughout the country. He eradicated all pagan idols and instituted a Passover that honored God more than any since the days of the Judges (2 Kings 23:22). So complete was his reform and so dedicated was his heart that Scripture says, "before him there was no king like him, who turned to the LORD with all his heart and with all his soul and with all his might, according to all the Law of Moses, nor did any like him arise after him" (2 Kings 23:25).

One would think that such circumstances would cause God to forestall the coming judgment on Judah. But the next verse tells us otherwise: "Still the LORD did not turn from the burning of his great wrath, by which his anger was kindled against Judah, because of all the provocations with which

Coaching Tip

This reading and the next contain a lot of genealogical lists. If you find it difficult to pronounce names as you read, it may help to listen to these lists being read through one of the many free online Bible programs, such as BibleGateway.com.

Manasseh had provoked him" (2 Kings 23:26). The four kings who followed Josiah were all evil. In 597 BC, the Babylonians swept down upon Jerusalem and captured it. A second attack occurred in 586 BC, and later that year the city, as well as its Temple were utterly destroyed.

What can we learn about the line of no return? Simply this: Don't cross it. And if you don't know where it is, stay far from it—keep it beyond your horizon. Rather than tempt fate by testing God's limits, follow God's commands and love God, ensuring that you'll never hear God say, "Enough." This applies to individuals, groups of people, and entire nations.

Respond

1. Can you think of any practical reason(s) why God finally sent His people into exile?

✱ 2. Do you think God judges nations today as He did Judah and Israel? Why or why not?

3. What steps might a person—or an entire nation—take to avoid ever experiencing God's "enough"?

Pray

Lord, be merciful. We live in a day and age when people question Your existence and have little concern about Your judgment. Turn our nation back to righteousness and the people of this land back to humility, love, truth, and obedience to Your Word. Amen.

Impact

The vision of Scripture Awakening is to assist, support, and work alongside God's people to help foster an awakening around God's Word. This is the surest way we can stand far from the spiritual danger zone where God says, "Enough." We hope you will stick with Scripture Awakening through the years to grow in your knowledge of the Word and to help others do the same!

Close

Do you realize that you have almost finished the first third of your 90-day journey through B90+? Feels good, huh? Congratulations! So, do you like lists? Apparently God does, as we'll see tomorrow on Day 29.

Session 5 • Overview

● REVIEW Days 21-28
History, Part 2: Division, Decline, Destruction

 Now is the time for your small group meeting to review the week's Scripture readings, cover the discussion questions, and watch the Essential Snapshot video together (or by yourself if reading alone). Point your mobile device's camera on the QR code to access the video entitled "Session 5: God's Presence". Or enter this link into your browser: **ScriptureAwakening.com/plus/**

- Discuss the questions marked by an asterisk (✱) from the **Respond** sections in Days 21-28, perhaps adding others if time permits.
- Watch the Session 5 video* (individually or with a small group).
    1. What insights from the video would you like to explore further?
    2. Do you often find yourself yearning to see more of God's glory? Why do you think God doesn't choose to reveal His full glory every day for everyone?
- Summarize the Preview (below) of what is coming next week, encouraging group members to read it on their own.

*Facilitators note: In order to watch the Essential Snapshot video with your group, you will need a large video monitor, if meeting in-person. If hosting a small group remotely, use Zoom (or similar service) to stream the video from your device to share with group participants.

● PREVIEW Days 29-35
History, Part 3: Return, Reconstruction, Restoration

Weekly Reading: 1 Chronicles 6:1 to Esther 10:3

Summary

The reign of David and Solomon over a unified kingdom climaxes in the construction of a magnificent temple. Tragically, Solomon's sin opens the way for the kingdom's division. The new southern kingdom of Judah is led by a succession of both "good" and "bad" kings, perpetuating its ultimate destruction by the Babylonians and the exile of its people.

Following the Persians conquest of the Babylonians, Zerubbabel, Ezra, and Nehemiah each lead a remnant back to Jerusalem. They rebuild the Temple, encourage the people to be faithful to God, and reconstruct the walls of Jerusalem. Strikingly, God uses the faithfulness of a young girl, Esther, and her uncle to thwart a diabolical plot against the Jews who remain behind in exile.

Books You'll Encounter This Week

1 Chronicles Overview (Conclusion)

Continuing our readings from last week, we see how David consolidates his reign over all the tribes. His military victories over neighboring enemies expand the kingdom and strengthen his rule. David's desire to build a permanent "house" for God is answered by God's promise to use his successor not only to build David's house but to establish his throne forever.

In preparation for the fulfillment of God's promises, David makes preparations for the construction of the Temple and organizes the Levites and priests to lead its worship. His reign concludes with the transition to Solomon's reign.

2 Chronicles Overview

2 Chronicles covers much of the same ground as 1 and 2 Kings. Like 1 Chronicles, it was written to encourage the returning exiles.

Focusing on Solomon and his successor's rule over the southern kingdom of Judah, the book emphasizes the "good" kings who model their reigns after that of David. The Temple is given a prominent role to reinforce the people's identity as worshipers of a Great God.

Ezra Overview

Cyrus becomes king of Persia and, fulfilling the plan of the Sovereign God of the Nations, releases the exiles to return to Jerusalem. The books of Ezra and Nehemiah recount three waves of returning exiles over the following one hundred years.

The first group comes back under the leadership of Zerubbabel and begins rebuilding the Temple. Local opposition delays the work until prophets Haggai and Zechariah exhort the people to trust in God and complete the job.

Ezra, a teacher "skilled in the Law of Moses" (Ezra 7:6b), arrives several decades later to discover that many Jews had intermarried neighboring peoples despite God's clear directives otherwise. He leads the people to repent and recommit to the Covenant.

Nehemiah Overview

Whereas Ezra was a teacher and scribe, Nehemiah was a skilled administrator and leader. Leading a third wave of God's returning people, Nehemiah organizes and inspires them to rebuild Jerusalem's walls. They miraculously accomplish the task in a short 52 days.

This Old Testament historical narrative concludes with a time marked by spiritual decline that harkens back to the era of the Judges. Despite the determined efforts of both Ezra and Nehemiah to unite the people around God's purposes, something more is clearly needed. The four hundred "silent" years which follow set the stage for the birth of the promised Messiah.

Esther* Overview

Set during the time between the return of Zerubbabel and Ezra, Esther describes events in the Persian capital. An enemy of God, Haman, plots to annihilate the Jews. Young Jewess Esther becomes queen and thwarts Haman's evil plan through God's intervention and the wise council of her uncle, Mordecai.

Things to Look for This Week

As you read, consider how:

1. Chronicles emphasizes God's spiritual rule through the enduring work of the Levites and priests in the Temple in contrast with the declining spiritual condition of the kings who bring the nation down.

2. The reconstructed Temple, gates, and walls of Jerusalem provide hope and encouragement to the returned remnant despite their lack of political autonomy.

3. Although God is never specifically mentioned in the book of Esther, His guiding hand is continually working behind the scenes to orchestrate events and to protect His people.

***Note:** The book of Esther is covered next week in Session 6.*

Day 29 · **Why All of the Lists?**

When we turn to 1 Chronicles, we are confronted with list after list after list. Twelve chapters of lists open the book, in fact. What benefit can possibly be derived from such long and tedious records? The answer can be summarized by two words, as we will see.

Read

You have two reading options: read the full selection of Scripture or a single overview chapter each day.

- Full Reading: 1 Chronicles 6–17
- Overview Chapter: 1 Chronicles 9

Reflect

You drive to the store with a list in your hands of things you want to buy. As you carry your list, you may not be thinking about the many lists around you that quietly help you to fulfill your task. Your car, for example, is comprised of thousands of parts. Each part is listed in parts warehouses and stores worldwide; otherwise, your car would be difficult to repair, and you may end up walking to the store instead. On your car's dashboard is an identification number that is listed on multiple databases through which police know your driving history. Without that number, you might have been less careful on the road and wrecked your vehicle long ago. You safely arrive to the grocery store where you intend to search for products that are listed in government and commercial databases for quality control and delivery system purposes. Without such databases, the shelves would be sparse.

The world functions on lists. The most important lists are of those that focus on people—such as lists of loved ones who have gone before us. This is what we find in 1 Chronicles. We can see why these lists are essential by pondering two words: *appreciation* and *verification*.

Appreciation. The names on the Biblical lists are not imaginary. These names belong to real people whose lives deserve to be remembered. Each person here has a story, and each story is a piece of the great puzzle of Israel's history. Without names, stories, and history, Israel would not exist today.

In the day of its writing, Chronicles carried the names of people whom others knew or had known personally. One reading Chronicles long ago might have been heard to say, "That was my uncle," or "Let me tell you more about great-grandpa." To read these lists in their day would be much like a person visiting a veteran's memorial today. We establish and visit monuments to show gratitude for those who gave life and limb to secure our liberties.

Coaching Tip

If you are doing the Bible overview mode, you might sometimes wonder how much you are missing by reading only one chapter a day. You always have the option of switching to the full Bible reading mode, whether on occasion, or for the remainder of your journey.

Those who visit such monuments may point with tear-filled eyes to the engraved name of someone they love. Lists are important.

Verification. The Hebrews influenced the world with their penchant for record keeping and historical verification. Why? Because, unlike the gods of the surrounding nations, Israel's God spoke into the future with promises and urged people to remember His past works. The nations surrounding Israel also kept lists but not with the strong sense that they were capturing actual space/time events involving people whose stories were part of a larger, chronologically-based plan. For this reason, the Bible is the most historically verifiable document of antiquity. From its earliest days, its stories were recorded and linked to verifiable local, national, and international events. Studies in archaeology and comparative literature have thus become strong supporters of Scripture's great and unbroken story of God's work throughout time. Without the lists in the Bible, Scripture would be considered merely a nice fabrication of what might have occurred in times past based on people's wishes and imaginations.

Respond

1. Think of some of the lists that are most important in your life. Are family genealogical records part of that list? Why or why not?

2. As you read through the lists in 1 Chronicles and in earlier portions of the Bible, what has been your reaction to them?

✱ 3. If someone told you, "Every genealogical list should be removed from the Bible," how would you answer them?

....

....

....

Pray

Lord, thank you for the lists in Chronicles and in other sections of the Bible. Help me to see more and more how true it is that all Scripture is inspired by You and useful for us. Amen.

Impact

Some people live by their lists. Others don't make lists at all. How about you? If you haven't done so for some time, consider making a prayer list of people and needs you hope to remember daily and another of people you hope to pray for weekly. Place it in your Bible and use it. Keep it updated and be sure to record answers to prayer.

Close

So today you discovered two important purposes in God's recording of lists. And on that note, we hope that B90+ has become a regular part of your daily list of priorities. Tomorrow's lesson will put it all in context.

Coaching Tip

Scripture was written by God to comfort the afflicted and to afflict the comfortable. As you read, be open to both of these aspects of God's work in your life that you might grow and mature in your faith.

Day 30 · **Catch the Context**

The question is often asked, "Why do 1 and 2 Chronicles repeat so much of what is already found in the Bible?" This question can challenge those who attempt to read the Bible in its entirety. Indeed, nearly 50% of the information in Chronicles is found in other portions of the Old Testament—especially in Samuel and Kings. When we look beyond the repetition in Chronicles to the reasons it was written, however, we find greater appreciation for the book. There is a force behind the book that, once seen and understood, makes Chronicles quite an interesting read. Clarification comes when we ponder the book's context.

Read

You have two reading options: read the full selection of Scripture or a single overview chapter each day.

- Full Reading: 1 Chronicles 18 – 2 Chronicles 1
- Overview Chapter: 1 Chronicles 28

Reflect

Why all of the repetition in Chronicles? And why is it also different from the material it appears to mimic? To understand, we must briefly compare Samuel and Kings with Chronicles, noting timing, emphasis, and application.

Timing. The narratives in Samuel and Kings were written during Israel's exile, around 550-560 BC. The Chronicles, however, were written sometime after the exile—around 450-300 BC—and therefore in a completely different context. In Samuel and Kings, for example, the people of Israel were given understanding as to why they finally had been judged by God. The author of Chronicles, on the other hand, wrote his account after Israel had returned to rebuild and inhabit Jerusalem; he sought to encourage them to live faithfully for God under their renewed covenant.

Emphasis. A person who is intentionally making choices that will harm others needs to be confronted; a person who really wants to do the right thing but struggles to stay the course, conversely, needs encouragement. Do we offer correction or comfort in a given situation? The answer is found in the context of a person's life.

The context for Samuel and Kings places Israel in the days before her exile; this was a radically different time than that of post-exile days and the writings of Chronicles. That explains the shift in tone from a message of confrontation to one of consolation. We see a similar shift in emphasis in other writings tied to this time period in the life of Israel. Isaiah, for example, had such a different tone and tenor in his writing before the exile than that focused after the exile that some scholars attempt to divide his book into two sections. The first 39 chapters provide correction while the remaining 27 offer the comfort of the Lord. In the New Testament, Paul learned about a corrupting influence in the Church and insisted the instigator be disciplined. Once the same person repented, however, Paul urged fellow believers to show compassion and to offer him comfort (2 Corinthians 2). Indeed, God's inspired Word is useful in both contexts (2 Timothy 3:16-17).

When we compare Samuel and Kings to Chronicles, the difference in emphasis becomes obvious. Samuel and Kings puts on open display the compounding sin problem in both the Northern and Southern Kingdoms. The writers warn God's people about the long-term consequences of disobedience. By contrast, Chronicles gives very little attention to the Northern Kingdom and shows reasons—based on the better lives of certain kings in the South—for God to give the nation opportunity to rebuild. King David and King Solomon are allotted some 29 chapters in Chronicles, with a more concentrated focus on father and son's successes than on their respective sins of adultery and idolatry. Solomon's son, Manasseh—described in Samuel and Kings as the man who brought the whole house of Judah down in the end—is shown in Chronicles to have repented later in life. Which of these accounts, Samuel and Kings or Chronicles, is correct? Both. Which is more viable to Israel's story? Both equally, based on the context.

Application. The narratives in Samuel and Kings, and Chronicles reveal a God who cares for us enough to do what is best for us in each situation. Seeing this helps us sympathize not only with the repetitive nature of Chronicles but with people in our lives who need more understanding and compassion. We are thus reminded that the books of the Bible are written for us, but they were not originally written to us. That is, once we see the context of Biblical books (whom they were written to), their contents make more sense for our own lives. Grasping this simple truth helps us to see clearly the relevance of the books to their original time period while at the same time rendering them more understandable and useful to our lives today.

Respond

✱ 1. Why is it important to understand the context of the books of the Bible?

2. Think of people you know who need to be confronted for their poor choices. If you were to bring a word of correction to them, what steps would you take?

....

....

....

....

3. Think of people you know who need encouragement to rebuild their lives. Consider how God might use you as an answer to their prayers. Record steps you hope to take.

....

....

....

....

Pray

Lord, thank you that You love me enough to discipline me if necessary, and to lift up my hands and strengthen me when I need it. Help me to be more like You as I relate to others—being slow to judge and seeking to understand the context of their lives. Amen.

Impact

Think of a person who irritates you. Then ask yourself whether or not you really understand the context of their life situation and story. What special history or what wound of the soul or body might be irritating that person? Ask God to give you His perspective that you might be less bothered and more compassionate toward him or her.

Close

Congratulations, you've just completed day 30 of Bible in 90 Days Plus. We are looking forward to the next 60 days together. We believe the first 30 days have blessed you, so why not share your experience with family and friends, and invite them to take the B90+ journey.

Day 31 · **Supernatural Support**

King Asa was one of Judah's "good" kings. He failed to trust God later in life, however, and made some serious mistakes. During a confrontation regarding these mistakes, the prophet Hanani spoke words that framed the promise of God's support, and he did so in a manner that has inspired people ever since:

> *For the eyes of the LORD move to and fro throughout the earth that He may strongly support those whose heart is completely His.* (2 Chronicles 16:9, NASB 1995)

Let's look more closely at this promise in the context of 2 Chronicles.

Read

You have two reading options: read the full selection of Scripture or a single overview chapter each day.

- Full Reading: 2 Chronicles 2–17
- Overview Chapter: 2 Chronicles 16

Reflect

1 & 2 Chronicles repeat a lot of stories and information that were provided in earlier portions of the Old Testament. They do so, however, in a unique manner: they provide a fresh demonstration of the supernatural support the Jews would need in order to return to Jerusalem and rebuild their Temple despite insurmountable odds.

Asa, the third king of Judah and sixth of David's house, is introduced as a king who "did what was good and right in the eyes of the LORD his God" (2 Chronicles 14:2). His story demonstrates the reality of God's supernatural support; it also shows us what happens when we lack it. For most of his life, Asa was serious about trusting God. As king, "He took away the foreign altars and the high places and broke down the pillars and cut down the Asherim and commanded Judah to seek the LORD, the God of their fathers, and to keep the law and the commandment" (2 Chronicles 14:3-4). In response to his righteousness, the Lord protected the people. When, for example, the king of Ethiopia and his overwhelmingly large army came against Judah, Asa cried out to the Lord. In turn, God granted Asa victory; years of peace followed.

In the twenty-sixth year of his rule, Asa was assaulted by Baasha, king of Israel. Rather than depend on God for protection, Asa formed an alliance with Syria. When Hanani, the seer, confronted Asa and reminded him that God's strong support comes only to those whose hearts are completely His, the king imprisoned Hanani. Judah's years of peace thus came to an

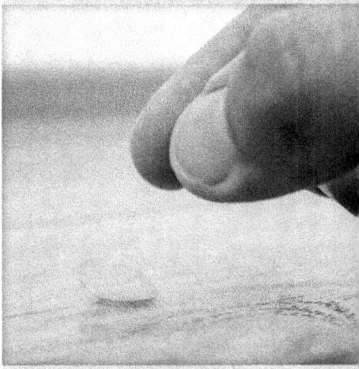

Coaching Tip

Scripture memorization comes through meditation. When you come across a favorite verse, write it out and reflect on it throughout the day. After a few days of enjoying a verse in this manner, it will become locked securely in your heart. As your list of favorite verses grows, review the verses at least once a month to retain them in your memory and to be enriched by their truths.

end, as did Asa's good health. His story reminds us of the great help available to us today through the King of the universe. It also reminds us of the foolishness of not depending on God for assistance in all of life's challenges.

God desires to be our support in both the big and small details of our lives. We tend to seek God only for what we consider to be the big things, thinking God will not bother Himself with the small details of our lives. But it is precisely because God is so great that He is not only able, He is also willing to be involved in what we consider the small issues of life. In fact, these small things—right down to the attitudes and decisions of our hearts—matter most. From the undivided heart comes the promise of God's mighty strength. Our quiet trust, childlike prayers of dependence, and an attitude of surrender create a channel through which God will show His supernatural support to us, always.

Respond

✱ 1. What is the most helpful learning point for you as you consider King Asa's life?

....

....

....

....

2. Do you tend to trust God with the small details of your life? Explain.

....

....

....

....

3. Read 2 Chronicles 16:9, found in the opening paragraph of this lesson. Write this verse out, reflect on it, and consider memorizing it.

....

....

....

....

Pray

Lord, thank you for Asa and many other characters and stories in the Bible that highlight the simple truth of 2 Chronicles 16:9. Help me to live by this verse. Amen.

Impact

Like Asa, every person needs God's supernatural support. Some can receive it best through another person. The Bible tells us, for example, to offer special care to the elderly and the widow. Pray for those in nursing homes and retirement centers who are using Bible in 90 Days and encourage any loved ones you know in such facilities to do the same.

Close

Humility. Easy to say. Difficult to embrace. No one is exempt from pride, from pawns to princes. Even those who start well with God can fall from grace into the pit of pride. Day 32 will reveal some hard but good lessons from the lives of Israel's and Judah's kings.

B90+

Coaching Tip

Humility is the correct posture of the heart for reading God's Word. For as we humble ourselves, the Lord is able to speak to us with clarity and conviction, confronting our sins and changing us.

Day 32 · **Humble Yourself**

As we read through the sad stories surrounding the demise of Judah, we cover a period of nearly 350 years involving 20 kings. Eight of these kings are said to have "done what is right in the sight of the Lord." But even these righteous kings had weaknesses that became apparent when they trusted more in themselves than they trusted the Lord. Think of examples like Solomon's idolatry, Asa's hardness of heart, Jehoshaphat's divided heart, Joash's unbelief, Amaziah's compromises, Uzziah's arrogance, Hezekiah's boasting, and Josiah's foolish decisions. While these defects did not dominate any of their lives constantly, they did leave a dark mark on their life stories. The lesson we can learn from one and all of them is stated well by Solomon, "Pride goes before destruction, and a haughty spirit before a fall" (Proverbs 16:18).

Read

You have two reading options: read the full selection of Scripture or a single overview chapter each day.

- Full Reading: 2 Chronicles 18–31
- Overview Chapter: 2 Chronicles 26

Reflect

Ironically, the universal problem seen in the lives of the kings is also the root cause of all sin: pride. Pride provoked Satan to rebel against God in the first place, and the final end of all evil will come when the last rebel, both angelic and human, is removed from God's presence. Humility is the safest way to live before God until that final day.

Had each of the eight righteous kings maintained an attitude of humility, none would have had far to fall. And had they stumbled, God would have kept them from landing on their faces (Matthew 23:12). For, "God opposes the proud but gives grace to the humble" (James 4:6b). When we humble ourselves, our place of greatest weakness and vulnerability becomes a source of God's enduring grace and strength. Pride, however, sets us up for failure.

Think about the story of King Uzziah. Also known as Azariah, Uzziah was the tenth king of Judah. Taking the throne at 16 years of age, he reigned for 52 years. Uzziah's reign was the most prosperous of Judah's kings next to that of Jehoshaphat, and—of course—Solomon. He engaged in agricultural pursuits, reorganized Judah's army, and fortified the kingdom. "His fame spread far and wide, for the Lord gave him marvelous help, and he became very powerful" (2 Chronicles 26:15c NLT). Yet in the very next verse we read,

But when he had become powerful, he also became proud, which led to his downfall. (2 Chronicles 26:16a)

Thinking himself above God's standards, Uzziah decided to take up the priestly duty of offering incense before God. When confronted by 80 priests, rather than humbling himself and repenting, the king became angry. He was immediately afflicted with leprosy. From that day on, his leprosy excluded him from the very Temple that he had hoped to control.

Each of us is called by God into service. You may be a teacher, an accountant, a pastor, an artist, a governor, a plumber, or a student. Regardless of your area of service or mine, we must each humble ourselves if we hope to bring glory to God. For in so doing, we will find God to be our intimate Friend, Guide, and Protector.

Respond

1. In your own words, complete this thought: "The most difficult part about humility is . . . "

✱ 2. Why is it essential that we humble ourselves before God?

3. According to James 4:10, what must we do to be exalted by God?

Pray

Lord, I cannot easily discern my own pride. Help me to see Your greatness that I might humble myself and that You might be glorified in and through my life. Amen.

Impact

Dawson Trotman, the founder of a Christian organization, The Navigators, was once asked, "How do you know if you are a servant?" He answered, "By how you react when someone treats you as one."[1] Ask God to enable you to respond with humility and kindness toward those who don't understand you and who oppose you.

Close

The Bible says that without faith, it's impossible to please God (Hebrews 11:6). And yet there are times when God chooses to touch our physical senses with His manifest presence, as you will see in tomorrow's lesson.

---

1 AZ Quotes. https://azquotes.com/author/24943-Dawson_Trotman.

Day 33 · **Why Church?**

The books of Chronicles and Ezra emphasize the presence of God. 2 Chronicles 5—a high point in the narrative—states that the priests literally cannot remain in a standing position because God's glory is so heavy upon them as they serve in the newly-constructed Temple (2 Chronicles 5:14). In the years that follow, though, the sins of God's people erode God's presence. In 2 Chronicles 29 & 30, Hezekiah finally purifies the Temple and commemorates Passover. His great grandson, Josiah, also strives to bring back the presence of the Almighty (2 Chronicles 34-35). Neither Hezekiah's nor Josiah's righteous lives and bold attempts to promote righteousness are sufficient, however, to prevent the downward spiritual spiral of the nation.

The Temple in Jerusalem remains central in the eyes of God's people until the Temple and Jerusalem itself are destroyed by invading Babylonians who carry the Jews into exile. Even in exile, however, the people long for God's presence and pray toward Jerusalem. Seventy years after the destruction of the holy city, Zerubbabel and Ezra lead the people of God back to Jerusalem to rebuild the Temple and re-institute the traditional observance of Passover (Ezra 1-7). With the Temple as a centerpiece, the wonderful truth that we are designed to dwell in God's presence dominates Chronicles and Ezra as a reminder that it should also dominate our lives.

Read

You have two reading options: read the full selection of Scripture or a single overview chapter each day.

- Full Reading: 2 Chronicles 32 – Ezra 7
- Overview Chapter: Ezra 7

Reflect

1 & 2 Chronicles describe the diminishing presence of God for Israel and eventually Judah, until the people finally lose God's protection and Jerusalem falls. After the people of God are taken into exile, God rekindles in their hearts a longing for home, for Jerusalem. Beginning with the story of Ezra, we see Jehovah guiding them to return to the holy city and rebuild the Temple that God's presence might once again be established in their lives.

Throughout the Bible, God's presence is the primary theme upon which all other narratives are set. It all begins in the Garden of Eden where Adam and Eve walk intimately with God. They turn away from the Lord God, however, and embrace the dark ways of Satan who takes the form of a wily serpent. Adam and Eve are removed from the Garden but not without hope. Their nakedness is covered by the skins of an animal—the first recorded instance of a blood sacrifice. From that point on, sacrifice will be needed for forgiveness that we might once again enjoy the presence of God.

Coaching Tip

At times you may come across Biblical truths that inspire you deeply. Don't keep those golden nuggets of insight to yourself. Find someone to share them with. And when you cannot find a listening ear, write them down and ask God to provide an opportunity to share your insights in His time.

As a result of Adam and Eve's fall from grace, the world becomes infected with sin and rebellion. The long journey of the Jews to Sinai prepares them to appreciate God's prescription for the Tabernacle, a blue print for entering God's presence once again. From the outer gate to the inner sanctuary, the worshipper repeatedly passed through single doors, each a symbol for Christ, the one way to the Father. Just inside the outer gate, for example, stood the brazen altar, a picture of Calvary too large to ignore. The Tabernacle's design, its furnishings, and the priest's clothing reminded God's people of the means by which we must enter God's presence.

The tabernacle's rich analogies and teachings were carried over to the Temple where the same design patterns were generally repeated but in larger proportions. It all prefigured the Church, the Temple God established under the New Covenant (Ephesians 2:19-22). The God who once dwelt within a structure has come to dwell *within us.* One day, the entire cosmos will be remade with God as its center. From that point on, He will be our dwelling place, for we will live *in Him* (Revelation 21:22). Thus, our experience of His presence will be fulfilled perfectly, fully, forever. Until that day, the Church remains the best expression of God's presence the world will ever see until the Lord returns to bring us home.

Respond

1. Can you think of anything God desires more than to have us in His presence forever, that He might give His glory to us and be glorified in us (Ephesians 1:6 & 12)? Explain.

....

....

....

....

✱ 2. How should an awareness of God's plan for us to be with Him forever impact our focus on His presence today?

....

....

....

....

3. Examine your life. Are there things about your life you should change to enable you to live more fully in God's presence? Explain.

....

....

....

....

Pray

Thank you, Lord, that despite our sin, You love us still. It is overwhelming and unfathomable to think that You desire to bring us home and to glorify us in Your presence. Help me to experience Your presence more each day as I continue to read Your Word and pray. Amen.

Impact

Throughout the Bible and through the history of the Church, God has revealed His presence in greater glory when His people humble themselves and pray. Take time today to pray for God's presence to be more obvious in your life and for you to be more desirous of His glory.

Close

If you long for God's glory, then you also need to prepare to face opposition. Moses did . . . so did David. And next, we will see how Nehemiah, who served God fully, resisted evil men to help preserve the glory of God.

Coaching Tip

At times you may find it difficult to keep your focus as you read Scripture and pray. God can help you to stay awake and keep focused as you ask Him for protection from distracting forces and for a fresh infilling of His Spirit.

Day 34 · **Rebuild for God**

Ezra and Nehemiah were likely one conjoined book until around the time of Christ. Spanning a period from the fall of Babylon to the fifth century BC, the text describes the mission to rebuild the fallen city of Jerusalem. Three waves of returned exiles engaged in the project that was led by Zerubbabel, Ezra, and Nehemiah respectively. Zerubbabel, Judah's governor, joined by Joshua, the High Priest, led the first group of 40,000 Jews back to their home. This group would rebuild the altar and lay the foundations of the Temple. Ezra, the scribe, led the second expedition to Jerusalem. His purpose focused on the rebuilding of the people's spiritual lives. Nehemiah, cup-bearer to Persian King Artaxerxes, led the third envoy and gave attention to the rebuilding of Jerusalem's walls. That feat was accomplished in an astounding 52 days.

Read

You have two reading options: read the full selection of Scripture or a single overview chapter each day.

- Full Reading: Ezra 8 – Nehemiah 9
- Overview Chapter: Nehemiah 2

Reflect

Each group of returned exiles faced its own challenges and oppositions, but none were fully deterred. In other words, each somehow tunneled through and fulfilled its task of rebuilding Jerusalem—beginning with the altar and Temple then working its way out to the protective walls of Jerusalem. From this example, we glean at least three applications for the rebuilding efforts in which God calls us to engage ourselves today. Some are personal while others are communal:

Deepening Devotion. The life of worship and devotion is represented by the prioritization given to the altar. This was the first thing the returned exiles sought to rebuild. Even as they did so, Nehemiah and Ezra challenged them to keep their hearts right with God lest all of their work be done in vain. Likewise, our hearts must also be set on pleasing God: without a heart of devotion, our entire focus on service to God will be wrong; our best efforts in life will be wasted.

Facing Opposition. Once we commit to obeying God, we too can expect opposition. Jesus said, "Remember the word that I said to you: 'A servant is not greater than his master.' If they persecuted me, they will also persecute you. If they kept my word, they will also keep yours" (John 15:20). Let us thank God for those who keep His Word and press in with the tenacity of Zerubbabel, Nehemiah, and Ezra as we face opposition.

Enjoying Protection. We can trust in God for the strength and protection we need every day when we remain fully separated from the world for Him and His will. The entire history of Israel proved the importance of this call to holiness; it's impossible not to link our protection to theirs—from the deliverance from Egypt, to the habitation of the land of promise, to the return from captivity, and beyond. Israel's failure to trust and stand in firm obedience to God directly caused its 70-year exile. In Ezra and Nehemiah, those rebuilt walls symbolized Israel's return and newfound protection—a protection that can be ours today.

Respond

✱ 1. What are your favorite parts of your reading from Ezra and Nehemiah? Why?

2. What are the most challenging parts of your reading from Ezra and Nehemiah? Why?

3. Which of the three areas mentioned above do you need to work on most: deepening devotion, facing opposition, or enjoying protection? Why?

Pray

Lord, help me to become more devoted and obedient to You each day as I read Your Word, even if opposition comes my way. As You guided and protected the people who returned to rebuild Jerusalem, be my Protection. Help me to remain true to You. Amen.

Impact

Jerusalem was rebuilt by more than prayer. Stones, cement, and willing workers were also required. Sometimes we mentally divide the world between the secular and the sacred. God wants us to invite Him into every aspect of our lives. As you go about your day, remember Paul's exhortation: ". . . whatever you do, do all to the glory of God" (1 Corinthians 10:31b).

Close

As we've just seen, Nehemiah stood strong in the face of opposition. Even so, in the story of Esther, we'll see that she too had to face wickedness, fear, and even death to save her own people. You will *not* want to miss Day 35 of "Esther: On Stage."

Day 35 · **On Stage**

The book of Esther shadows tension between Heaven and earth. It records an account of the same ongoing spiritual warfare that is happening even as you read these words. And—like it or not—you are part of this great eternal narrative. As you read Esther, think about the way God works quietly in the world and the essential role you and I serve toward its imminent outcome.

Read

You have two reading options: read the full selection of Scripture or a single overview chapter each day.

- Full Reading: Nehemiah 10 – Esther 10
- Overview Chapter: Esther 7

Reflect

Following the exile, the Persians conquered Babylon and held vast regions of land in the Middle East. The book of Esther is set in Susa, one of the Persian capitals, during the reign of King Ahasuerus, whose Greek name was Xerxes I (486–464 BC). Some exiled Jews had already returned to rebuild Jerusalem, but—unaware they faced greater danger by remaining in Babylon—the majority refused to take the journey home. The return trip to Jerusalem of more than 1,600 miles required passage through many dangerous territories.

The Storyline. The great irony of Esther is that it never mentions the name of God, even though its unfolding narrative shows His mighty hand at work from beginning to end. The storyline of the book creates a fitting parallel to the experience of the Jews in exile: God seemed to be at a distance; and yet God was still working in the details of their lives.

The Plot Thickens. In commemoration of the book of Esther and its timeless message, the Jews celebrate Purim to this day (Esther 9). Reading of the book aloud is an essential part of the Purim festivities. Christians likewise appreciate and celebrate Esther not only for its historic relevance in God's Word but also for the present-day applications it holds. It teaches us, for example, about the spiritual warfare that surrounds us as long as we live in this world (Ephesians 6:10-18).

Our archenemy, Satan, seeks to destroy us in much the same manner as Haman sought to annihilate the Jews of Susa (1 Peter 5:8). The Apostle Paul says that Christ, the King of Kings, has all authority (1 Timothy 6:15). Much as the king is the only one who can extend the scepter of grace in Esther, Christ is the only One whose grace can deliver us from our ever-present danger and eternal destruction. But in order to claim our deliverance, we must do our part. Similarly, Esther made a choice; she approached the king

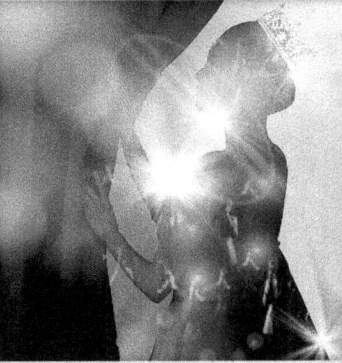

Coaching Tip

Remember that the Bible is an entire library with various genres: history, poetry, wisdom literature, prophecy, etc. Some Biblical books may combine genres, much as writers do today. Nevertheless, each book, every page, is inspired by God. As you read, try to discern the genre that is before you to enhance your appreciation and insights about the text.

to request the protection and preservation of her people, saying, "If I perish, I perish" (Esther 4:16e). Her petition was a fitting picture of the kind of intercession needed today before the throne of God.

The Climax. The book of Esther is a call to unity among God's people. Esther was not alone in her prayers; the people of God prayed and fasted for three days per her instruction (Esther 4:16). And once the decree to annihilate the Jews was nullified by another decree allowing God's people to protect themselves, they went into battle. So it is today: in order to be victorious over the dark powers that seek to destroy us, believers must rise up and fight, first in prayer, and then by taking up the truth of the Word, the sword of the Spirit (Ephesians 6:17). The book of Esther also reminds us that no matter how overwhelmed we may feel in our encounter with the dark powers of the world around us, God is quietly and sovereignly working out His purpose in our lives and on our behalf.

Respond

1. From your reading of Esther or the above commentary, what do you think is the main purpose or theme of the book of Esther?

2. Does this story encourage you? Explain.

✱ 3. The book of Esther supports the Biblical promise that no matter how bad things seem on the world scene, God is working out His eternal purpose. Do you believe this? Explain.

....

....

....

Pray

Lord, thank you that You reign over the affairs of humanity. Help me to trust You more and to participate in Your call for believers to pray together even as they did in the book of Esther. Amen.

Impact

The warfare described in Esther involved both spiritual and physical battles. We must remember those who fight on both fronts today. Scripture Awakening's Bible in 90 Days outreach impacts troops in the military, assisting them as they read, study, and live the Bible. Do you know anyone in the military? Consider sharing with them about B90+ and how it has impacted your life.

Close

Wasn't that a great story? As you continue this journey through the Bible, there is even more in store: adventure, wisdom, and sometimes suffering . . . but not without a purpose. Tomorrow we dive into the woes—and joys—of Job.

Session 6 • Overview

● REVIEW Days 36-42
History, Part 3: Return, Reconstruction, Restoration

 Now is the time for your small group meeting to review the week's Scripture readings, cover the discussion questions, and watch the Essential Snapshot video together (or by yourself if reading alone). Point your mobile device's camera on the QR code to access the video entitled "Session 6: God's Presence". Or enter this link into your browser: ScriptureAwakening.com/plus/

- Discuss the questions marked by an asterisk (✱) from the **Respond** sections in Days 36-42, perhaps adding others if time permits.
- Watch the Session 6 video* (individually or with a small group).
    1. What insights from the video would you like to explore further?
    2. Our readings give us a sense that God is accomplishing His plan, even when it is unseen. Do you believe that as you trust and rest in the Lord your moments will be filled with eternal purpose? Why or why not?
- Summarize the Preview (below) of what is coming next week, encouraging group members to read it on their own.

*Facilitators note: In order to watch the Essential Snapshot video with your group, you will need a large video monitor, if meeting in-person. If hosting a small group remotely, use Zoom (or similar service) to stream the video from your device to share with group participants.

● PREVIEW Days 43-49
Poetry, Part 1: Suffering, Worship, Prayer

Weekly Reading: Job 1:1 to Psalm 102:28

Summary

This week transitions from the historical narrative in the first 17 books of the Old Testament to the 5 Poetical Books. Whereas the Pentateuch and Historical Books focused on the past, the Poetical Books focus on living in the present and address many issues of contemporary concern.

Hebrew poetry is not primarily based on meter or rhyme but on parallel structure. This writing style creates reinforced, complemented, contrasted, or restated thoughts often through the use of imagery, helping us to more fully appreciate the intent and feelings of the original authors.

Job, one of the earliest books in the entire Bible, considers the problem of apparently unjust suffering. It contrasts man's limited human perspectives and misconceptions about evil with God's divine wisdom and sovereignty.

The book of Psalms provides an anthology of prayers and hymns, often set to music, for individual or corporate worship.

Books You'll Encounter This Week

Job Overview

Scholars believe that Job was a contemporary of the patriarchs. In this philosophical discourse, God allows Satan to test Job by causing Job to tragically lose his wealth, family, and health in rapid succession. In three cycles of heated debate, Job and his friends dispute the cause of his suffering and God's administration of justice. God concludes the discourse by challenging the debaters to trust the wisdom of His sovereign rule over the cosmos, the details of which are beyond their limited comprehension.

Psalms Overview (Introduction)

One of the best-loved books of the Bible, Psalms is a collection of 150 hymns and poems, authored over a period of hundreds of years. Divided into five sub-books, the individual psalms can be categorized a number of ways: by book, type, author, function, or size. This week's daily commentaries provide additional insights into these categorizations.

Covering the full range of human emotion, from deepest despair to joyous praise, the Psalms reflect the personal nature of our relationship with God. They offer a variety of perspectives on what it means to truly worship Him through prayer and song.

As you move through the Psalms at your normal Bible in 90 Days reading pace, mark the ones you want to revisit at a later date that you might appreciate them even more fully.

Things to Look for This Week

As you read, consider how:

1. The book of Job is really more about trusting in God's sovereign rule than about the suffering of the righteous.
2. Many of the same themes from the Historical Books (trust, kingship, God's sovereignty, etc.) are repeated and emphasized in the Psalms.
3. Even though many of the Psalms are *example* prayers, they are not meant to serve as *model* prayers for every situation and generation. Instances of "invoking divine judgment (curses) on one's enemies," for example (such as Psalm 79), must be balanced against Christ's call for us to love and bless our enemies.

Coaching Tip

When reading through the entire Bible, you are likely to come up with far more questions than answers, and that is okay. Questions—and even doubts—are stepping stones to understanding and growth.

Day 36 · Asking Why

Preschool children love to ask, "Why?" And frustrated parents sometimes shut them down. It is helpful to remind ourselves, from time to time, why it is that children have a propensity to ask, "Why?" The simple answer, of course, is that they are wired to be inquisitive. Their minds are filled with wonder as they explore the world. When we take time to listen to them and grapple with their questions, we are encouraging them in their journey of learning and growth. But what about the answers they are not yet ready to comprehend? And what about the answers we don't have? Even our acknowledgment of such unknowns is an essential part of their learning process.

Regardless of our age, the Bible calls us to become like children to enter the Kingdom of God; to maintain the childlike curiosity that promotes learning and growth all of our days. For example, when faced with the problems of suffering and evil, we are invited to ask questions. And it is okay for us to acknowledge that we may never fully comprehend God's answers. The book of Job was written to help us come to terms with this challenging task.

Read

You have two reading options: read the full selection of Scripture or a single overview chapter each day.

- Full Reading: Job 1–19
- Overview Chapter: Job 1

Reflect

If God is perfectly good and all-powerful, why do the righteous suffer? This question has been with us from the beginning of recorded history. The account of Job is a worldwide classic because it's recognized as one of the earliest books in recorded history to deal with this complex issue head on. And it does so with all of the wisdom we have come to expect from God's Word.

A carefully crafted composition, the book of Job addresses the problem of evil from both Heavenly and earthly perspectives. It begins and ends with the courtroom in Heaven, while its middle section carries us through the theological confusion we each face on earth. From Heaven, we recognize God's loving and eternal purpose in testing and trying and refining the righteous. We grow through our trials and are rewarded for our faith. From the world's vantage point, however, everything seems to be turned on its head by human misery and tragedy. And we ask God, "Why." Most of the time, like Job's friends, we attempt to solve the complex problem of evil with simplistic answers.

Job reminds us that our first step toward solving the problem of evil is to bring our questions to the Father of all that is good. In so doing, we are quickly reminded that God's ways are higher than our ways "as the heavens are higher than the earth" (Isaiah 55:9). Ultimately, Job teaches us that the problem of evil is resolved in the goodness of God; the God whose very person defies and will one day eradicate evil altogether. In God's presence, our "why" finds its answer in a "Who." This "Who" is an all-powerful and all-loving God who not only promises to use evil for good, but who also delivers on that promise.

God's Word calms our hearts with the promise that human suffering meets its match at the foot of the Cross. There we see that the only One who is perfectly righteous takes the suffering we deserve upon Himself. His death and resurrection remind us of an important fact: even if we cannot solve the problem of evil, we can still know without a doubt that God loves us and has solved the problem for us. Looking up, we can therefore declare with Job that,

> *I know that my redeemer lives, and that in the end he will stand on the earth. And after my skin has been destroyed, yet in my flesh I will see God; I myself will see him with my own eyes.* (Job 19:25-27a NIV)

Respond

1. Do you believe that we humans will ever have a complete answer to the problem of evil? Explain.

2. Are you excited about learning the things of God or has your childlike enthusiasm been dulled by your experiences in life? Why?

✱ 3. How might you rekindle the childlike curiosity that is fitting for children of the Most High God (Matthew 19:14)?

....

....

....

....

Pray

Lord, as I read Your Word, instill in me once again the budding excitement about Your truth that ought to be the experience of every child of God. Amen.

Impact

Consider people you know who, like Job, have had or currently face great suffering. Pray about ways you may come along side them, encourage them, and show them you care enough to listen.

Close

As we will see tomorrow, Job doesn't get the answer he wanted, but the one God knew he needed. As God's children, many questions will go unanswered, but one thing surely remains: the steadfast love of our heavenly Father.

Day 37 · **Behind the Façade**

On the surface, the book of Job seems to address one particular question: "Why do the righteous suffer?" But by the time we reach the conclusion of the book, we realize that we have been asking the wrong question. We begin the book reasoning that God is not administering justice on earth; we end the book recognizing that there is a flaw in our logic. Justice is expected to be meted for the just, we assume. But what if Scripture is correct in telling us that no one is truly righteous? Once we cease justifying our own behavior and recognize God alone is just, we are ready to uncover new insights that can strengthen our faith.

Read

You have two reading options: read the full selection of Scripture or a single overview chapter each day.

- Full Reading: Job 20–36
- Overview Chapter: Job 23

Reflect

The Book of Job is another reminder to us that the Old Testament serves as a vital foundation for the New Testament. Thought to be the oldest book in the Bible, Job carries current insights about the nature of God that put philosophical conundrums such as "the problem of evil" in perspective. Consider, for instance, that:

1. **God is the Source of Comfort.** Job challenges us, through extended dialogues with his "friends," to realize that humans tend to be shortsighted. We often avoid a Biblical worldview, a view that brings God into the picture and invites us to measure temporal things against God's eternal purposes. Once we do so, however, we find wisdom and comfort to face the conundrums of life. Job reminds us of our need to center our theology on God. When we filter the Bible to fit our own agendas, we miss the very truths that might enable us to enjoy life in its fullness. It all begins by accepting that God is good and the source of comfort in our lives.

2. **God Works Evil for Good.** In order to find God's comfort, we must be careful not to create a caricature of God that defies the Biblical account. In seeking to justify themselves and to quiet Job's complaints, for example, Job's companions reveal their personal misconceptions about the character of God. Three cycles of speeches—delivered by the first three of Job's friends—attempt to solve the problem of evil by saying that Job is suffering because he is not truly righteous. If this were the main issue, would not all suffer all of the time?

Coaching Tip

When reading the Bible, it's important to distinguish between what people say and what God says. Context is the key. When Job and his friends dialogue about their understandings of God, for example, they are in the process of learning about God. When God speaks, whether at the end of this book or through a prophet in other books, we are not only learning with men but hearing from God.

Similarly, the disciples of Jesus asked about a blind man, "who sinned, this man or his parents, that he was born blind?" (John 9:2). Jesus chided them for embracing the assumption that all suffering is caused by personal sin. The world is filled with evil and darkness; all of us are affected by it. As the Author of goodness, however, God promises to use all of our suffering for our good and for His glory if we will only trust in Him.

3. **Like Job, We Must Trust God in Order to Find Our Reward.** The book of Job invites us each to make a choice: rather than blame God for evil, we can look to God for its eradication and thank God for goodness. Looking to our Lord's righteousness rather than to our own, we can stand amazed at the undeserved love our God showers upon us. Job—whom God declared more blameless and upright than his friends—suffered for a time but was eventually rewarded mightily for his faith (Job 1:8; 42:10-17; James 5:11). How much more should we accept our trials and tribulations even as we trust God for His grace and the forgiveness offered through the sacrifice of Jesus Christ, the only One who is truly righteous?

Job leaves us with one ultimate question. It isn't why evil exists in the world but why goodness exists. Why are any of us blessed? If we are quick to question God about the very suffering we're rightly due; why then are we so slow to thank God for the endless blessings we do not deserve? We may call this the "problem of goodness," a problem we all must face as we ponder the character of God.

Respond

1. What new insights have you drawn from your reading from Job or the commentary above?

2. The Lord alone is righteous. He is also just. What are the implications of these two Biblical truths?

✱ 3. Do you know anyone who has rejected God because of evil in the world? If so, do you think that person's perspectives are justified? Explain.

....

....

....

....

Pray

Lord, thank you for Your mercy and kindness. If we were judged according to perfect standards of justice, we would all fail. But You took the hit Yourself, on the Cross. Help us, then, to cease judging You and to thank You forever for Your never-ending mercies. Amen.

Impact

A societal drift away from Scripture in the Western world has caused a significant increase in the number of people who reject God simply because there is evil in the world. There is nothing simple about the problem of evil, but the Word of God brings us back to the source of life: God Himself. Encourage your friends and family to engage in the B90+ program that they might become refreshed by the hope found in God's Word.

Close

Remember when we first started Job? Blessed at the beginning—then immense suffering—followed by abundant joys at the end because God gave him perspective. We will see you tomorrow.

Coaching Tip

It is good to pause once in a while and to remember the reason for which you are doing this read through the Bible. Psalm 1 describes that reason beautifully. Reflection on the whole of God's Word will bring happiness, joy, and blessing to the whole of our lives. Take a few minutes to ponder some of the blessings that have come to you thus far through your readings.

Day 38 · **Planted to Grow**

The Psalms are some of the most widely read and beloved portions of the Old Testament. They call us to worship God from the heart and to keep our lives rooted in the Scriptures. Psalm 1 opens describing a person who is rooted like a tree planted by water, one who can expect significant spiritual growth and good success in life. Written from a desert climate, this analogy would be striking to its original audience who was familiar with long hot journeys through arid terrain and the joy of coming across an oasis. Psalm 1 illustrates the oasis.

Read

You have two reading options: read the full selection of Scripture or a single overview chapter each day.

- Full Reading: Job 37 – Psalm 17
- Overview Chapter: Psalm 1

Reflect

If the book of Job concluded with a description of the wonderful blessings placed on Job because of his faith, the Psalms open with instruction on how to live in such blessings all of the time. God's abundant blessings are promised to those who delight in God's Law (Psalm 1:1). *Torah*, the ancient Hebrew word for "Law," suggested to Israel both the five books of Moses (Genesis to Deuteronomy) and the teachings of God in general. Christians today use the word "Scripture" to refer to the whole Word of God, including promises and commands to encourage and correct.

Psalm 1, for example, reminds us of the great benefit received from reading God's Word.

It is not enough to just read it, however; the Psalmist calls us to *meditate* on Scripture (Psalm 1:2). *Hagah*—the Hebrew word for "meditate"—connotes a murmur or sigh; it suggests a reflection on truth that stirs one's spirit. The Psalms are written for the heart, and the Psalmist is reminding us that God's Word is meant to penetrate our inner being. Much as water and nutrients are drawn by capillary action into the heart of the tree, so must we plant ourselves into God's Word to draw from its life-giving truths in order to receive nourishment of heart and soul.

The promise of "fruit in season" is amplified by the Psalmist's mention of good success in all of our endeavors (Psalm 1:3). *Fruit in season, success in life . . .* these are the *blessings* of God that rest on those who pattern their lives after Scripture. The word the author uses for "blessing"—*ashar*—refers to happiness, joy, pleasure, well-being. It also connotes "walking the straight path."

In the deserts of the Middle East, a person who gets off of the main path might wander aimlessly, desperate for water, eventually to be attacked by bandits—hence the warning to those who veer from Scripture. Referenced by the Psalmist as "the wicked," this group misses the available blessings of God and will eventually perish. We can do better. We will be known by God and blessed of God when we remain rooted in God's life-giving Word (Psalm 1:6).

Respond

1. What do you like most about the book of Psalms?

2. In your own words, how is the practice of reading and meditating on Scripture like planting your soul in the flow of life-giving water?

✱ 3. Psalm 1 promises fruitfulness in season for those who remain connected with God through His Word. Record one or more reasons why that might be true.

Pray

Lord, thank you for Your Word and for giving us the privilege of drawing nourishment from it daily. Help me to be changed by Your truth and to live by it. Guide those around me to do the same. Amen.

Impact

God's Word is full of promises for the faithful believer. Make time in your busy schedule to pause, meditate on Scripture, and offer up praise for the work Good is doing in your life—especially through these daily readings.

Close

As we grow physically or intellectually, we don't always perceive any changes because such growth occurs incrementally over time. So it is with spiritual growth. As we read God's Word day by day, we grow in our knowledge of God, His purposes in the world, and His purposes for our lives. Let's rejoice in the hope that we will also grow closer *to* Him.

Day 39 · **God's Big Net**

The book of Psalms is made up of five sub-books, or sections, that draw us into the presence of God like a big net. Each section is demarked by a closing doxology, giving praise to the God who loves us and wants us to enter into relationship with Him (Psalms 41:13; 72:18–19; 89:52; 106:48; 150). The potential of such a relationship is highlighted by the thematic flow of the books in a direction that moves its focus from one person to the world's populace. Beginning with Book One, the emphasis flows from the man David (Book 1: Psalms 1-41), to David's kingdom (Book 2: Psalms 42-72), to the end of the Davidic dynasty (Book 3: Psalms 73-89), to the honoring of God as King (Book 4: Psalms 90-106), to the final triumph of God's Kingdom (Book 5: Psalms 107-150).

David's name is attached to 73 of the Psalms. Thirty-seven of David's psalms reside in the first book (Psalm 1 to 41). We will focus on Psalm 19 as it is central to Book 1 and illustrates beautifully the concept of God's big net. If the whole of the Psalter is cast before us like a large net, in other words, Psalm 19 closes its fibers around us and tightens the threaded arguments for God's existence from general to specific.

Read

You have two reading options: read the full selection of Scripture or a single overview chapter each day.

- Full Reading: Psalm 18–37
- Overview Chapter: Psalm 19

Reflect

Fishermen used three kinds of nets in the time of Christ: the *seine*, the *circular*, and the *trammel*. The seine net was several hundred feet long and as much as 20 feet high. Dropped from boats while several hundred yards offshore, floats kept its upper edge on the water's surface and sinkers pulled the other edge to the bottom. The seine net would be dragged to shore, closing in around everything in its path.

This is the net Jesus used to describe the Kingdom of Heaven (Matthew 13:47-48). Known for its grand scope and ability to funnel everything into its clutches, it was a fitting illustration for the drawing power of the revelation of God: from general, to special, to personal.

Central to Book 1 of the Psalms, Psalm 19 draws us into God's clutch of grace through a big net. It reminds us never to underestimate the power of God's Word to bring people to Himself. Psalm 19 moves us from general reasons to believe in God, to the specific revelation of God, to the realization of God on a personal level. Beginning with *The world* (Psalm 19: 1-6), it nar-

Coaching Tip

When you sometimes wonder whether it is worth taking time every day to read Scripture, reflect on the truth that faith comes by reading and hearing God's Word, and ponder the great benefits of a growing faith (Romans 10:17).

rows the lens of insight to *The Word* (Psalm 19:7-11), finally closing in on *Our words* (Psalm 19:12-14). We will look briefly at each section.

The World. The Psalmist often recognizes the Creator through the cosmos. If in Psalm 8, David sees God's majesty in the night sky, in Psalm 19, he is impressed by the power of the sun as it fills the day sky. Through the sun's light, the earth has life. Whether observing this correlation with the naked eye or through the most advanced instruments and theories of science, humanity at large has always been touched by the nagging sense that there must be a Creator who set it all into motion. But there is more.

The Word. The movement from the world to the Word, from God's general revelation to God's special revelation, tightens the net. Creation, or the world itself, suggests—but does not reveal—God to us. The revelation of the Bible as the Word, however, brings us closer. Using five synonyms for God's Word, David expresses a sense of endless gratitude for God's written teachings and instructions for our lives. They are God's law, testimony, precepts, commandments, and rules. By reading the Word, we come to understand who God is and what God does. As we respond to Scripture, we begin to experience what God can do in and through each of us. For this, we must also consider our words.

Our Words. God is not satisfied for us to perceive Him through the world or even to experience Him through the Word. He thus draws the net tighter until we know Him so well that we cannot help but honor Him with our words. We see how David has been captured by God's love through the words he chooses to close his Psalm:

> *Let the words of my mouth and the meditation of my heart be acceptable in Your sight, O Lord, my Rock and my Redeemer.* (Psalm 19:14)

Respond

1. What idea from the Scripture reading or the commentary especially encouraged or challenged you? Explain.

2. Why do people need more than the Creation (God's general revelation) to really know and follow the Lord?

✸ 3. How does the reading and hearing of Scripture help our faith and the faith of others to grow (Romans 10:14-17)?

Pray

Lord, thank you for the Psalms, a treasure chest of spiritual riches for the Christian life. Teach me to love Your Word as King David did and to love others enough to share the riches. Amen.

Impact

The Word of God is able to capture people with the truth of God. Think about natural and loving ways you can encourage others to read, reflect on, and respond to God's Word. For some, it may be a word of encouragement based on Scripture, for others a note, for others a tract or written verse, and yet others may, for a time, only be able to receive your silent prayers on their behalf. Regardless of how God leads you to encourage others, remember God's promise that His Word does not return empty (Isaiah 55:11).

Close

Guess what? You're almost halfway through B90. Today you reached another milestone by completing Day 39 of B90+! Congrats! Keep it up, and you too will have the satisfaction of having read through the entire Bible.

Coaching Tip

When we base our faith on emotion, it becomes as fickle as the weather. When we base our faith on Scripture, it becomes as solid as the ground on which we stand. Our emotions may fluctuate, but faith is meant to lead us into greater stability despite how we feel. Pray for the Word to inform your faith and for your faith to inspire your life—emotions and all.

Day 40 · **Dealing with Depression**

As we saw yesterday, the book of Psalms is divided into clusters or sub-books. We can also categorize them by somewhere between 5 and 20 types. Why so many possible types? The answer is as simple and complex as is the array of human emotions, for the Psalms are a canvas on which all of the colors of emotion are expressed—from laughter to lament, from rest to rage, and from exuberance to exhaustion. As you read the Psalms, let them reveal the state of your heart and emotions.

Read

You have two reading options: read the full selection of Scripture or a single overview chapter each day.

- Full Reading: Psalm 38–60
- Overview Chapter: Psalm 42

Reflect

We are called to love God with all of our heart, soul, and mind (Matthew 22:37). The Psalms show us how to do so, both individually and communally. This act of loving begins by recognizing that God loves us as we are, even when we are overwhelmed by emotion. We in turn can learn to love Him with our whole being, emotions and all—including the emotions we typically label as negative, such as depression. Psalm 42, for example, uses two repeated verses (5 and 11) to show us how to deal with the depressed state of mind based on two levels of our awareness:

Self-awareness. The author twice asks himself the question, "Why are you cast down, O my soul" (Psalm 42:5, 11)? The experience of being downcast or depressed is one of the great challenges faced by people today. Less common is the self-awareness needed to address one's depression in a meaningful and healthy way. This is especially true in certain circles, such as within the average Christian church, where it seems to be anathema to admit to depression. Yet, doesn't the very book from which we draw exuberant praise songs also call us to be as honest as David about our experiences of depression? Through his poetry, the shepherd-king grants us permission to experience the entire palate of human emotions and to own them as part of our Christian journey.

God Awareness. Psalm 42 also calls forth an awareness that God is with us, even when we are depressed. It reminds us from the start that we must seek the presence of God with the very intensity by which a thirsty deer would seek out a fresh stream of crystalline water. When we choose to seek God in this manner—even when we don't feel like doing so—we can be honest about our times of depression. And we can know that, even in that honesty, God loves us still. Such reflection on God positions us to remember that we are made in the image of God. Our emotions, rightly understood and expressed through a heart of worship, are part of that image. It is this choice to focus on God, no matter how we feel, that brings us hope. And hope lifts us out of the pit of despondency. Thus, the repeated statement mentioned above ends with the words, "Hope in God; for I shall again praise him, my salvation and my God" (Psalm 42:5, 11).

When you experience depression, read Psalm 42 and give special focus to verses 5 and 11. Remind yourself that even the great Psalmists experienced depression. It is not sinful to do so. The sad and sinful thing is for us to close God out and to refuse His love, to remain in the dark valleys while God is waiting to lead us into higher pasture lands.

Respond

1. Do you sometimes experience depression? If so, how do you cope with it?

2. What are the negative consequences of failing to see that God loves us as we are, emotions and all?

✱ 3. What can we learn from Psalm 42 about receiving God's strength and help in times of doubt, depression, or even despair?

Pray

Lord, help me to see and believe that You love me, even when my emotions overwhelm me. And when I am depressed, continue to hold me by the hand, protecting me from a fall. I trust in You and Your love. Amen.

Impact

Depression and anxiety impact millions of lives, and many sufferers think there is no way out. Scripture Awakening seeks to bring hope through media, encouraging people with the promises of Scripture. Pray for the impact of Scripture Awakening's media outreach to grow exponentially as part of the Scripture-based awakening that is so desperately needed in our day.

Close

Psalms is the most widely read and highly treasured book in the Bible. It's poems, hymns, and prayers resonate with the wide range of human experience and emotions. If you can, we encourage you to read the full text of Psalms during Bible in 90 Days Plus.

Day 41 · **Praise in Hard Times**

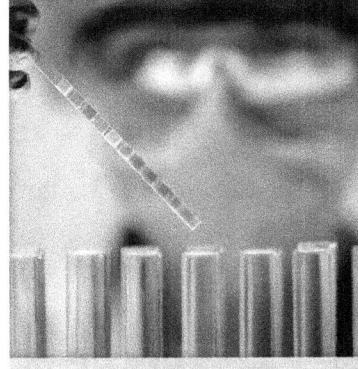

Litmus paper is one simple way to determine the pH of a solution today. It was developed in the fourteenth century when scientists discovered that a mixture of colored organic compounds—derived from lichen—turned red in acid solutions and blue in basic solutions. One dip of the paper and you have your answer. So it is with Psalm 73. Its simple words show us much about the condition of our souls against the mirrored truth of Scripture.

Read

You have two reading options: read the full selection of Scripture or a single overview chapter each day.

- Full Reading: Psalm 61–78
- Overview Chapter: Psalm 73

Reflect

We have noted that the longest book in the Bible by number of verses—the Psalms—is broken into 5 groupings or sub-books. We have also seen that specific psalms may be grouped by type. A third way one might recognize the rich variety in the Psalter is to categorize them by author. Nearly half of the psalms, 73 in total, are ascribed to David. Additionally, 12 are attributed to Asaph, 11 to Korah, 2 to Solomon, 1 to Moses, and 1 each to Ethan and Heman. Authors of the remaining 50 psalms are anonymous, with no name attached.

Reflection about the authors of each of the psalms helps us appreciate the aspirations behind them. Consider Psalm 73, for example, written or transcribed by Asaph. Likely the lead Levite singer in David's court, Asaph is said to be the author of Psalms 50 and 73-83. When we ponder the *context*, *content*, and *corrective* guidance in this psalm, Asaph's rich understanding of worship becomes a litmus test for our lives.

The Context. The third grouping of the Psalms, which begins with Psalm 73, was written primarily by Asaph. It focuses predominately on how to worship God, even in difficult times. It is likely that the psalms in this grouping were composed in response to the tragic decline and fall of David's house that led to the exile—one of the most trying times in Israel's history.

What difficulties are you facing today? Are there challenges you have faced in life that are difficult to forget? Or people who are hard to forgive? God understands. He desires to buffer your acidic memories and to heal your painful wounds. It all begins by realizing you are not alone. Asaph writes to help us understand that hardships are a part of life, even for a child of God. And God strengthens us in them when we learn to look to Him.

> **Coaching Tip**
>
> The Psalms invite us to express the full range of our heart's emotions to God. As we do so, let us remember that God is always worthy of praise, no matter how we feel and no matter what we face. As we praise God, we can see Him for who He really is, and Scripture will come to life.

The Content. The Asaphites were Temple musicians (1 Chronicles 6:39; 15:17-19; 16:4-7; 2 Chronicles 29:30). Berachiah's son, Asaph, had the special privilege of ministering in God's presence before the Ark of the Lord. His position before God gave him fresh perspective on the importance of praise in our lives, even when circumstances and people are against us. Asaph's faith and faithfulness are expressed clearly in the closing of Psalm 73:

> *Whom have I in heaven but you? And there is nothing on earth that I desire besides you. My flesh and my heart may fail, but God is the strength of my heart and my portion forever* (Psalm 73:25-26).

The Correction. Throughout the Scriptures, we learn that it is important to praise God, even in hard times. Our circumstances may be challenging, but God never changes. Nehemiah reminded the Israelites when they returned from exile to cheer up, saying that, "the joy of the LORD is your strength" (Nehemiah 8:10c). Paul, describing the key to his endurance in difficult times exhorts us to "rejoice in the Lord always" (Philippians 4:4a). James teaches us to rejoice even in our trials for they are used by God to develop character (James 1:2-4).

These and other human authors of Scripture remind us, with Asaph, that praise is a choice. When we see God for who He really is, we can praise Him with confidence, even when we feel confused, confounded, or crushed. God is with us, and His love will never fail.

Respond

✱ 1. Do you think the level of praise in our hearts is a reflection of what we believe about God? Explain.

2. Do you tend to praise God even in hard times? Why or why not?

3. In what way might the Psalms help you to be more like Asaph, a man who praised God when life was easy and when it was difficult?

....

....

....

Pray

Lord, the Psalms are like litmus paper, revealing the attitudes of my heart. Forgive me for the times I allow jealousy, resentment, and even bitterness to live inside of me like acid in a test tube. Neutralize these attitudes by Your love and grace, and lead me to become a person of praise. Amen.

Impact

We are all called to praise God all of the time—even when life is difficult. As we lift our burdens to God, He takes them on that we might be free to serve Him and to serve others as we follow Paul's admonition: "Bear one another's burdens, and so fulfill the law of Christ" (Galatians 6:2). Give your burdens to God today and ask Him to show you someone you can bless today by making their burden a little lighter.

Close

The Psalms are alive and speak to the issues of the human heart over and over again. Today's lesson was about difficulties. Tomorrow lesson will be about abandon—that is—earnest worship!

Coaching Tip

Scripture may confront us, convict us, correct us, or confirm us. No matter how it impacts our lives, it always leads us into lives of worship. As you read, think of reasons to give thanks and praise to God.

Day 42 · **Earnest Worship**

We have considered various ways to categorize the Psalms: by book, type, or author. We may also categorize psalms by their function. Whether used to assist prayer, to aid liturgy, to glean wisdom, to enhance pilgrimages, to console the weary and oppressed, or to offer God thanks, psalms serve as practical tools for our spiritual lives. The most substantial and overarching function of the Psalms is to call us into earnest worship, whether for individuals or entire congregations. Psalm 100 serves as a classic example of this call.

Read

You have two reading options: read the full selection of Scripture or a single overview chapter each day.

- Full Reading: Psalm 79–102
- Overview Chapter: Psalm 100

Reflect

"The Old 100th," also known as "All People That on Earth Do Dwell" arose in the time of the Reformation as one of the best-known melodies in all Christian musical traditions. The verses of this song were taken from an early translation of Psalm 100. When we read and think about this Psalm, we can understand why; it summarizes, like a blueprint, the heart and life of worship. Its seven imperatives, in fact, lead us into earnest worship experiences:

1. **Make** *a joyful noise to the* LORD, *all the earth (Psalm 100:1)!* At times, the Psalms call us to be still before the Lord. On other occasions, such as in the first verse of Psalm 100, they exhort us to praise God with an exuberance that cannot be contained. When Jesus entered Jerusalem in triumph and the Pharisees insisted that He quiet the praises of the surrounding throngs, the Lord answered, "I tell you, if these were silent, the very stones would cry out" (Luke 19:40). Psalm 100 envisions such praises filling the whole earth.

2. **Serve** *the* LORD *with gladness (Psalm 100:2a)!* Ancient Hebrew words for worship emphasize active praise: lying prostrate, kneeling, lifting the hands, spinning with joy, shouting, singing, boasting in the Lord. Each word for worship reminds us that we must praise God not only with our lips but with our lives. In whatever way we serve the Lord, our service becomes true worship when we serve Him from our hearts.

3. **Come** *into His presence with singing (Psalm 100:2b)!* Although God is present everywhere, not everyone is aware of His presence. We must make a deliberate act to draw near to God and to live in His presence.

4. **Know** *that the* LORD, *He is God (Psalm 100:3a)!* Worship is built on solid thinking and sound theology. If we do not know God, however, we will not be motivated to worship Him. God is above all others and worthy of our praise forever and ever.

5. **Enter** *His gates with thanksgiving, and His courts with praise (Psalm 100:4a)!* The people of ancient Israel entered the Temple to worship. Today, the Church is God's Temple. Psalm 100's call to enter into worship is as vital now as it was in the day this Psalm was written. Everyone who calls on the name of the Lord would do well to be part of a worship community.

6. **Give thanks** *to Him (Psalm 100:4b)!* Our worship is enhanced by thanksgiving, which in itself is a form of worship. If we develop the habit of giving thanks to God every day, our days will become enriched with earnest worship.

7. **Bless** *His name!* "For the LORD is good; His steadfast love endures forever, and His faithfulness to all generations" (Psalm 100:4c-5). Our ultimate reason to give thanks to God is God Himself. No matter how our circumstances work against us, God is always for us. For this reason, we can bless and praise His name, now and always.

The average person changes jobs numerous times during their career. When we step into Heaven, however, we will have one primary occupation for all eternity: worship. It will not be work for us but a joyous response in our hearts to God's overwhelming goodness. If earnest worship is to be our lot for all eternity, why not get started today?

Respond

✱ 1. Psalm 100 gives us seven essential imperatives for a life of worship. Which of the seven do you connect with most readily? Why?

2. "Worship can be hard work." Do you agree? Explain.

3. What can you do to develop a deeper and stronger life of worship? As a start, write out Psalm 100. Consider memorizing it.

Pray

Lord, You are worthy of praise, and You will have it for all eternity. Help me, as I continue to read Your Word, to know You better that I might fully develop a life of worship. Amen.

Impact

Many people around the world do not know God, much less worship Him. *Beyond Words Radio*, a ministry of Scripture Awakening, aims to reach the unreached and to encourage the faithful. Pray for those who listen to be built up in their faith, and pray for the expanding work of God's powerful Word.

Close

You've probably heard the adage: "Worship isn't for us, it's for Him." We hope B90+ has helped you draw closer to the Lord. May these daily lessons become part of your daily worship of Him.

Session 7 • Overview

● REVIEW Days 35-42
Poetry, Part 1: Suffering, Worship, Prayer

 Now is the time for your small group meeting to review the week's Scripture readings, cover the discussion questions, and watch the Essential Snapshot video together (or by yourself if reading alone). Point your mobile device's camera on the QR code to access the video entitled "Session 7: Facing Evil". Or enter this link into your browser: **ScriptureAwakening.com/plus/**

- Discuss the questions marked by an asterisk (✱) from the **Respond** sections in Days 35-42, perhaps adding others if time permits.
- Watch the Session 7 video* (individually or with a small group).
  1. What insights from the video would you like to explore further?
  2. If someone asked, "How can you believe in a supposed all-powerful and all-loving God when there's so much evil in the world?"—how would you answer them?
- Summarize the Preview (below) of what is coming next week, encouraging group members to read it on their own.

*Facilitators note: In order to watch the Essential Snapshot video with your group, you will need a large video monitor, if meeting in-person. If hosting a small group remotely, use Zoom (or similar service) to stream the video from your device to share with group participants.

● PREVIEW Days 43-49
Poetry, Part 2: Wisdom, Vanity, Love

Weekly Reading: Psalm 103:1 to Isaiah 14:32

Summary

This week's readings conclude the Poetical Books and transition to the Prophetical Books with the first of the Major Prophets.

The book of Psalms appropriately concludes with five grand Hallelujah (Praise the Lord) psalms highlighting one of its overall themes—praise. Proverbs, Ecclesiastes, and Song of Songs, primarily authored by King Solomon, show us how to live wisely and purposefully in the world, how to express love in marriage, and how to honor the God whose love transcends even that found in the best of marriages.

The Prophetical Books provide God's perspective on many of the events from the historical narrative. As those who "speak for God," the prophets uniquely provide God's evaluation of the current situation (*forthtelling*) and offer insight into God's intended future blessings and judgments (*foretelling*). As the first of the major prophets, Isaiah offers a power message of imminent judgment along with the promise of future salvation through the ministry of the coming Messiah.

Books You'll Encounter This Week

Psalms Overview (Conclusion)

This week's readings include all of the Psalms' fifth sub-book which emphasizes the coming Messianic King and His Kingdom. This sub-book also includes the Hallel (used during annual Jewish celebrations) and the Songs of Ascents (used by pilgrims traveling to Jerusalem). Because of the richness of this book, we recommend that you mark specific Psalms you may want to revisit later to more fully appreciate them.

Proverbs Overview

A book of timeless and pithy maxims, the Proverbs highlight general principles to help us live wisely in the world. The wise life, personified by "Lady Wisdom," is contrasted against the life of foolish choices, illustrated by the "Adulterous Woman" who entices and ensnares the unwary.

Ecclesiastes Overview

Written by a wise "Teacher," Ecclesiastes is primarily a discourse on the vanity of life without God, even for the world's most privileged. Seeking personal fulfillment through wisdom, pleasure, projects, and wealth, the Teacher found his pursuits to be as empty as smoke or vapor—here one minute and gone the next. Finally, he acknowledges reverence for God and keeping His commandments to be the only true source of hope and purpose.

Song of Songs Overview

Whereas the wisdom of Ecclesiastes contains some deep and even depressing implications for the unbeliever, the celebration of love in the Song of Songs may be uplifting and encouraging for any marriage and especially for the people of God. This collection of love sonnets has been variously interpreted as a love poem between lovers, as a general illustration of God's love for His people, and as a representation of Christ's love for the Church. Within the pages of this book is found some of the Bible's most sexually explicit imagery and poetry.

Isaiah Overview

Set during the reigns of the later kings of Judah, Isaiah offers messages of condemnation and consolation. Its 66 chapters thematically mirror the

Old and New Testaments. In the first 39 chapters, Isaiah warns friends and foes alike of God's imminent judgment. In the final 27 chapters, he foretells the coming of Christ, praises the Lord's faithfulness, and offers comfort for God's people.

Things to Look for This Week

As you read, consider how:

1. Wise choices frequently require delayed fulfillment while foolish ones seek immediate gratification and are often accompanied by adverse, long-term consequences.

2. Living a self-centered life apart from God leads to disappointment, discontentment, disillusionment, and despair. It's not enough to be wise, you have to act wisely.

3. Romantic love helps us understand and better appreciate the perfect love God has for us.

Coaching Tip

One of the great evidences that the Bible is inspired by God and motivated by God's love lies in its unified message. It was written by 40 human authors from three continents and languages over a span of two thousand years. As you read, take note of themes that are woven together like golden threads, from beginning to end.

Day 43 · God's Love Letter

Not long after my wife Lin and I met, we knew we wanted to get married; but we agreed to wait a year. We wrote letters back and forth every day, and I visited her when I could. One day, I pulled into her graduate school dorm's parking lot after a long overseas trip; she came running out, excited to see me. Then she paused, turned, and reached into her mailbox to see if there was a letter from me. I laughed at the thought; she was so accustomed to reading my love letters that she wanted to have my letter in hand as she greeted and hugged me. Looking back, I realize this is exactly how the Lord wants us to view the Bible. We could even call it God's love letter to us.

Read

You have two reading options: read the full selection of Scripture or a single overview chapter each day.

- Full Reading: Psalm 103–119:72
- Overview Chapter: Psalm 119

Reflect

The Psalms can be categorized not only by book, type, and author, but also by size. This designation becomes most pronounced when we reach Psalm 117, the shortest of the Psalms. This psalm is followed shortly after by Psalm 119 which is more than twice the length of every other psalm. Was the author trying to make a point in Psalm 119 by writing at such great length?

Robert Ripley reported in his *Old Time Radio Show* that in 1875, Parisian painter Marcel de Leclure sent a love letter to his sweetheart, Magdalene de Villalore. Marcel's letter contained the French words "I love you" written 1,875,000 times. Marcel spoke the words as a scribe took dictation. He aimed for length to prove the depth of his love. The Bible was spoken to us by God through some 40 authors over two thousand years. When we read it, we cannot help but see "I love you" written on every page.

Deeply moved by God's love and His Word, the author of Psalm 119 responded to God, writing the longest chapter in the Psalter which would become the longest chapter in the Bible. The author wrote long and reached deeply. The words of Psalm 119 are carefully thought out, like a love letter, each of its words etched with emphasis and forethought. Divided into 22 stanzas of 8 verses, the Psalmist highlighted each stanza by 1 of the 22 letters of the Hebrew alphabet. Every verse within each stanza begins with its designated letter; thus do the first 8 verses of the Psalm begin with "Aleph." And each verse of the next stanza begins with the second Hebrew letter, "Beth."

So determined was the author to express his love for God and for the Bible that he laced each of the Psalm's 176 verses, with the exception of verse 122, with a Hebrew synonym for "Scripture." Like a master craftsman, he placed these synonyms like sparkling diamonds on the felt display of the Psalter. Looking back, we can ponder each synonym to rekindle our love for the Bible and its true Author, God:

We find in Psalm 119 that Scripture is:

1. God's **"Word"** (*dābār*—a general word for God's revelation), and we believe it;

2. God's **"Law"** (*tôrâh*—meaning "instruction"), and we heed it;

3. God's **"Testimony"** (*'ēḏâh*—a declaration of God's will), and we celebrate it;

4. God's **"Statute"** (*ḥūqqîm*—meaning "things inscribed"), and we embrace it;

5. God's **"Commandment"** (*miṣwâh*—an authoritative command), and we obey it;

6. God's **"Judgment"** (*mišpoṭ*—a judicial decision or a binding law), and we respect it;

7. God's **"Precept"** (*piqqûḏîm*—i.e., injunctions), and we study it;

8. God's **"Saying"** (*'imrâh*–which is sometimes translated "promises"), and we listen to it;

9. God's **"Way"** (*derek*—the way of life established by God's Word), and we live by it;

10. God's **"Path"** (*ōraḥ*—a metaphorical word suggesting the right path), and we follow it.

Respond

1. Sometimes Christians are accused of being "bibliophiles," lovers of Scripture. Is that a bad thing? Is it possible to love the Word but not love God? Explain.

✱ 2. Some Christians claim to love God, but do not believe or follow Scripture. Is it possible to love God without loving God's Word? Why or why not?

....

....

....

....

3. Write a short prayer to God—a psalm from your heart—thanking God for giving you His love letter, designed to guide your life.

....

....

....

....

Pray

Lord, thank you for Your Word. Help me to love it as did the author of Psalm 119. Amen.

Impact

The Bible is God's love letter to the world. Help us get as many people as possible to read His love letter. Your suggestions and advice on how to improve or expand the B90+ program are an important part of the process. You can email your feedback to: info@scriptureawakening.com.

Close

Ever met a person who was a "know-it-all"? We probably all have. But then there's God, the truest "know-it-all" ever! And instead of that being an irritant, God's omniscience can be of great assurance and comfort to us. So tune in tomorrow.

Day 44 · **God Knows All**

Psalm 139 shows us God's intimate care, constant companionship, and profound knowledge of the details of our lives—right down to our every thought. Once we know this truth as its author David knew it, we find fresh inspiration to live for God no matter what challenges may come our way.

Read

You have two reading options: read the full selection of Scripture or a single overview chapter each day.

- Full Reading: Psalm 119:73–146
- Overview Chapter: Psalm 139

Reflect

When we begin to think that God doesn't know, doesn't care, or cannot help us, Psalm 139 calls us to think again. In it, David describes:

- God's **Omniscience:** He knows everything (Psalm 139:1-6);
- God's **Omnipresence:** He is everywhere (Psalm 139:7-12); and
- God's **Omnipotence:** He can do anything (Psalm 139:13-16).

The final stanza—Psalm 139:17-24—shows David's response to the greatness of God. Overwhelmed by God's personal care, power, and all-pervasive presence, he declares:

> *How precious to me are your thoughts, O God! How vast is the sum of them! If I would count them, they are more than the sand. I awake, and I am still with you.* (Psalm 139:17-18)

Aware of God's unlimited power, David asks for vindication from his enemies (vv. 19-22). Aware of God's continual presence and perfect knowledge, David asks God to search him and to correct any thoughts or attitudes that are not right before God (vv. 23-24). As we read and reflect on this Psalm, we may find ourselves doing the same. For God knows all.

Take time to read through Psalm 139, pondering its paragraphs, sentences, and ideas. Look at it overall, and think about its parts individually. What does it say to you? The realization that God is constantly with you, knowing you perfectly, loving you intimately, and protecting you relentlessly is supported by the whole of Scripture but perhaps nowhere so clearly as in this Psalm. Jesus once said,

> *Are not two sparrows sold for a penny? And not one of them will fall to the ground apart from your Father. But even the hairs of your head are all numbered. Fear not, therefore; you are of more value than many sparrows.* (Matthew 10:29-31)

Coaching Tip

When David and other Biblical authors wrote the Psalms, their words were profound even though their lives were not perfect. So it is for us. Each day as you read, ask God to work through your life. You may not consider yourself incredibly capable; God only asks that you be fully available.

Psalm 139 was written to help us move beyond doctrine to practice, beyond concepts *about* God to conversations *with* God. When we believe, like David, that the all-knowing, all-powerful God is with us always, we find incentive to honor Him through thick and thin, when we are inspired and when we are tired.

Respond

1. What is your favorite part of Psalm 139. Why?

....

....

....

....

2. What portion of Psalm 139 do you need to reflect on and embrace more fully? Describe.

....

....

....

....

✱ 3. If you really believed the words of Psalm 139, in what ways might your life be changed?

....

....

....

....

Pray

Lord, You have given us the Psalms to help us pray and to show us Your ways. Let my heart be in tune with Your heart, and my steps aligned with Your steps. Amen.

Impact

God knows all. But more than half of the world has yet to know God—the God of the Bible. Consider using a prayer guide, such as the online Joshua Project (JoshuaProject.net) to guide your prayers for people who do not have access to Bibles and the Christian message.

Close

Tomorrow we will finish up Psalms and enter the Biblical landscape of Wisdom. Most of Proverbs was penned by the wisest man who ever lived: King Solomon. Treasures ahead! See you then.

Coaching Tip

God's Word is chock-full of God's wisdom. In order to fill our lives with it, we must partake every day. Ingesting divine wisdom is much like enjoying a good meal; we must chew slowly and take time to enjoy the texture and taste of every bite. If we rush through our reading of Scripture, we may develop indigestion.

Day 45 · **Wisdom Speaks**

The opening chapters of Proverbs call us to embrace God's wisdom, which comes to us through godly counsel and speaks to us as a good friend. Personified as a woman, wisdom is worth more than knowledge, riches, pride, or position. She is the result of a humble reliance on God and a respect for God's laws. And her fruit is a fulfilling life in the world. Wisdom has been around since the earth first spun on its axis, and she will be here still when the world comes to an end. Her help is as close to us as is our next thought, but we must learn how to access her insights in order to enjoy their benefits in our lives. The book of Proverbs shows us how to do this.

Read

You have two reading options: read the full selection of Scripture or a single overview chapter each day.

- Full Reading: Psalm 147 – Proverbs 11
- Overview Chapter: Proverbs 1

Reflect

Proverbs can be divided into three areas: an opening (chapters 1-9), middle (chapters 10-29), and closing (chapters 30-31). The opening section—our focus today—features advice from a father to his son (Proverbs 1:1-19; 2-7), and portrays wisdom as a lady (Proverbs 1:20-33; 8-9). These opening chapters set the stage for the presentation of the profound, pithy, and priceless proverbs that pack chapters 10 to 29. The closing two chapters remind us, once again through both a male and female voice, that wisdom is necessary for a good life (Proverbs 30:1-31:9; 31:10-31). This unique blending of voices shows us that wisdom is for both genders, for young and old—for everyone. Without it, no one can reap the full benefits life has to offer. Consider then wisdom's *provision*, *principles*, and *protection* that you might reap its benefits in your life.

The Provision of Wisdom. The lady in the opening and closing of Proverbs personifies wisdom to help us believe that we can embrace it personally, much like practical advice from a caring mother or a close friend. Lady Wisdom is but a personification of the insight that comes from God, the true source of all wisdom (Proverbs 2:6). As we mature in our understanding of God and the world, we come to see that all wisdom is ultimately "from above" (James 3:17), and we learn to trust and respect God. In other words, the "fear of God" captivates us. The fear described in Proverbs is not one that causes us to run from God; it is, rather, a healthy sense of reverence and veneration that invites us to draw near because "the fear of the LORD is the beginning of wisdom" (Proverbs 9:10a).

The Principles of Wisdom. The book of Proverbs was not given to us as a treasure chest of divine promises that guarantee life will go easily for us. It is rather a rich collection of the principles by which life functions best. We can better appreciate the benefits and limitations of Solomon's proverbs by holding them up against two related Old Testament books of wisdom: Job and Ecclesiastes. Focusing on the norms we might expect in a life filled with God's wisdom, the book of Proverbs leaves Ecclesiastes and Job to cover the exceptions. Job describes the injustices that will prevail on earth even as we live wisely, and Ecclesiastes reminds us that nothing in this world is lasting or perfect, not even the results that come from wisdom on earth. The Proverbs, importantly, are not an ironclad promise that when we do the right thing and follows God's course, life will always go our way. They tell us, rather, that when we follow God's course our chances of good success in life increase exponentially.

The Practice of Wisdom. As you read the Proverbs, ask God for the humility needed to live by God's wisdom the rest of your days. Solomon drew wisdom from God to establish his kingdom, and he became the author of some 3,000 proverbs including the majority that fill this book. When his heart became proud, however, he fell away from God and acted foolishly. His mistakes carried Israel from her era of peace and prosperity into a future of ruin and disgrace. We must learn, then, not only from Solomon's words but also from his life. Even the wise may fall away from God and act foolishly. But the fear of God will hold us fast and keep us true to Him.

Respond

✱ 1. If you could have more knowledge or more wisdom which would you choose? Why?

2. Is it possible to be a genius but not at all wise? Explain.

3. According to Proverbs 1 and the other opening chapters in the book, what is the key to obtaining wisdom?

....

....

....

....

Pray

Lord, thank you that You make wisdom available to all who ask. I ask for it, Lord. I humble myself and depend on Your guidance and counsel by which I might live well while on earth all of my days. Let it be, and may You be glorified in me. Amen.

Impact

Knowledge is easily accessed from the world, but wisdom's primary source is from God and His Word. Make a list of areas in which you seek wisdom for your life. Ask God to give you His insights through Scripture, prayer, and the advice of wise counselors.

Close

In case you missed it, today is the official halfway point in Bible in 90 Days Plus, which means you have completed reading through half of the Bible! Celebrate this week with some small but significant reward . . . did someone say *ice cream!*?

Day 46 · **Gleaning Wisdom**

Do you know why the Bible is better than a dictionary? The dictionary has words, including verbs, but the Bible has *PROverbs*. The Bible's proverbs are action oriented. Like verbs, they move us forward. As you read, make note of the proverbs that especially motivate you in a positive direction. Record your favorites.

Read

You have two reading options: read the full selection of Scripture or a single overview chapter each day.

- Full Reading: Proverbs 12–22
- Overview Chapter: Proverbs 12

Reflect

The middle section of the book of Proverbs—chapters 10 to 29—contain a wealth of wisdom that instructs us in nearly every aspect of our lives. To illustrate this, I have randomly selected 20 verses, 1 from each of these chapters in sequential order, categorizing them with 1 word, then summarized in a short statement. Take notice of each summary word to get a sense of how God's all-encompassing wisdom flows through the book and benefits your life. Most importantly, take time to read and reflect on the Proverbs not only today but all of your days. You may find it helpful to write out specific proverbs. Consider also attempting to re-write key proverbs in your own words. The aim in doing so is not to replace Scripture but to reflect on it; not to change God's Word but to cherish it more fully that your life might be changed.

Proverbs 10:20	**Values**:	Wise values are found in our words, which can impact the world.
Proverbs 11:3	**Integrity**:	Live with integrity and show justice; God is watching you!
Proverbs 12:2	**Behavior**:	God blesses righteous behavior.
Proverbs 13:3	**Words**:	Control your tongue and improve your life.
Proverbs 14:4	**Tenacity**:	God gives strength for big tasks but with it may come changes and new challenges.
Proverbs 15:5	**Chastening**:	Discipline from God and parents is an opportunity for growth.
Proverbs 16:6	**Focus**:	The one who consistently speaks truth and shows love will stay on track.

Coaching Tip

Some sections of the Bible, such as the Proverbs, are like thick steak; they are difficult to digest quickly. Read through them at a natural pace and plan to come back to this book from time to time after you complete your read through the Bible in order to digest its wisdom more fully.

Proverbs 17:7	**Honor**: You are a prince or princess of the King of Kings; live and speak like it!
Proverbs 18:8	**Gossip**: You can do inestimable good or harm to another by your words.
Proverbs 19:9	**Honesty**: Don't lie about another; it will come back to bite you.
Proverbs 20:10	**Fairness**: Those who cheat others must reckon with God.
Proverbs 21:11	Wisdom: Those who are wise receive instruction and become wiser still.
Proverbs 22:12	**Truth**: Speak the truth, and God will establish your words.
Proverbs 23:13	**Discipline**: Train your child in love, and your child will later love you for it.
Proverbs 24:14	**Future**: Glean wisdom today to create a better tomorrow.
Proverbs 25:15	**Patience**: By the art of gentle persuasion, you can move a king.
Proverbs 26:16	**Sloth**: The lazy person's heart is fat with arrogance.
Proverbs 27:17	**Excellence**: People of character build on each other to create excellence.
Proverbs 28:18	**Stability**: Walk rightly before God, and He will establish your steps.
Proverbs 29:19	**Persuasion**: People need more than words to be motivated.

Respond

1. Which of the above statements speaks most to you? Look up the corresponding verse in the Bible and reflect on how it applies to your life.

....

....

....

....

....

2. Write down another verse or two from your reading of Proverbs that especially challenged you. Explain why or how it applies to your life.

....

....

....

....

✱ 3. Complete this thought, "I need God's wisdom because without it . . ."

....

....

....

Pray

Lord, fill my mind and heart with Your wisdom that Your wisdom might be reflected in my life. Amen.

Impact

You—a reader of Scripture and lover of God—have full access to God's wisdom. Ask God to make you a better listener and an instrument of wise counsel in time of need to a specific person, as God leads.

Close

My wife and I read, reread, and rotated through Proverbs every month for four years. The results were amazing! We had a deep well to draw from which benefited our personal lives, parenting, and ministry for years to come.

Coaching Tip

The aim of Bible in 90 Days is for us to "read each word thoughtfully." If you have been rushing through your readings, slow up and pray for God to help you glean insight and fulfillment in what you read. As you do so, your daily time in the Word can become the richest, most fulfilling part of your day.

Day 47 · **The Fulfilled Life**

Five books in the Old Testament are commonly referred to as wisdom literature: Job, Psalms, Proverbs, Ecclesiastes, and Song of Solomon. Job provides wisdom about suffering; Psalms about worship; Proverbs about making choices; Song of Solomon about love; and Ecclesiastes about finding fulfillment in life. The book of Ecclesiastes opens by describing the empty life, using the Hebrew word *hebel* 37 times. *Hebel* is translated "emptiness," "vanity," "meaninglessness," "vapor," or "breath." Ecclesiastes shows us how fleeting our pursuits are without God. It also points the way to a fulfilled life.

Read

You have two reading options: read the full selection of Scripture or a single overview chapter each day.

- Full Reading: Proverbs 23 – Ecclesiastes 5
- Overview Chapter: Ecclesiastes 1

Reflect

Ecclesiastes focuses on teachings from a sage called "Teacher." Traditionally, the book is understood by Jews and Christians to have been written by King Solomon in his later years. This teacher had the opportunity to seek fulfillment in the things that motivate the populace: wisdom, wealth, pleasure, and productivity. After pursuing each area with gusto, the teacher came up empty; yet through his pursuits, he was filled with insight that the world needs today.

Wisdom (Ecclesiastes 1:12-18; 2:12-16): We sometimes assume that if we could gain enough wisdom and knowledge our lives would come together to give us true satisfaction. But we can never seem to get enough; in fact, the more we know about the world, the more depressed some of us feel. After seeking and finding more wisdom than the kings who proceeded him in Jerusalem, the Teacher concluded that "in much wisdom is much vexation, and he who increases knowledge increases sorrow" (Ecclesiastes 1:18). For him, the accumulation of much learning was nothing more than "a striving after the wind" (Ecclesiastes 1:17b).

Wealth (Ecclesiastes 5:18-6:12): The world tells us that if we have enough money, our lives will be complete. But how often has a person won the lottery or achieved fame and fortune only to feel empty? The Teacher, one of the world's richest people in his day, summarizes that "He who loves money will not be satisfied with money, nor he who loves wealth with his income; this also is vanity" (Ecclesiastes 5:10).

Pleasure (Ecclesiastes 2:1-3): Our culture promises happiness and fulfillment through indulgence in worldly pursuits. Temporary pleasures, however, cannot satisfy our deepest needs. The Teacher, illustrating the point, said to himself, "Come now, I will test you with pleasure; enjoy yourself." He sought to fulfill himself with every type of pleasure. Wine and laughter, women and wealth were all his without limit. Even so, he concluded, "But behold, this also was vanity" (Ecclesiastes 2:1).

Productivity (Ecclesiastes 2:4-26; 3:9-4:16): We sometimes believe that if we can advance just a little further in our jobs or add a notch to our prestige or position in life, we will be content. But even such positive benefits are short-lived. In the Teacher's words, they are a mere "striving after the wind" (Ecclesiastes 2:26). He built houses, planted vineyards, developed parks, owned herds and flocks, increase productivity, and amassed a great treasury. Still, he was not satisfied.

Each of these areas—wealth, wisdom, pleasure, and productivity—left to themselves do not fulfill us. But there is One who does. His name is God. When we come to know Him and invite Him into the details of our lives, we can find fulfillment regardless of our circumstances, position, financial security, or prestige.

That is what our read through the Bible and the programs of Scripture Awakening are all about. As we read the Word, we come to know God. As a result, when we accumulate wealth, we find purposeful ways to use and share it (Ecclesiastes 5:8-6:12). As we grow in wisdom, we can most easily accept that life isn't perfect (Ecclesiastes 7:1-29). With God in the picture, our lives take on new meaning; even the thought of death motivates us to live better lives (Ecclesiastes 9:1-18; 11:7-12:8).

In summary, God's Word shows us the way to the fulfilled life (Ecclesiastes 12:13-14).

Respond

1. The Teacher, as described above, sought fulfillment in at least four ways. How do you seek fulfillment?

✱ 2. Read the conclusion of the book: Ecclesiastes 12:13-14. Do you agree with the Teacher's assessment? Explain.

3. How can knowing God bring us fulfillment even when things on earth do not?

Pray

Help me, God, to find my fulfillment in You alone, that all of life might become more meaningful to me once again. Amen.

Impact

The world offers us fulfillment in things we cannot keep. The Word offers us fulfillment in things we cannot lose. Pray for people you know who would benefit by reading God's Word daily. If God opens a door, invite them to give B90+ a try.

Close

God's Word brings us fulfillment. B90 participant Suzanne Larson says it well: "WOW! I thought I would get a good overview of the Bible but didn't expect more. I was wrong! Reading the Bible this way showed me context like I never imagined. This has been such a powerful experience for me!"

Day 48 · **Real Love**

Many people are confused about the meaning of love. In today's culture, for example, various concepts are attached to the one word "love." New Testament authors, borrowing from riches in the Old Testament, constructed a solid and specific description of God's love and how it works itself out in our lives. This Biblical comprehension is enhanced for us as we come to know the Old Testament foundations on which it is built. The Song of Songs—also called the Song of Solomon—is a perfect place to start.

Read

You have two reading options: read the full selection of Scripture or a single overview chapter each day.

- Full Reading: Ecclesiastes 6 – Isaiah 1
- Overview Chapter: Song of Solomon 8

Reflect

Understanding the Song of Songs. Hebrew interpreters of the Song of Songs recognized the book as an analogy of God's covenant of love with the people of Israel. Christian theologians built on that concept and expanded it to suggest the Song of Songs provides a metaphor of Christ's covenant of marriage to the Church, which includes believers throughout history. In our modern era, a new and more human-centered approach has been suggested and taught, suggesting the love poetry in Song of Songs can serve as God's instruction manual for romance, sex, and marriage.

Which of these interpretations is the right one? Biblically, all three are correct. Marriage and romance are described in the Bible as pictures of God's love offered to each of us. This illustration is seen initially in His covenant with Israel, then more fully through Christ's coming as the Bridegroom of the Church (Ephesians 5:22-33). At the same time, the Bible as a whole—and Song of Songs in particular—contains rich Biblical insights revealing God's intention for human marriage and sexuality. Considering the fact that God created marriage and sex, we should not be surprised to discover that as our primary instruction manual from God, the Bible contains insights for this important aspect of our lives.

Understanding God's Love. Seen in this broader context, the Song of Songs tells us much about love from God's perspective. The Bible teaches that God's love is selfless, consistent, and complete. When such love is brought into human marriages, they function as they were intended. In order for matrimony to excel, both partners need to give themselves fully to each other in love. This idea carries the narrative in the Song of Songs, making it both a fitting manual for marriage and a divine forecast of Christ's coming for His Bride, the Church (Revelation 19:6-10; 21:9-14).

Coaching Tip

As you read the Scriptures, remember that the overarching theme of the Bible is God's love. It is His love letter to you; He longs for you to know His heart and His covenant of love. This simple and profound understanding sheds light on every story and teaching in the Bible.

God's love is perfect; ours is imperfect. When we invite the Lord into our lives, however, His love fills our hearts and our love for others grows. The Song of Songs shows this progression working itself out in the love between a man and a woman, a shepherd and one working in the vineyards. Whether the romancing shepherd was actually King Solomon may be debated, but we really should not miss the progression of love shown in the book. It moves from a selfish love to one that is selfless. This deepening love is evident, for example, in the three parallel phrases the woman uses to describe her growing devotion and commitment to her bridegroom (Song of Songs 2:16, 6:3, 7:10).

Growing in God's Love. Real and lasting love is built on commitment. It grows not through passion or emotion but through selfless acts of kindness and devotion. Such love endures the storms of life, builds perseverance, and strengthens relationships. Built on commitment and self-sacrifice, it sustains friendships and creates a safe haven for maximizing romance. The very experience that so much of the world strives for—sexual fulfillment and pleasure—is enhanced and maintained when this Divine understanding of love is embraced by individuals and whole societies.

Respond

1. As you read the Song of Songs, do you feel that it is too graphic and sexual to be in the Bible? Explain.

✱ 2. In what ways do you think our modern culture has lost the true meaning of love?

3. Examine your heart and relationships. Does God's love, true love, inspire your relationships? How might you improve in this regard? Be specific.

....

....

....

....

Pray

Great and gracious Lord, thank you for loving us enough to die for us. When we fail You, You love us still. Fill us with Your Spirit and with Biblical understanding, that we might display Your matchless love in the world. Amen.

Impact

The world is looking for love, and Christians are connected to love's source. We have an opportunity—largely untapped—to show the world how great and unending is the supply of love available to anyone who comes to the Lord. Some people may never see God until they experience His love through your life and mine. Think of someone you know who needs to be loved, and ask God for wisdom about how you can make a difference in his or her life.

Close

If we really love God, we will want to know God, even see God. Tomorrow we will actually see a vision of God.

Coaching Tip

If you are having a difficult time reading because the font is too small in your Bible, consider using a large print version, whether hard cover or online.

Day 49 · **A Vision of God**

Isaiah is the prophet who saw and spoke of Jesus more than did any other. The amazing thing about his writings is that they bring us an understanding about our Lord that is every bit as detailed and clear as what is written of Him in the New Testament. And Isaiah was written hundreds of years before His birth. Quoted by more New Testament authors than any other Old Testament book, Isaiah's prophecy instructs us still today. In fact, the authors of the New Testament relied on what Isaiah saw to help them describe what they experienced when God showed up in the person of Jesus Christ. By reading Isaiah, we can see God in a new and clarified light.

Read

You have two reading options: read the full selection of Scripture or a single overview chapter each day.

- Full Reading: Isaiah 2–14
- Overview Chapter: Isaiah 6

Reflect

As a young man, Isaiah was commissioned by God through a dramatic vision. The prophet's friend and strong supporter—King Uzziah—had just died, and Isaiah saw another on the throne. This new king was God, who was "high and lifted up; and the train of his robe filled the temple" (Isaiah 6:1b). This simple vision of the Almighty, described in a mere 13 verses, set Isaiah on the pathway of his prophetic calling. His calling can change our lives and strengthen our own sense of calling as well.

He saw the Lord's Holiness. As Isaiah looked at the throne of God, he saw mighty angels standing above the Lord, calling out, "Holy, holy, holy is the Lord of hosts; the whole earth is full of his glory!" (Isaiah 6:3). Three times God's holiness was mentioned, suggesting the three persons of the Trinity and the unending reality of God's perfection and glory: past, present and future.

Until we see God's holiness, we do not really know or understand God. When Jesus began His ministry, He often quoted Isaiah to remind the people that He was fulfilling the prophet's visions and words from long ago (see John 12:37-43). Jesus, the eternal Son of God, is truly holy. The word *holiness* means "to be set apart." It cannot be fully defined by a set of rules, as the Pharisees attempted to do. It is defined by a relationship of intimacy and obedience to the Living God. Like Isaiah, we are called and set apart for God's purposes in the world.

Isaiah recognized his personal unworthiness. As the vision of the Lord on His throne was revealed, the Temple shook and the prophet cried out, "Woe is me! For I am lost; for I am a man of unclean lips, and I dwell in the midst of a people of unclean lips; for my eyes have seen the King, the Lord of hosts!" (Isaiah 6:5). Every time in Scripture when God appears in His glory or an angel reflects His glory, humans who are present become overwhelmed with a sense of their sinfulness and unworthiness. Once we understand who God is and that this same Lord is with us always, we begin to live in a state of true humility and awe before God; we lose all fear about people's opinions of us. John Wesley said it well: "Give me one hundred preachers who fear nothing but sin, and desire nothing but God, and I care not a straw whether they be clergymen or laymen; such alone will shake the gates of hell and set up the kingdom of heaven on Earth."[1]

The prophet was forgiven and commissioned. The prophet was forgiven his sins and sent to God's people with a message. Though most would reject his message, a remnant would receive and be refined by it (Isaiah 6:8-13). An educated author and skilled poet, Isaiah's message is contained in 66 chapters for each of us to read. When we do so, we too are confronted by God's holiness. As we humble ourselves and repent, we too will find our sins atoned for. And we will hear the gentle voice of God's Spirit commissioning us to go into the world with the Gospel message of truth, hope, and joy.

Respond

1. Have you ever had a vision of God, whether through a spiritual encounter or a keener understanding of Scripture? If so, how did it impact you?

....

....

....

....

2. What particular details from Isaiah's vision most parallels your own understanding of God? Explain.

....

....

....

....

---

[1] Mark Williamson, *A Blueprint for Revival: Lessons from the Life of John Wesley* (Studies in Christian History and Thought) (United Kingdom: Authentic Media, 2011).

✱ 3. As we see God more clearly and tell others about Him, should we expect the world to gladly receive our message all of the time (John 12:37-43)? Why or why not?

....

....

....

....

Pray

Lord, help me to see You and to know You more as I read the book of Isaiah. Reveal Yourself to me in such a manner that I cannot help but be Your witness in the world. Amen.

Impact

Isaiah's vision deeply changed his life. The great need of our day is for Scripture to similarly impact our lives. If time allows or once you've completed this study, check out the free podcasts at BeyondWordsRadio.org, covering hundreds of topics to help you understand how to live out the Scriptures in a world that does not know God.

Close

A Beyond Words radio listener contacted us saying, "I imagine you are not fully aware of the impact you have. My husband Jeff and I listen and are dedicated to your broadcasts. Your informative programs reach into our lives for our Lord God." — Mary (Tampa, FL)

Session 8 • Overview

● REVIEW Days 43-49
Poetry, Part 2: Wisdom, Vanity, Love

 Now is the time for your small group meeting to review the week's Scripture readings, cover the discussion questions, and watch the Essential Snapshot video together (or by yourself if reading alone). Point your mobile device's camera on the QR code to access the video entitled "Session 8: The Best Life". Or enter this link into your browser: **ScriptureAwakening.com/plus/**

- Discuss the questions marked by an asterisk (✻) from the **Respond** sections in Days 43-49, perhaps adding others if time permits.
- Watch the Session 8 video* (individually or with a small group).
    1. What insights from the video would you like to explore further?
    2. Do you believe the Bible shows us how to live our lives to their fullness? Why or why not?
- Summarize the Preview (below) of what is coming next week, encouraging group members to read it on their own.

*Facilitators note: In order to watch the Essential Snapshot video with your group, you will need a large video monitor, if meeting in-person. If hosting a small group remotely, use Zoom (or similar service) to stream the video from your device to share with group participants.

● PREVIEW Days 50-56
Major Prophets, Part 1: Condemnation, Salvation, Confrontation

Weekly Reading: Isaiah 15:1 to Jeremiah 31:22

Summary

Isaiah, considered by many to be "the Shakespeare of the prophets," continues his prophetic ministry. This week's readings conclude Isaiah's prophecies to the nation of Judah while prophetically looking ahead to the future restoration of the kingdom under the Messiah. A half-century after Isaiah, God calls Jeremiah to minister to the nation of Judah in her final days. The growing power and ambition of the Babylonians has become the latest threat to the nation. Despite Jeremiah's impassioned pleas for national repentance, her leaders refuse to either listen or respond, breaking his heart.

Books You'll Encounter This Week

Isaiah Overview (Conclusion)

Isaiah continues his series of prophetic messages of condemnation against the surrounding nations before zeroing in on both Israel and Judah. He then offers a historical narrative of the attack by Assyria against Judah and God's miraculous deliverance. In the book's final 27 chapters, Isaiah changes both audiences and messages. Speaking to Jews during and following the exile, he offers a message of hope through the work of the coming Messiah. Isaiah concludes his book with prophecies of a glorious future, not just for Israel but for the entire world.

Jeremiah Overview (Introduction)

Jeremiah is a reluctant prophet who, unlike Jonah, allows God to use him despite significant opposition and persecution from God's people. Among other challenges, God commands Jeremiah to inform the people of Judah that God will allow their capture by Nebuchadnezzar and their subsequent exile in Babylon for 70 years. After his call to ministry by God, Jeremiah delivers a series of 10 sermons concerning Judah's willful sinning and continued violations of the Covenant. His continued messages of judgment, condemnation, and the sadness he carries in his heart mark him historically as "the weeping prophet." He reveals how, like a hardened pot, the peoples' hearts are no longer pliable in God's hands, and now they must be completely broken. Jeremiah declares that while the nation's leaders are unfit to rule, a righteous King will come in the future—pointing to the coming Christ.

Things to Look for This Week

As you read, consider:

1. The contrast between the faithlessness of King Ahaz (who trusted in his alliance with Assyria) with that of faithful King Hezekiah (who led the nation in repentance and sought the Lord's help during his moment of crisis resulting in a great deliverance).

2. Isaiah's theme of the ideal future king from the line of David who, as the obedient servant of the Lord, will faithfully execute God's plan for salvation of His people and restoration of the nation.

3. The role of Jeremiah as Covenant mediator between the people and the Lord, as he calls them back into a right relationship with God based upon heart-felt obedience rather than superficial religious practices.

Supplemental Material

As you read this week, review the *Putting the Prophets in Their Place* chart in Appendix 4 on page 328.

Day 50 · **The Naked Truth**

The world is perishing for lack of truth; yet God will always have a witness. In Isaiah's time, for example, God's people were so hardened in their sin and rebellion that God warned Isaiah they would not listen to him (Isaiah 6:9-10). Nevertheless, the prophet would need to speak the truth, sharing God's heart with the people, even if he felt naked and exposed as he did so. At one point in his ministry, he was directed to strip down to his underwear as a sign of the poverty rebellious nations would soon experience if they did not repent. As we ponder the prophet's life of obedience, we may ask ourselves if we are similarly willing to obey God and proclaim the truth whatever the cost.

Read

You have two reading options: read the full selection of Scripture or a single overview chapter each day.

- Full Reading: Isaiah 15–29:10
- Overview Chapter: Isaiah 20

Reflect

Truth and Hope. The book of Isaiah's main theme coincides with the meaning of the writer's name, "The Lord is Salvation." His is a book of hope. Why then do the first 39 chapters of this great book of prophecy place so much emphasis on judgment? The answer is simple: salvation requires that we be saved from something. Isaiah lived from approximately 740 to 698 BC and saw the reign of four of Judah's kings: Uzziah, Jotham, Ahaz, and Hezekiah. He was told by God that judgment was coming on Israel for her sins and that there was no escaping it, but that there was hope. Isaiah watched the invasion of Assyria against Israel, and he warned about the soon coming invasion of Babylon against Judah. He also predicted with astonishing accuracy the return of a remnant of God's people to rebuild Jerusalem.

Truth and Judgement. The warnings of God's coming judgement were not only for Israel and Judah but for the surrounding nations—a demonstration of God's concern for all the peoples of the world. God chastens nations, and He also restores them. And whether or not people in nations near or far listened to God's message, it was Isaiah's responsibility to proclaim it. Much like the prophet Ezekiel, Isaiah would sometimes be called to illustrate his messages with outward signs. In Isaiah 20, for example, he was told to preach to Egypt and Ethiopia (Cush) with his outer garment and sandals removed as a sign that these two nations would be stripped bare by invading Assyria. The prophet walked about in this humiliating manner—in his underwear—for three years.

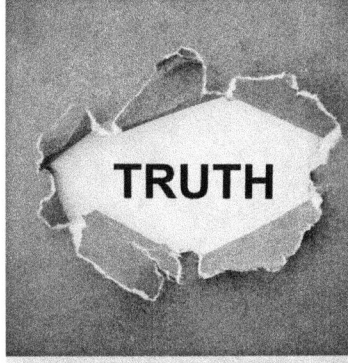

Coaching Tip

You have heard the adage, "If you don't use it, you'll lose it." When you learn a new truth in the Scripture, write it down and ask for God's help to live it out.

The Naked Truth. Some scholars think he was actually told by God to walk about naked, for those being warned would soon be stripped naked and dragged into exile. Either way, the awkwardness experienced by Isaiah as he obeyed God's call may be accentuated by the fact that he was well educated, possibly of a priestly or even an aristocratic line. His language demonstrates the finest classical Hebrew writing with a passionate poetic flair. Nevertheless, Isaiah was called to humble himself before the world so that by his life he might speak of God's coming judgement with a clarity that transcended words.

We may, at first, think of God as rather cruel to ask Isaiah to humiliate himself in this manner. Upon further reflection, however, we realize how incredibly merciful God is to have warned even these distant nations of the coming judgement. God's wish is for all to be saved (1 Timothy 2:3-4). So it is today that God's servants carry the message of His salvation throughout the world amid great hardship, simply that the world might know there is a God who loves them and who offers them salvation. It is this love that motivates them—and should motivate us—to speak the truth regardless of the awkwardness we experience.

Respond

1. The Western world has become Postmodern, believing there is no absolute truth. How does this drifting away from truth and God's Word impact your life and our culture?

✱ 2. Do you find it hard to speak the truth in love to others? Explain.

3. Which do you consider more impressive about Isaiah: the accuracy of his prophetic predictions or his willingness to proclaim God's truth to those who would not listen? Why?

....

....

....

....

....

Pray

Lord, thank you that You left us more than words on a page. You are with us in person through the Holy Spirit whom You promised would lead us into all truth and empower us to proclaim it. Do Your work in me as I continue to read Your Word and grow in Your truth. Amen.

Impact

Scripture Awakening seeks to lead people into the truth. We thank you for praying for this mission as God leads you. You are helping us to impact our Postmodern, Post-Christian culture so that people might turn back to the truth, one person at a time.

Close

Did you know that 90% of Christians have never read through the entire Bible? That's what Bible in 90 Days is all about, helping people become Biblically literate. What a marvelous accomplishment for you when you complete this Bible reading journey!

B90+

Coaching Tip

Isaiah declared the words he heard from God, no matter what the personal cost. He prepared the way for Christ, who now sends us. As you read and learn, don't contain the blessing. Be sure to share what you have gleaned with someone else.

Day 51 · **Supernatural Comfort**

Isaiah 40 marks a change-point in Isaiah's prophecy. The first 39 chapters focus generally on God's confrontation of Israel for her sin but chapter 40 begins with God's promised comfort. So clear is this theme that some scholars describe Chapter 40 as the beginning of a second portion of Isaiah, a portion sometimes referred to as "The Book of Comfort." In Isaiah 40, we can learn how to receive God's comfort for our own lives in times of need.

Read

You have two reading options: read the full selection of Scripture or a single overview chapter each day.

- Full Reading: Isaiah 29:11–41
- Overview Chapter: Isaiah 40

Reflect

Isaiah 40 opens with the words, "Comfort, comfort my people . . ." It then shows us the preparation and Person that brought comfort to Israel. On the same basis, God's comfort can be ours today as we serve "the God of all comfort" (2 Corinthians 1:3c).

Preparation (Isaiah 40:1-8): Isaiah 1-39 gives the background: Israel's sins lead to her demise and Assyria conquers the Northern Kingdom—Israel. Chapter 39 ends with a warning that Babylon will soon conquer Judah. Isaiah 40 then brings a shift; a message of comfort for the people after they've suffered their full measure in exile and received double for all their sins (Isaiah 40:2). This phrase is an idiom for "full measure"; it does not literally mean Israel received more punishment than she deserved. The word can be used of a paper being folded exactly in half, doubled over until one side mirrors the other. In other words, God's punishments are commensurate with our need for correction. And after we have received such correction, He then comforts us.

What hardship or difficulties are you facing today? Paul promises that God will use them to prepare you for His grace and mercy that you might soon comfort others (2 Corinthians 1:4). This is all made possible through Christ, who came into the world to take the punishment we deserve and received double for all of our sins. John the Baptist, who was sent to "prepare the way of the Lord," cleared the pathway for Jesus. His mission was to proclaim God's unchanging Word, as foretold by Isaiah (John 1:19-23; Isaiah 40:6-8).

Person (Isaiah 40:9-31): The remainder of Isaiah 40 describes God as the only Person who can bring us comfort, no matter our situation in life. Isaiah 40 is one of the greatest statements in the Bible about the sovereignty of God; we are wise to meditate on it and live accordingly.

God will carry us close to Him in our times of difficultly as a shepherd carries sheep (Isaiah 40:11). And we can always trust Him. Set against His greatness, our idols and even the nations of the world are as nothing (Isaiah 40:12-26). He promises, through His matchless power, to uphold and strengthen us always (Isaiah 40:27-31). Isaiah's poetic descriptions of God's promise to comfort us remain unsurpassed in the Bible. They are worth placing in our hearts and posting in our homes:

> *Have you not known? Have you not heard? The LORD is the everlasting God, the Creator of the ends of the earth. He does not faint or grow weary; his understanding is unsearchable. He gives power to the faint, and to him who has no might he increases strength. Even youths shall faint and be weary, and young men shall fall exhausted; but they who wait for the LORD shall renew their strength; they shall mount up with wings like eagles; they shall run and not be weary; they shall walk and not faint.* (Isaiah 40:28-31)

Respond

1. What trials or challenges do you now face or have you faced for which you need the comfort of the Almighty God?

....

....

....

....

✸ 2. List all of the promises you see in Isaiah 40:28-31 (see above).

....

....

....

....

3. According to the above text, our part is to "wait" on the Lord. What, in the context of your life, might such waiting look like today?

....

....

Pray

Lord, help me to know You through my reading of Isaiah. And teach me to wait on You that I might find Your comfort and the strength to live for You. Amen.

Impact

If we could see inside people, we would probably discover that every single person is in need of comfort and consolation for some difficulty they have had to face in life. Ask God to give you a supernatural sensitivity today to someone who needs the comfort of God.

Close

We hope today's lesson revealed more deeply the Spirit of our God who is our Comforter. In tomorrow's lesson, Isaiah will take us "back to the future," so to speak, so watch for it. Until then, may the rest of your day be blessed.

Day 52 · **Reading Backward**

The regathering of the nation of Israel was prophesied in the Bible hundreds of years before it occurred. At no other time has an ancient nation been scattered and regathered in such a significant manner; hence, their unique status as a Middle Eastern people using a language with such ancient roots. The ancient Semitic languages, like 11 other languages today, are read from right to left, which most of the world considers "backward." Isaiah read backwards, however, in an entirely different manner, as we will see.

Read

You have two reading options: read the full selection of Scripture or a single overview chapter each day.

- Full Reading: Isaiah 42–52
- Overview Chapter: Isaiah 45

Reflect

Isaiah often saw and spoke about the future. More than two hundred years after the prophet lived and preached, many of his predictions had already come to pass. Isaiah seems to read time backwards, writing about future events as though they had already occurred. He not only foretold the end of Israel's exile (Isaiah 40, 44) but repeatedly stated the name of the as yet unborn king, Cyrus, who would release the nation (Isaiah 45). So exacting and specific are Isaiah's words about the future that some scholars assume his statements to be the additions of later writers. But are they?

When we look at Isaiah's writing as a whole, we find his tendency to read time backward fills the pages of his book. Not only does he make accurate predictions about Cyrus and the Persians but about other nations, about Israel, about the Church, and about Christ. The predictive threads in his writing are complex and thoroughly interwoven with the rest of the Bible, challenging the notion that later Biblical authors and editors could have fabricated his predictions. The long-held traditional understanding that Isaiah and the other Biblical prophets were enabled by the Almighty God to see into the future is not only a sound option but a more logical explanation for the wealth of Biblical predictions that have come to pass through the ages.

There are numerous reasons for us to accept Isaiah's prophecies as true and accurate predictions given by God. Consider, for example, Isaiah's predictions about the coming Messiah. The New Testament references more than 70 of Isaiah's predictions about the coming Christ:

- His lineage (Isaiah 11:1-5/Romans 15:12; Revelation 22:16)
- His virgin birth (Isaiah 7:14/Luke 1:27,34; Matthew 1:20)

Coaching Tip

Issues surrounding Biblical interpretation can take years to sort out and understand. As we are doing so, it is essential that we build a foundation for such understanding by simply reading God's Word, allowing the whole of Scripture to give us perspective about its parts.

- His role as Messiah (Isaiah 9:6-7/Matthew 1:18-25)
- His Messianic impact as a stumbling stone and cornerstone (Isaiah 8:14; 28:16/Matthew 21:42-44; Romans 9:32-33; 1 Peter 2:8; Ephesians 2:19-22)
- His Messianic suffering (Isaiah 53/Matthew 8:14-17; John 12:37-38; Luke 22:37; 1 Peter 2:21-25; Acts 8:30-35; Romans 10:16)

When one takes time to unpack these and other predictions about Christ in Isaiah, written several hundred years before the Lord's coming, their accurate portrayals of what actually occurred are amazing. With this in mind, it is not that difficult to believe Isaiah would also predict the decree of Cyrus.

Isaiah's gift for seeing into the future fits into the tenor of the Bible as a whole. Predictions and their fulfillments fill the pages of nearly a third of the Biblical texts. Speaking ahead of time to His servants, God makes hundreds of statements about future events involving Israel, the Church, the nations of the world, and Christ's birth, life, death, resurrection, ascension, second coming, and the end of the ages. It may be easy for the casual reader to dismiss some of these predictions as vague, general, and open to reinterpretation. But when we study the context of the predictions and their fulfillments as well as the abundance of specific predictions and the strength of their interwoven messages, we are faced with an overwhelming demonstration of the trustworthiness of Scripture. No other book of antiquity carries a similarly rich and prophetic narrative.

The goal of Biblical prophecy is not merely to teach us to read time backward, like Isaiah but also to inspire us to look forward to Christ's return. It isn't primarily to give us a road map for tomorrow as much as a faith in God's guidance today. When we realize that God has a plan and is never taken by surprise, we can more completely surrender our lives to Him.

Respond

1. How would the predictions of the prophets have challenged or encouraged the Israelites when they were taken into captivity?

....

....

....

....

✱ 2. Do you have any favorite verses or passages that contain prophetic elements? If so, which?

....

....

....

....

3. In what way does Biblical prophecy encourage or challenge you today?

....

....

....

....

Pray

Lord, give me grace to worry less about the future as I simply believe You have the future in Your hands. Amen.

Impact

Not all of us have visions about the future as Isaiah did. But we can each draw insights from our readings for our lives today. If you are meeting in a weekly small group to discuss your readings with friends, whether face to face or online, be sure to share insights God has given to you. Pray also for each member of the group to grow in their faith.

Close

The specificity and accuracy of Isaiah's prophecies are astounding, as you will see on Day 53. Get ready to be motivated like never before!

Coaching Tip

The Word of God becomes alive to us when we have surrendered our lives to the Lord. His Spirit guides us and teaches us. If you have not yet given your life to Christ, make this the day of decision.

Day 53 · **The Great Motivator**

Isaiah 53, when read with careful understanding, becomes a great motivator for us to trust God more. It takes the predictive elements of prophecy—as seen in our previous lesson—and makes them personal. No matter whether a person is rich or poor, proud or humble, highly educated or barely educated, it places each of us at the foot of the cross. There we see our Savior suffering for us as He dies for our sins. When we then pause to look at the evidence that this suffering was part of God's established plan, we come to appreciate more than ever the amazing love of God.

Read

You have two reading options: read the full selection of Scripture or a single overview chapter each day.

- Full Reading: Isaiah 53–65
- Overview Chapter: Isaiah 53

Reflect

Isaiah 53 contains a stark description of a suffering person, one who gives Himself as a sacrifice for the sins of others. It contains imagery that—along with Psalm 22—has long been understood by Christians to be a prophetic foreshadowing of the crucifixion of Christ. Orthodox Jews, however, have suggested the suffering servant in Isaiah 53 may simply be a personification of the suffering nation of Israel. The former interpretation is clearly the more logical and Biblical choice. Consider that:

1. The verbiage of the text fits hand-in-glove with Christ's crucifixion but does not fit as well with the idea of a whole nation becoming a suffering servant. The personal pronouns in Isaiah 53 are singular and the descriptions of the Cross are specific. This chapter, combined with Psalm 22, have thus understandably turned countless unbelievers—even Jews—into followers of Christ. Such an interpretation does not minimize the suffering that Jewish people have experienced through the ages. It is rather an appeal to the obvious and plain reading of the text, bringing to us the realization that the terrible suffering God's people have experienced through the ages has not been in vain but instead has been part of God's greater purpose to bring eternal hope to Jews and Gentiles alike.

2. Isaiah 53 is but a leaf of insight floating down the river of Scripture's prophetic promise. Every book in the Bible points to Christ; every sacrifice offered foreshadows His death and resurrection. A person who seriously studies the whole revelation of God with an open mind and heart will find it difficult to avoid this glaring reality. Our Lord died, for example, on the day of Passover to fulfill several of the hundreds of prophecies

about His death. Such prophecies, including those embedded in Isaiah 53, relate thematically to the entire sacrificial system of the Old Testament and point unmistakably to God's eternal plan to provide His Son as a sacrifice for our sins. As if this were not enough, each of the prophecies about our Lord's death are inseparably interwoven with a myriad of additional prophecies foretelling His life, ministry, resurrection, and second coming.

3. Some people, striving to find a rational explanation for this prophetic element of Scripture, have suggested that New Testament fulfillments came about through people's manipulation of circumstances and Biblical texts. A simple analysis of the facts, however, refutes this supposition. First, the Dead Sea Scrolls and other archaeological and manuscript evidence demonstrate that Isaiah 53 was in print and part of the Bible hundreds of years before these things occurred, making the description of Christ's death and resurrection all the more astounding. Second, the disciples did not expect the crucifixion and did not understand its significance until after it had occurred. Third, a multitude of witnesses testified to the occurrence of both the crucifixion and the resurrection. Extra-Biblical writings corroborate such events. Had the death and resurrection of Christ been contrived, the Christian message could have been stopped cold in its tracks by its many opponents.

When one puts the pieces together, Isaiah 53 becomes a great motivator for unbelievers to analyze Scripture more closely to see if these things might be true. And it should motivate all who read the Biblical message to live more boldly for the God who gave His Son for us as an expression of His immeasurable love.

Respond

✱ 1. Which verses or ideas from Isaiah 53 are most challenging or encouraging for you? Why?

....

....

....

....

2. Do you believe that Isaiah 53 was written to foreshadow the sufferings of Christ on the cross or was it only about the nation of Israel as God's suffering servant? Explain.

....

3. Jesus said all that is required to receive the gift of eternal life is faith in His finished work (John 3:1-21). What is preventing you from believing in Him and entrusting your life to Him today?

Pray

Lord, thank you for dying the death that I deserved on the Cross two thousand years ago. Please forgive everything in my life—past, present, and future—that You call sin. Come live in me and guide my life now, granting me the eternal life and the forgiveness of sins that You promised. Amen.

Impact

Today's lesson invites you to receive Christ as your Lord and Savior. If you do so, be sure to seek the fellowship of other Christians. Attend a church that teaches God's Word. Find some strong believers who can mentor you in your faith. Invite them to take the B90+ journey.

Close

Do you sometimes think that you are too young to be used of God? Or too old? If God is calling you today, that is His invitation to trust Him to do through you whatever His calling requires. Tomorrow we will look at the life of Jeremiah who, though he was young, obeyed God at a critical time in Israel's history.

Day 54 · **Not Too Young**

Jeremiah faced the difficult task of proclaiming God's Word in a world experiencing radical and difficult change. Judah and Jerusalem were about to be ransacked by Babylon, and nobody wanted to believe it could or would happen. Jeremiah was positioned strategically by God to warn and prepare the people and to give them hope in God's sovereign care. The great need today is for young people, like Jeremiah, who are chosen and called by God to similarly bring God's hope to the world today.

Read

You have two reading options: read the full selection of Scripture or a single overview chapter each day.

- Full Reading: Isaiah 66 – Jeremiah 8
- Overview Chapter: Jeremiah 1

Reflect

Jeremiah was still living with his family in Anathoth—a Levitical town nestled in the foothills three miles north of Jerusalem—when God called him. He likely planned to serve as one of the Levitical priests like his father. But God's call would radically alter things. At a young age, Jeremiah found himself standing before dissenting prophets to confront an entire nation prior to its fall to invading powers. By studying his life, we can learn tips about living for God today, regardless of our age. Note that:

He was Chosen. We read in Jeremiah 1 that the prophet was chosen by God even before he was born:

> *Before I formed you in the womb I knew you, and before you were born I consecrated you; I appointed you a prophet to the nations.* (Jeremiah 1:5)

God chooses us before we know Him. And when we are old enough to think about God, we may find ourselves choosing Him. As an adult, for example, David came to realize that God had chosen and destined him for a specific purpose before he was born (Psalm 139:13-18). Similarly, Paul, in his adult years, understood that he had been chosen by God when he was still in the womb (Galatians 1:15). Amazingly, the Scripture declares that everyone who believes in Christ has been chosen by God in Christ before the world began (Ephesians 1:4).

He was Called. Jeremiah received his call at about 21 years of age. The societal understanding at his time was that neither priest nor prophet was mature enough to function in their formal duties until the age of 30. This helps us to understand Jeremiah's hesitation to act on God's call. The LORD

Coaching Tip

God is less concerned about your current age and ability than about your personal growth and your intimacy with Him. You may be young or old or in-between—it makes no difference—God wants to use you. Keep this in mind as you read and reflect on Scripture, asking God to speak to you and to guide you every day.

responded, "Do not say, 'I am only a youth'; for to all to whom I send you, you shall go . . ." (Jeremiah 1:7). The prophet teamed up with King Josiah, only 10 years his senior, who had also known the call of God at a young age. Just 8 years old when he took the throne, Josiah began to boldly confront Judah's idolatry by the age of 16. One is never too young to be chosen or called by God.

He was Commanded. The command came for Jeremiah to get busy doing God's work. He was not to wait until his message was perfectly polished or his hair tinted by a shade of grey. God challenged him, ". . . whatever I command you, you shall speak. Do not be afraid of them, for I am with you to deliver you, declares the LORD" (Jeremiah 1:7b-8).

Do you sometimes think of yourself as too young to be used of God? Or too old? If God is calling you today, this is the time to obey Him. To delay may in itself be an act of disobedience.

Respond

1. What inspires you about Jeremiah's life?

2. Do you think God uses young people today? How about older adults who may seem beyond the productive years of their lives? Give examples if you can.

✱ 3. Do you think we need more people who will proclaim God's will amid great opposition, like Jeremiah, for our day? Why or why not? If you believe we do need such people, ask the Lord to raise them up in our day.

....

....

....

Pray

Lord, call and commission an army of young people in our day to fulfill Your purposes in the world. You did it in the Bible, and You can do it again today. Even the 12 disciples were relatively young when You, Jesus, called them to follow You. Help me also to follow You wherever and however You lead. Amen.

Impact

Remember that people of all ages, physically and spiritually, are using Bible in 90 Days resources. Also realize that regardless of your age or perspective, what God is doing in your life is a valuable experience to share with your family, friends, or coworkers.

Close

In the late 1950s, Pete Seeger penned the famous the song "Turn! Turn! Turn!" The song lyrics have their origin in Ecclesiastes: "To everything (turn, turn, turn) / There is a season (turn, turn, turn) / And a time to every purpose, under heaven." So tomorrow on Day 55, we'll look at "A Time to Weep."

Coaching Tip

There might be times as you are reading when you feel a need to stop and pray to get your heart right with God. Do it! It is God's will. Remember that God's great commandment, to love Him with your whole being, was given to remind you of what matters most to God.

Day 55 · **A Time to Weep**

Western society is marked by a spiritual decline that parallels the situation in which Jeremiah ministered. In our age of Postmodern thinking, the majority of those who claim to be Christian do not believe in absolute truth. Approximately 9 out of 10 have never read the Bible through, even once. Rampant sexual immorality, the disintegration of marriage, and the decline of the family are staunch indicators of a nation that has drifted from God. These patterns were evident in Israel before the exile some three thousand years ago. Let's look deeply into Jeremiah's writings to glean insights for our day.

Read

You have two reading options: read the full selection of Scripture or a single overview chapter each day.

- Full Reading: Jeremiah 9–20
- Overview Chapter: Jeremiah 9

Reflect

Jeremiah 9 opens with the words:

> *Oh that my head were waters, and my eyes a fountain of tears, that I might weep day and night for the slain of the daughter of my people!* (Jeremiah 9:1)

In this passage, the young prophet was weeping for at least three reasons.

1. **The people did not honor God.** Jeremiah lived and prophesied during the reign of Judah's final five kings: Josiah (640–609 BC) Jehoahaz (609 BC), Jehoiakim (609–598 BC), Jehoiachin (598–597 BC) and Zedekiah (597–586 BC). The people had become so wicked through the span of Jeremiah's ministry that at one point God challenged him to find even one righteous person in Jerusalem (Jeremiah 5:1). The city and nation had become so spiritually corrupt that God finally warned Jeremiah that if even "Moses and Samuel stood before me, yet my heart would not turn toward this people" (Jeremiah 15:1). Even after righteous King Josiah purged the land of idols, the people were so steeped in wickedness that the nation could not be saved. They were destined to destruction.

2. **The people did not know God.** There was ultimately only one reason for the exile: the people no longer knew God. Having ignored Scripture, they lost all fear of God and chose to worship idols. God told Jeremiah, ". . . falsehood and not truth has grown strong in the land . . . they have forsaken my law that I set before them, and have not obeyed my voice or walked in accord with it" (Jeremiah 9:3b,13).

3. **God loved the people too much to leave them that way.** Even as God finally brought judgement on Jerusalem, He told them why: He was disciplining them in love. God's heart was broken and He used His prophet—Jeremiah—to express His feelings. The young prophet was both poetic and passionate, a fitting vessel for such a difficult time. Known today as "the weeping prophet," Jeremiah prefigured our Lord, who would later weep over Jerusalem before it would be destroyed once again in AD 70 (Luke 19:41).

If Jeremiah and Jesus both wept for God's people, should we not do the same? It all begins by seeing God's people as God sees them—loved by God too much to be left in a state of spiritual compromise.

Respond

✱ 1. Do you think that in some ways the Church of today faces challenges similar to those faced by believers in the Old Testament before the exile? Explain.

2. How would you answer the question, "Why is Jesus weeping over the Church?"

3. If we hope to have a positive impact on Church and society, do you think it is important that we learn to weep over God's people as Jeremiah and Jesus did? Explain.

Pray

Lord, show me what moves Your heart as You consider the Church of our day. Help me to see what You see and to feel what You feel, so that like Jeremiah, I might be a faithful vessel of Your purpose in the world. Amen.

Impact

Sin has run rampant since time began. Now more than ever, it's critical to keep our hearts right with God and remain in His Word daily. In doing so, pray that the Lord will use you to help those compromised by sin or unbelief.

Close

So then, there is a time for everything. Today was about sorrows and the correct response to it. Tomorrow's lesson will also present insights about the times we live in.

Day 56 · **Chaos, Chronos, or Kairos?**

Jeremiah lived in a chaotic time. Storms were brewing: the nations of Egypt, Assyria, and Babylon appeared on the horizon of western Asia, poised to bring their wrath down on small states such as Judah. A greater storm fomented in the prophet's heart as he downloaded warnings from Heaven about God's coming judgment; yet, following on the heels of God's warnings came promises of hope. God showed Jeremiah how the people would eventually get right with God and return to the land to rebuild Jerusalem. By pondering these events we can glean insights about God's propensity to turn even our chaotic moments into opportunities for our growth and for His glory.

Read

You have two reading options: read the full selection of Scripture or a single overview chapter each day.

- Full Reading: Jeremiah 21–31:22
- Overview Chapter: Jeremiah 25

Reflect

Jeremiah was a tender soul. Even so, he was given the heavy task of predicting and proclaiming the downfall of Jerusalem. And he did not shirk his duties. His unfolding ministry, as described in the book of Jeremiah, reads like a disjointed patchwork of narratives. The book's halting linear progression may bother the Western reader; we like everything to fit into a chronological framework. The disrupted flow of the book, like a stream working its way around huge boulders and deep crevices, reflects the time in which Jeremiah lived. Chaos abounded.

But *kairos* won the day. The Greek word *kairos* refers to divine opportunities and moments through which God's unseen plans unfold. We may not always see God at work, but when we sometimes catch glimpses of it, we relax and realize once again that God is in control even if we are not. Such kairos moments are sprinkled throughout the book of Jeremiah. Even as false prophets, prideful kings, and angry crowds hated Jeremiah's words, he proclaimed the truth without reservation. And he suffered for it. In chapter 25, for example, he spoke of coming judgment with a stark clarity; in the next chapter, his listeners sought to take his life.

Jeremiah 25 contains the clear and unambiguous warning that Israel would be brought into exile by Babylon for 70 years. So specific was this warning that Daniel, nearly 70 years after the deportation from Jerusalem, would read Jeremiah's words afresh and inquire of God about its fulfillment (Daniel 9:1-3). This becomes a kairos moment for us when we realize that God required the 70-year exile to compensate for the 70 years of the Sabbaths

Coaching Tip

About this point in the journey, it is easy to look at the length of the major prophets and the number of books left in the Old Testament and to feel overwhelmed. In reality, you are nearly 2/3 of the way through the entire Bible! You're doing great!

the Jews had ignored. It was all part of God's redemptive reset for the nation, a call for the people to turn their hearts back to Him (2 Chronicles 36:21). God's people would be taken out of their comfort zone and into what seemed like true chaos that they might leave their idols behind and begin seeking God once again; only then would they find true rest.

Does your life seem chaotic? Remember that even when we are not in control, our God still reigns. Nothing goes awry in His great plan. Our responsibility is to look for the divine opportunities He puts before us daily. A kairos moment may appear in the midst of a disruption in your busy schedule or in circumstances that break apart your preset plans. These kairos moments often become apparent when we pray as did Jeremiah and Daniel, listening to God and gleaning insight about how God is at work even in the chaos.

Respond

1. Jeremiah teamed up with King Josiah to bring reformation in the land, but it didn't last. The people were soon dragged into exile for their sins and rebellion. Does this mean the efforts of the king and prophet were in vain? Why or why not?

....

....

....

....

✱ 2. Do you generally assume things are out of control around you, or do you believe God is in control even when you cannot understand why or how? Explain.

....

....

....

....

3. What things can you do to better recognize God's kairos moments amid your earthly chaos?

....

....

....

....

Pray

Lord open my eyes to see how You are working in and around me when life is normal and when life seems to go crazy. Help me to so know Your love and sovereignty that I might trust You as Jeremiah did, even in the bleakest of circumstances. Amen.

Impact

Kairos moments are the divine opportunities that come to us, often unplanned and unexpected, to help us better understand God's heart and God's plans. Ask God to make you more sensitive to kairos moments today.

Close

Enduring: "en·dur·ing; adjective; continuing or long-lasting." The Bible states that "the word of the Lord remains forever" (1 Peter 1:25). Coming up: God ensures that what He says will remain—forever—despite what men may say or do to prevent it.

Session 9 • Overview

● REVIEW Days 50-56

Major Prophets, Part 1: Condemnation, Salvation, Confrontation

 Now is the time for your small group meeting to review the week's Scripture readings, cover the discussion questions, and watch the Essential Snapshot video together (or by yourself if reading alone). Point your mobile device's camera on the QR code to access the video entitled "Session 9: The Best Life". Or enter this link into your browser: **ScriptureAwakening.com/plus/**

- Discuss the questions marked by an asterisk (✱) from the **Respond** sections in Days 50-56, perhaps adding others if time permits.
- Watch the Session 9 video* (individually or with a small group).
    1. What insights from the video would you like to explore further?
    2. What truth or promise from the video teaching most encouraged you to trust that God has the future in His hands? Explain.
- Summarize the Preview (below) of what is coming next week, encouraging group members to read it on their own.

*Facilitators note: In order to watch the Essential Snapshot video with your group, you will need a large video monitor, if meeting in-person. If hosting a small group remotely, use Zoom (or similar service) to stream the video from your device to share with group participants.

● PREVIEW Days 57-63

Major Prophets, Part 2: Lamentation, Restoration, Sovereignty

Weekly Reading: Jeremiah 31:22 to Daniel 5:30

Summary

Jeremiah chronicles how, following the death of good King Josiah, Judah's next four kings refuse to respond to God's messenger or his message, leading the nation to its ultimate doom and destruction. Providing warnings of God's imminent judgement, Jeremiah suffers intense persecution and finally witnesses the downfall of Jerusalem and its magnificent Temple. He then composes a series of mournful laments, expressing the deep anguish and grief experienced by all of God's people.

Meanwhile, among the captives already in Babylon, Ezekiel and Daniel minister to the exiled Jewish community and the Babylonian king. Despite their adverse circumstances, these prophets proclaim that God is still in control, fulfilling His plan.

Books You'll Encounter This Week

Jeremiah Overview (Conclusion)

Jeremiah's trials continue as the nation and her leaders reject him and his message. The people's perpetual disobedience to the Law reveals their need for a new covenant, one written in their hearts and minds. The prophetic promise of such a hope, however, does not divert God's people from their present calamity. To make the point clear, Jeremiah describes the fall of Jerusalem twice in great detail. After the great city falls, the rebellious remnant disobediently drags the prophet with them into Egypt. Jeremiah also prophesies against the surrounding Gentile nations. His book concludes with a symbol of hope as the exiled king of Judah, Jehoiachin, is released from captivity and given a place at the Babylonian king's table.

Lamentations Overview

Lamentations is a book of poetic laments concerning the destruction of Jerusalem. The author, whom Jewish tradition claims was Jeremiah, anguishes over the complete and utter desolation of both the Temple and Jerusalem. In the midst of it all, however, the writer sees hope for the future, proclaiming that God's mercies are new every morning, for He is forever faithful (Lamentations 3:22-23).

Ezekiel Overview

Ministering to captives in Babylon, Ezekiel's initial prophecies warn of the coming fall of Jerusalem. Using visions, symbolic acts, and parables, he informs his fellow Jews that deliverance for the city will not come, and their exile will not be brief. After the fall of Jerusalem, he offers oracles of hope for restoration with a new Temple in a new land where the Spirit of God will return to live among His people. Like a valley of dry bones, the dead nation will be miraculously brought back to life by the power of God.

Daniel Overview

Contemporaries of Ezekiel, Daniel, and his three friends remain faithful to God while serving as exiles in the court of the Babylonian king. Inspired by God's Spirit, Daniel reveals God's prophetic plan for the Gentiles and the secession of coming regional powers.

This week's readings conclude with the eerie warning of the imminent fall of Babylon through the vision from God of a hand writing words of final judgment on the wall of the great Babylonian banquet hall.

Things to Look for This Week

As you read, consider:

1. How Jeremiah's initial message of coming judgment transitions to one imploring the nation to accept God's punishment and submit to the Babylonians—a message considered treasonous by many.

2. That Ezekiel's vision of God's Spirit (His presence) departing the Temple is symbolic of the spiritual condition of the people. God is no longer in their midst, and they do not even realize it.

3. How Daniel's moral excellence and uncompromising devotion to God were essential to his seven-decades long ministry—the longest of any of the prophets.

Day 57 · God's Enduring Word

Jeremiah was once instructed by God to write all of the prophecies he had received through the years (Jeremiah 36). Calling his trusted assistant and secretary, Baruch, Jeremiah began dictation. What happened afterward is a graphic reminder of the enduring power of God's Word.

Read

You have two reading options: read the full selection of Scripture or a single overview chapter each day.

- Full Reading: Jeremiah 31:23–44
- Overview Chapter: Jeremiah 36

Reflect

Jeremiah dictated the prophetic messages he had given through the years to preserve them in writing. Prohibited from going to the Temple, the prophet asked his assistant, Baruch, to read the completed scroll aloud in Jerusalem. The timing was especially good as the people of Judah were gathering in the Temple for a day of fasting; they were likely pleading for God's mercy because the Babylonians threatened to storm the city. Faithful Baruch stood in front of the gathered crowd and read Jeremiah's warnings of imminent danger and judgment. The king's officials listened, took the scroll from Baruch, and told him to leave.

The officials brought the scroll to King Jehoiakim. As he sat in front of his firepot, the king had the scroll read aloud to him and—using a scribe's knife—he cut off each section as it was being read. Piece by piece, he dropped the scroll into the flames until then entire document was consumed. In response, God instructed Jeremiah to "take another scroll and write on it all the former words that were in the first scroll, which Jehoiakim the king of Judah has burned" (Jeremiah 36:28). Thus was the Word of God preserved for generations to come, even for our benefit today.

This incident is one of many recorded in the annals of human history in which those who oppose God have attempted to destroy His Word. But the Word of God has always endured. Antagonists have outlawed it, shredded it, burned it, and buried it; but they have not been able to prevent its impact in the world. Whether written or spoken, God's Word always has been and always will be a realistic force to be reckoned with because it proceeds from the mouth of God. Those set on destroying the Word might destroy the world in their efforts, but still the Word will remain. As Jesus said, "Heaven and earth will pass away, but my words will not pass away" (Matthew 24:35).

The Word of God is sealed and secured in the heart of God. And He will ensure that it is proclaimed as long as there is even a modicum of hope for

Coaching Tip

David described God's Word as more desirable than even "much fine gold" (Psalm 19:10). Those who pan or dig for gold must work for it. They do so with excitement because of the great value in every bit they discover. Keep this image in mind as you read.

people to heed its truth. Jeremiah understood God's heart on the matter and was bold to proclaim it. At God's command, he recreated the scroll and continued speaking the truth. His motivation was unwavered. As he told Baruch,

> *It may be that their plea for mercy will come before the Lord, and that everyone will turn from his evil way, for great is the anger and wrath that the Lord has pronounced against this people.* (Jeremiah 36:7)

Do you know a person, a community, or a nation that is not heeding God's Word? If, like Jeremiah, you know the heart of God, will you seek to proclaim it nevertheless? People's opinions may change, but God's unchanging Word will endure. As Isaiah said, "The grass withers, the flower fades, but the word of our God will stand forever" (Isaiah 40:8).

Respond

✱ 1. If you were put behind bars for your faith and were prohibited from having any books or any portions of Scripture, do you think you would come to appreciate God's Word in a new way? Explain.

2. If you knew you had one year before the scenario described in question 1 above were to come to pass, what would you do to prepare? Would you spend more time meditating on and memorizing Scripture?

3. What might be the benefits of living by your answer to question 2 above each day of your life, even though you may never be imprisoned for your faith?

....

....

....

Pray

Lord, thank you for giving us access to Your enduring Word. Help me to treasure it, to hide it in my head and heart, and to live according to Your commands and promises. Amen.

Impact

God's Word endures, and it enables us to do the same. Think of the perseverance and endurance Jeremiah exhibited as he kept on preaching even when the entire nation seemed to be against him. In what ways have you given up on a person who needs God or on a ministry that was just too difficult? Ask God to show you if you need to repent, soften your heart, and view that person or opportunity with more of His compassion.

Close

Coming up: on Day 58, we shall see the tragedy of not heeding God's Word. In fact, God doesn't just hold His people accountable for their words and actions but even nations that don't know Him. Tomorrow: "Alas Babylon."

Coaching Tip

When big interruptions such as sickness and unexpected responsibilities threaten to break your reading schedule, remember that your daily time with God provides the solace and strength you need to face such interruptions ... just keep reading!

Day 58 · **Alas Babylon**

In Jeremiah's time, Babylon was the superpower that came against the wayward people of God. Israel and Judah had long been protected by God, but generations of utter disregard for God and His Word finally landed them into exile. Babylon thus became God's instrument for judgement. We cannot blame God, however, for the arrogance of spirit, idolatry of heart, and selfishness in policy that guided Babylon. We should rather thank God for bringing justice in the end even to Babylon as it was conquered by the Medes and Persians. This was Jeremiah's viewpoint for people in his day, and it may guide the thinking of those alive at the end of time when a worldwide system of oppression—in the spirit of Babylon—comes against the people of God with yet greater fury.

Read

You have two reading options: read the full selection of Scripture or a single overview chapter each day.

- Full Reading: Jeremiah 45–51
- Overview Chapter: Jeremiah 51

Reflect

Jeremiah 45 to 51 contain prophecies against the nations that surrounded Judah. Egypt, Philistia, Moab, Ammon, Edom, Damascus, Kedar, Hazor, and Elam each received their rebukes from the prophet. But Jeremiah's words reach a climax when denouncing Babylon in chapters 50 and 51. With some reflection, we can discover reasons for his vehement denunciations of Babylon, the combined force of which provides insights for our lives in a world of difficulty today.

1. **Finding Justice.** Babylon was the superpower that needed to be brought to justice for her treatment of Judah and Jerusalem. She was God's willing instrument to punish the people of God for their sins as Jeremiah and other prophets forewarned would happen. But the prophets also foretold the punishment that would come upon Babylon once the Jews repented for their sins, sought God afresh, and were ready to return to Jerusalem and rebuild it. In 539 BC, the Medes and Persians became the instrument God used to conquer Babylon for her pride and injustices.

2. **Future Justice.** When we read the words of the prophets against Babylon and see how they fit into the context of the entire Bible, we get a sense that what Jeremiah predicted and Daniel witnessed—the fall of Babylon—will be repeated once again on the world scene, but this time on a larger scale. In Genesis 10 and 11, Babylon's early history was established by Nimrod as he inspired the building of the Tower of Ba-

bel, a symbol of independence and rebellion against God. That same spirit dominated Babylon when, in Jeremiah's time, she was set on conquering the nations of the Middle East. The Bible predicts a day when a world government will arise with the same kind of pride and arrogance, once again set against God and His people. And her day too will come to an abrupt end. Revelation 17 and 18 describe her overthrow by the Lord Himself, as a precursor to the revelation of God's glorious Kingdom.

3. **Final Justice.** Christians around the world are suffering for their faith. According to Scripture, such suffering will eventually be accentuated and localized everywhere through a superpower that reigns with the dominating haughtiness that once filled the breast of previous Babylonian rulers from Nimrod to Nebuchadnezzar. If and when that occurs, we can turn back to Jeremiah's words and once again trace the narrative of Babylon from the early pages of the Bible to its end. And we must remember that our God still reigns. We can trust that as before, at the right time, God will once again punish and remove the final Babylonish power from its pedestal—but this time forever. And as God once released the Jews from oppression that they might rebuild their Temple, God will likewise set us free. This time, however, we will be freed for an eternal reward and for the enjoyment of the Temple that God Himself will construct as our eternal dwelling.

Respond

1. When you hear the word Babylon, what comes to mind?

✱ 2. Can you envision a world government forming on the global scene in this generation? If so, do you think it will be sympathetic toward Christians and Jews? Explain.

3. What *comfort* can we find in the Biblical teaching about Babylon?

Pray

Lord, nothing takes You by surprise. You predicted both the rise and fall of Babylon. And as nations rise and fall with the passing of time, You remain on Your throne—unmoved. Help me to capture this truth in deeper measure as I read Your Word so that no matter how the world changes in my lifetime, I might know Your peace in my heart. Amen.

Impact

Many people are rattled and shaken by changes on the world scene and headlines in the news. How about you? Pray for the Lord to give you His perspective on the world, that you might walk in peace. Then encourage others to do the same.

Close

God uses trials to test us. Charles Spurgeon, known as the "Prince of Preachers," wrote these words: *"Trials teach us what we are; they dig up the soil, and let us see what we are made of."*[1] Today's lesson reminded us of trials that may come our way. Tomorrow we will gain insights to help us grow in hard times, even in our grief.

---

[1] Charles Haddon Spurgeon, *The Complete Works of C.H. Spurgeon: Volume 2: Sermons 54-106* (Fort Collins, CO: Delmarva Publications, Inc., 2012), 233.

Day 59 · **Growth Through Grief**

Western cultures tend to bury their grief, only to find it rising again in new and unhealthy forms. Rather than face our grief head-on, we attempt to patch our pain and suffocate our sorrows. But it never works; grief festers inside and isolates us from each other and from God. We can learn from books like Lamentations on how to grow through our grief to become a healthier, stronger, and more compassionate people.

Read

You have two reading options: read the full selection of Scripture or a single overview chapter each day.

- Full Reading: Jeremiah 52 – Ezekiel 6
- Overview Chapter: Lamentations 3

Reflect

Lamentations, written as a funeral dirge, is one of the most profound expressions of grief in the Bible. Provided as a guidebook for people crushed under the indescribable horror of a demolished Jerusalem, it also provides for us a touch-point with God in our darkest valleys. The book tells us that God will be with us in every experience of life, even when it seems that God has abandoned us. Crafted with great care and precision, the Hebrew poetry undergirding Lamentations shows us that—when we hit bottom and think that all of life has ended—we can find ourselves standing on a rock, connected as never before with the Source of life.

The book opens with four chapters that, like Psalm 119, are acrostics; but Lamentations is written in a meter called *qinah* (lament), normally with three beats followed by two. The fifth and final chapter, with its own unique 22-line acrostic form, is bested only by Chapter 3. Twice the length of the other chapters, the middle chapter of Lamentations rises before us as the mountain peak of spiritual insight and reminds us that when grief takes us down, we can look up still to the God who is forever good. It proclaims the truth that,

> *The steadfast love of the LORD never ceases; his mercies never come to an end; they are new every morning; great is your faithfulness. "The LORD is my portion," says my soul, "therefore I will hope in him."* (Lamentations 3:22-24)

Lamentations teaches us to trust God in our grief. God experiences our grief with us and invites us to use it to draw closer to Him. Each of the prophets seemed to understand this truth as they spoke about God's judgment and mercies—often in the same breath. In the modern Western world, some people think it inappropriate to cry out to God with an honest expression

Coaching Tip

Our human tendency is to avoid emotions we consider to be negative. For this reason, we also tend to avoid Scriptures we don't like. But all Scripture is inspired by God and God wants to be close to us in every aspect of our lives. As we believe and read with this truth in mind, we position ourselves for a greater intimacy with God and growth in our faith.

of doubt, depression, or despair. Lamentations, however, reminds us when we obey God's call to love Him with all of our heart, we should bring to Him even the parts that hurt.

The book closes with the glorious reminder that one day God will replace our sorrow with eternal celebration. Aware of this, we can rejoice in God's mercies and faithfulness today. And we can face our grief head-on as did the Jews in their time of lament. As we trust God, even our dark valleys will become pathways to higher mountaintops and grander vistas than we have ever known.

Respond

1. Are you experiencing sorrow and grief today? What steps might you take to grow through your grief?

✱ 2. Read Psalm 56:8 and Hebrews 4:14-16. Do you believe that God is with you in your times of sorrow? Why or why not?

3. When you meet people who are dealing with grief, do you tend to show kindness and understanding toward them, or do you tend to cut them off? How can you grow in this part of your life?

Pray

Lord, thank you for Lamentations which reminds us that You carry our sorrows and share our grief. Help me to trust You even if I face difficulty without or despair within. May Scripture guide my grief so that I can grow through it and become a minister to others who suffer in it. Amen.

Impact

Sometimes those facing grief just need a friend. Rather than hearing our words of advice, they long for a caring heart and a listening ear. Pray for people you know who are grieving. Ask the Lord to show steps you can take to support them.

Close

C.S. Lewis wrote: *"We were even promised sufferings. They were part of the programme. We were even told, 'Blessed are they that mourn,' and I accepted it. I've got nothing that I hadn't bargained for. Of course it is different when the thing happens to oneself, not to others, and in reality, not in imagination."* [1]

---

1 C.S. Lewis, *A Grief Observed* (New York: Harper One, 2001), 36.

Coaching Tip

Have you ever run track? The only way to run the distance is to set a pace and to conserve some energy for the final sprint at the end. It is good to do the same thing as you read the Bible in 90 days. Relax. Keep your rhythm. Enjoy, rather than push yourself so that you can go the distance.

Day 60 · **By All Means**

In 597 BC, Ezekiel and ten thousand other Jews were forced into Babylonian exile. During the first seven years of his ministry there—described in Ezekiel 1-24—Ezekiel had the difficult task of warning the Jews that Jerusalem, which was several hundred miles away, would fall to the Babylonians. He was also to teach God's people that even though the Temple would be destroyed, God would be with them. The prophet was called by God to use dramatic and creative illustrations to communicate to a people who otherwise may not listen. Much like the Apostle Paul who wrote, "I have become all things to all people, that by all means I might save some" (1 Corinthians 9:22b), Ezekiel used every means to effectively communicate God's will and warnings to the people.

Read

You have two reading options: read the full selection of Scripture or a single overview chapter each day.

- Full Reading: Ezekiel 7–20
- Overview Chapter: Ezekiel 16

Reflect

Ezekiel was of a priestly line; he likely had been serving as a priest when he was taken into Babylonian captivity. There, he received the call of God to serve as a prophet during a tumultuous time. His message would need to be stark and startling to capture the attention of the Jews in exile. And Ezekiel was a willing servant. By noting his use of vision sharing, prophetic signs, and visual analogies, we can be challenged to likewise seek and serve God to the best of our ability, by all means.

Vision Sharing. God spoke to Ezekiel in visions and dreams and the prophet was bold enough to declare them. Taken as a whole, the visions God gave Ezekiel are so graphic and vivid that they become almost three-dimensional to the reader. His *vision of God's glory* opens his book (Chapter 1) and his *vision of the future Temple* (Chapters 40 to 48) closes it. These two visions acted as bookends for all of the others which together show how the glory departed from Israel and how the people were to regain it. In today's readings, for example, we note the *vision of Jerusalem's abominations* in Chapter 8, the *vision of the slaughter* in Chapter 9, and the *vision of God's glory departing* from the Temple in Chapter 10.

Prophetic Signs. Ezekiel was called by God to dramatize his prophetic insights with signs that would capture the attention of the people. God told him to lay on his left side for 390 days in front of a small model of the coming siege, living on ceremonially defiled bread. Then he was to lay on his other side for an additional 40 days. He was also commanded to shave his head and beard and to use the clippings as yet another sign of the coming siege (Ezekiel 5). In Chapter 12, he was told to carry out his baggage at night, not through his door but by cutting a hole through the wall of his house. This strange behavior served as yet another sign and warning of imminent exile. Even if the people never fully accepted his message, it would be difficult for them to miss its meaning.

Visual Analogies. Ezekiel was also given visual analogies to make his prophecies clear. His analogies were as vivid as his visions and as detailed as his illustrations. We see in our current reading, for example, the analogy of the vine (Ezekiel 15), of the prostitute (Ezekiel 16), and of the two eagles (Ezekiel 17). A word picture can be a powerful teaching tool, and Ezekiel was guided by God to use them well. His description of wayward Israel in Chapter 16, for example, builds on a theme common to the Old Testament: Israel is in covenant with God much as a husband and wife enter a covenant through marriage. Ezekiel's exposition of what this means for our lives is drawn out through an expanded storyline that is unparalleled in the rest of the Bible. He knew how to drive a point home!

When we look at Ezekiel's life, we cannot help but look at our own. Each of us has spiritual gifts and endowments given to us uniquely by God. When we are serious about serving God in love, like Ezekiel, we will put our whole heart into such service. This fits with the words of Paul, who reminds us that whatever we do, we should "do all for the glory of God" (1 Corinthians 10:31b).

Respond

✱ 1. As you read from the book of Ezekiel, does the prophet seem a bit off to you? Or might it be that the world around him was spiritually off, and his seemingly extreme measures were necessary to get their attention? Explain.

2. What do you perceive to be your main calling or task in life from God?

3. If you were to apply yourself in your occupation, business, ministry, or volunteer services to serve with your whole heart for God's glory, would it make a difference? If so, how?

Pray

Lord, thank you that Ezekiel was faithful to You even in such a difficult time and with such a difficult task. Help me to learn from his life and to be bolder and more consistent as I serve You in the place You have me living and working today. Amen.

Impact

Like Paul and Ezekiel, we should reach people "by all means." Thankfully, we receive stories every week from various parts of the world of changed lives and people who are growing in their faith. Your participation in this program is helping to create a movement to impact the world. Thank you for helping to make this possible!

Close

To our senses, Ezekiel appears peculiar. But "peculiar" is a word whose meaning has changed over time. It doesn't mean that Christians are odd or unusual. It means we are people who belong to God . . . as His own possession. And for that, we can rejoice.

Day 61 · **The Greatest Fall**

When reading the Old Testament prophets and Psalms, there are occasions when Messianic prophecies suddenly pop up and surprise the reader. But what about Satan's opposition? If the goodness and grace of God are shown to us through prophecy, is there ever a time when the darkness and deceptive ways of Satan are also revealed—along with a description of his fall from Heaven? Ezekiel 28 is a good place to start.

Read

You have two reading options: read the full selection of Scripture or a single overview chapter each day.

- Full Reading: Ezekiel 21–31
- Overview Chapter: Ezekiel 28

Reflect

Ezekiel 28 is the third chapter of an extended denunciation of Tyre. One of the oldest continually inhabited cities in the world, Tyre is situated on the Mediterranean coast about 25 miles south of Sidon. Its history in Biblical times was conjoined with great wealth, in part because of its alliance with Israel. When King David and King Solomon drew from its vast resources of timber and skilled laborers to construct Jerusalem's Temple, Tyre benefited greatly. As a result, trade routes from Tyre opened into Egypt, Arabia, and Mesopotamia. The Babylonians in Ezekiel's time saw the great wealth of the city and deemed it worthy prey to be devoured by its vicious military.

Due to its advantageous location along the sea, Tyre has been seen as a prize jewel to surrounding nations since its founding in 2750 BC; it therefore changed hands from one conquering empire to the next. Beginning with the ancient Egyptians, it was taken by the Macedonians, Romans, Greeks, Byzantines, Crusaders, Mamelukes, and finally the Arabs. In the era of the Babylonians, however, the people of Tyre were able to withstand assaults in their island fortress. Following a failed 13-year siege of Tyre, Nebuchadnezzar left it alone. It was Alexander the Great who would next conquer the city, fulfilling the vision Ezekiel had of its demise.

In Ezekiel 26-28, the prophet highlighted the arrogance of Tyre and its king as well as its eventual demise. Most striking is the poetic imagery of Tyre's king:

> *You were the signet of perfection, full of wisdom and perfect in beauty. You were in Eden, the garden of God . . . You were an anointed guardian cherub . . . you were on the holy mountain of God; in the midst of the stones of fire you walked. You were blameless in your ways from the day you were created, till un-*

Coaching Tip

Pride is insidious and may lurk inside any of us under religious coverings. If by learning more about the Bible you sometimes find yourself becoming prideful about what you know rather than becoming humbler because of Who you know, then read Ezekiel 28 or Isaiah 66:2 once again.

righteousness was found in you ... you were filled with violence in your midst, and you sinned; so I cast you as a profane thing from the mountain of God (Ezekiel 28:12b-16).

Christians all the way back to Tertullian in the second century AD have often viewed this as a prophetic statement about Satan. The blameless perfection of one who was an anointed angel of the highest order and in whom unrighteousness was found fits the description. The rejection of this "anointed guardian cherub" from God's presence seems to confirm it.

Regardless of whether or not one links this profound poetic imagery with the devil, the principles and parallels between the fallen king of Tyre and the fallen angel of rebellion can be made. And with this parallel, we are reminded of a simple truth: even the most powerful, protected, and prideful will fall. Ultimately every knee will bow before the Lord of Lords and King of Kings (Philippians 2:10-11).

Respond

1. Do you think the lament of Ezekiel 28:12-19 relates to Satan? Why or why not?

✱ 2. The Proverbs tell us that, "Pride goes before destruction, and a haughty spirit before a fall" (Proverbs 16:18). How might this truth be applied to your life? Be specific.

3. What things can you do to keep a humble spirit before God and others?

Pray

Lord, my tendency to become prideful crops up from time to time, unexpectedly. Help me to humble myself before You as I read Your Word daily and recall how great You are. As You see fit, lift me up and use me as according to Your plan. Amen.

Impact

True humility isn't something we can work up in our hearts. It is rather the natural response to one who truly perceives the greatness of God. As you walk through the day today, think about God, and praise Him for His greatness, asking Him to build humility into your life on a deeper level.

Close

John Climacus, a seventh century monk, wrote: *"An angel fell from Heaven without any other passion except pride, and so we may ask whether it is possible to ascend to Heaven by humility alone, without any other of the virtues."*[1]

---

[1] Saint John Climacus, *Ladder of Divine Ascent*, trans. Archimandrite Lazarus Moore (New York: Missionary Society of St. Paul the Apostle in the State of New York, 1982).

Coaching Tip

As you read through the Bible, you will be caught up in major themes that carry you from the beginning to the end, such as today's focus on God's glory. Make note of such themes for future study; when you come back to them in years to come, you will be greatly blessed. A good way to do so is through *The Amazing Journey*, a year-long study of the great themes of Scripture, available through Scripture Awakening.

Day 62 · **God's Manifest Presence**

Historians of revival describe increasing levels of God's presence. Once we become more aware of these levels, we may long to see more of God's glory; for when the Lord appears in increasing glory, everything changes—even our lives. As God manifests Himself, we become humbled and repentant, and we get right with God. We are then empowered to live for God with great joy and courage. Much like believers in the days of the early Church, we begin to experience God's glory in deeper ways and bring it out to the world. We can see this reality in the book of Ezekiel.

Read

You have two reading options: read the full selection of Scripture or a single overview chapter each day.

- Full Reading: Ezekiel 32–42
- Overview Chapter: Ezekiel 40

Reflect

Our reading takes us into the opening descriptions of Ezekiel's Temple as the main focus of this lesson. Covering the final nine chapters of the book of Ezekiel, the vision of the Temple also brings us back to the book's beginnings—the point where the glory of God is first revealed to the prophet. God's glory is a central theme in the book of Ezekiel; it should also be a primary focus in our lives.

Scholars have long debated the meaning of Ezekiel's Temple vision with all of its intricate details and measurements. Was his vision a depiction of the Temple that we will see during the time of the Millennium? Or is it solely a symbolic representation of God's glory, meant at the time to inspire the Jews to return to Jerusalem and rebuild the Temple? If so, Gentiles under the New Covenant might likewise be inspired by Ezekiel's vision to live in the world as God's Temple (1 Corinthians 3:16-17, Ephesians 2:19-22, 1 Peter 2:5). Or might the prophet's Temple vision be given to help us focus on the future day when the world will be remade and we will be surrounded by God's glory—the day when He will be our Temple (Revelation 21:22)?

No matter how we interpret Ezekiel's Temple vision, it always symbolizes the manifest presence of God for the Temple has always been the place where God meets with His people. Larger and more glorious than the temples built by Solomon, Zerubbabel, or Herod, the Temple in Ezekiel's vision calls us to understand and pursue God's glory in three ways:

1. **God's general presence.** Whether people recognize God or not, He is in the city and in the country; on each mountaintop and in every dark valley; in the quiet of one's bedroom and in the bustle of a shop-

ping mall: God is present everywhere (see Psalm 139:1-12). When Ezekiel and 10,000 others were swept into exile, they might have assumed God wouldn't go with them since the Temple remained in Jerusalem. In the opening of the book of Ezekiel and in its close, however, God's presence and the Temple became the main focus as a reminder to Ezekiel and the people that God was with them—even in a foreign land.

2. **God's cultivated presence.** During the first seven years of his ministry, Ezekiel challenged the people to cultivate God's presence. The Temple, which the Jews thought necessary for drawing near to God, was then destroyed and Ezekiel's message focused on future judgments and their hope of God's deliverance. This culminated in a vision of the new Temple, with the people and God dwelling together. That flow of thought reminds us that until the day we are in the new world—in God's unshielded presence—we should learn to cultivate the presence of God in our lives (Psalm 42:1-2). We don't have Ezekiel and the prophets to provoke us, but we do have Scripture, prayer, worship, and other means to guide us as we draw near to God.

3. **God's manifest presence.** The book of Ezekiel shows us a digression and then a progression of God's glory. The vision in Chapter 1 depicts a throne that is mobile, reminding us that God can manifest Himself to anyone at any time. After the prophet provides warnings of the destruction of the Temple in Jerusalem, he receives visions of the digression of God's presence. The glory of God departs from the Temple's threshold (Ezekiel 9:3; 10:4), moves out to the east gate of the city (Ezekiel 10:18-19), and settles over a mountain east of Jerusalem, likely the Mount of Olives (Ezekiel 11:22-23). Finally, the word comes to Ezekiel that the Temple in Jerusalem is demolished (Ezekiel 33:21). At this point, his preaching centers on Israel's future hope, which culminates in Chapters 40 to 48 with the new and more glorious Temple and the glory of God returning in manifest presence (Ezekiel 43:1-12).

The presence of God has always been the longing and hope of the believers in Israel, and the Temple is the symbol of His manifest presence (Exodus 40:34-38; 2 Chronicles 7:1; Acts 4:31). It was this glorious hope that inspired the rebuilding of Solomon's Temple. The same hope was brought to a new dimension when Jesus, the manifestation of God's glory, came to establish the Church. Still, we all long for something more. Like Moses, we cry to God from our hearts, "Please show me your glory" (Exodus 33:18).

Respond

1. Describe one or more ways God's *general* presence may be recognized (in Creation, through the love of a parent, etc.).

2. Do you long to *cultivate* God's presence more fully in your life through reading the Word, praying daily, fellowshipping, and worshipping with other believers? How specifically might you press in to cultivate this presence?

✱ 3. What do you think might cause God to *manifest* His presence yet more fully in your life or in the world? It may help to think of stories in the Bible, such as those in the book of Acts.

Pray

Lord, thank you for reminding us about Your glory in the book of Ezekiel. Help me to seek Your presence in fuller measure, until the day I see You face to face. Amen.

Impact

Scripture Awakening is committed to helping you grow in your faith and knowledge of God to the point that you become God's instrument of renewal, touching the lives of others in yet greater ways. Following our read through the Bible, you will be introduced to other resources that, should you so choose, can help you take the next step in your journey of faith. As you continue to read to the end of the Bible, think and pray about someone you can mentor by bringing them on the journey with you.

Close

Some truths come to us easily, even intuitively. Other truths require study and reflection before they are retained in our minds. The topic we will explore in our next lesson is a little of both. We may accept it intuitively, but we cannot embrace it fully without studying books like Daniel. The topic? "God is in control."

Day 63 · **God is in Control**

The book of Daniel dramatizes the sovereignty of God's Kingdom on the stage of life. It does so through stories about God's protection over the humble and His judgments on the prideful. Those who somehow think the account of Daniel lacks unity may have missed this great theme and its flow within the book. Lessons drawn from stories in the first half of the book play out in the world through prophecies in the second half. We read of Nebuchadnezzar's dream in Chapter 2; of the deliverance of Daniel's three friends from the fiery furnace in Chapter 3; and of Nebuchadnezzar's humiliation in Chapter 4. Through each story we mount a summit of insight that illuminates one central truth even in the darkness of exile: *God is in control!*

Coaching Tip

Have you noticed how often your Bible readings and prayers help you get through your daily challenges? Sometimes it may almost seem that God is orchestrating your devotional time. Maybe He really is.

Read

You have two reading options: read the full selection of Scripture or a single overview chapter each day.

- Full Reading: Ezekiel 43 – Daniel 5
- Overview Chapter: Daniel 4

Reflect

The idea that God reigns sovereign over the world's affairs becomes pronounced for those who read Daniel in its original composition. Daniel was written in both Hebrew and Aramaic. Chapter 1 introduces Daniel and his friends through Hebrew—the language of the Jews. Chapters 2 to 7 are composed in Aramaic—the common language of the Babylonians and Persians—and focus on God's plan for the nations. Finally, Chapters 8 to 12 switch back to Hebrew as the book describes God's plan for the Jews. Daniel thus welcomes us into his book with an introduction in Chapter 1 and follows up with two related mountains of insight: the first written in Aramaic for the nations; the second in Hebrew for God's people.

The Aramaic section of Daniel, Chapters 2 to 7, and perhaps the Hebraic section, Chapters 8 to 12, follow a classic poetic structure found in ancient literature and often in the Bible, the *chiastic* format. The word *chiasm* is derived from the Greek letter *chi*, which looks like an "X." It creates a parallelism between the halves of a piece of writing that come together in the middle to highlight the central point of a text. Chiastic structure creates a foundation for many sections and stories of the Bible. Modern western dramas, whether on the screen or in a book, typically build toward a climax that peaks near the end of the plot. Ancient cultures liked to place a story's climax in the center, with the beginning and end paralleling each other like the sides of an "X." Thus we see in the Aramaic section of Daniel a climatic center surrounded by mirror-like parallelism:

Chapter 2: God's eternal Kingdom overcomes in Nebuchadnezzar's dream.

Chapter 3: Daniel's friends are delivered from the fiery furnace.

Chapter 4: God judges Nebuchadnezzar.

Central Focus: 4:37: The king declares God's sovereignty.

Chapter 5: God judges Belshazzar.

Chapter 6: Daniel is delivered from the lions.

Chapter 7: God's eternal Kingdom overcomes in Daniel's dream.

Daniel and those who edited his work would have us know with a certainty what Nebuchadnezzar finally declared at the center of this chiasm: "Now I, Nebuchadnezzar, praise and extol and honor the King of heaven, for all his works are right and his ways are just; and those who walk in pride he is able to humble" (Daniel 4:37). Chapters 8 to 12, written in Hebrew, also appear to have been composed in chiastic format; they focus not on the secular king who is humbled but on the Messiah who is to be exalted.

As we read Daniel, we are reminded how drastically Daniel's world was turned upside down when he was captured and brought into exile. We are challenged to realize that even then God was in control; and we are invited to embrace this wondrous truth for our lives today.

Respond

1. Describe a time or experience in your life when you really knew that God was in control.

2. Do you tend to turn to God and trust God more when life is easy or when it is difficult? Explain.

✱ 3. Which story in the first half of Daniel encourages or challenges you the most? Why?

....

....

....

....

Pray

Lord, help me to rest in the confidence that even when the world seems to turn dark around me, still Your light shines, and You are working everything for good. Amen.

Impact

Say out loud, "God is in control." Offer this truth as a prayer and praise to God throughout the day, asking God to give you His insight about what He is up to.

Close

It's easy to believe God is in control when our faith is encouraged. It can be difficult to trust God, however, if we are taught that the Bible is merely the words of human beings. The next lesson will provide some valuable insights to help us trust in God and His Word even when the world tells us otherwise.

Session 10 • Overview

● REVIEW Days 57-63
Major Prophets, Part 2: Lamentation, Restoration, Sovereignty

Now is the time for your small group meeting to review the week's Scripture readings, cover the discussion questions, and watch the Essential Snapshot video together (or by yourself if reading alone). Point your mobile device's camera on the QR code to access the video entitled "Session 10: Against the Odds". Or enter this link into your browser: ScriptureAwakening.com/plus/

- Discuss the questions marked by an asterisk (✱) from the **Respond** sections in Days 57-63, perhaps adding others if time permits.
- Watch the Session 10 video* (individually or with a small group).
    1. What insights from the video would you like to explore further?
    2. Do you find predictive Biblical prophecy to be convincing evidence that the God of the Bible is for real? Why or why not?
- Summarize the Preview (below) of what is coming next week, encouraging group members to read it on their own.

*Facilitators note: In order to watch the Essential Snapshot video with your group, you will need a large video monitor, if meeting in-person. If hosting a small group remotely, use Zoom (or similar service) to stream the video from your device to share with group participants.

● PREVIEW Days 64-70
Minor Prophets: Judgment, Deliverance, Restoration

Weekly Reading: Daniel 6:1 to Matthew 23:39

Summary

The readings this week conclude the major prophets and continue through all the minor prophets. The writings of the minor prophets address four primary audiences (Judah, Israel, Assyria, and Edom) during three different time periods (before the exile, during the exile, and after the exile). Despite their distinct emphases, the minor prophets share common themes: they confront sinful practices, call the people back to their Covenant relationship with the Lord, alert the nation of coming judgment, and prepare God's people for the coming Messiah.

Books You'll Encounter This Week

Daniel Overview (Conclusion)

The book of Daniel concludes with Daniel's ministry under the Persians during which he offers several prophetic messages establishing a chronological framework for future events.

Hosea Overview

God calls Hosea to marry a woman who is unfaithful to him and then commands the prophet to remain true to her. Hosea's life thus supports his message to faithless Israel, calling her back to the God who has loved her despite her unfaithfulness.

Joel Overview

A devastating plague of locusts serves as an object lesson concerning the Lord's eminent judgment and the coming "day of the Lord" (Joel 2:1).

Amos Overview

The Lord sets a plumb line against His derelict people, Israel, sparing them no longer but promising future restoration.

Obadiah Overview

Obadiah prophesizes God's judgment against Edom and her ultimate destruction for her arrogant attitude and aggression against Judah.

Jonah Overview

Jonah is commonly remembered as the story of a prophet who was swallowed by a big fish. The primary theme of the book, however, is God's mercy to a nation that fully repents and turns to Him. Jonah, finding it difficult to accept God's mercy toward the repentant Assyrians, becomes a reminder to each of us that if we claim to follow God and accept His mercy, we must also show mercy toward others.

Micah Overview

A contemporary of Isaiah, Micah reveals God's concern for social justice in Israel and Judah.

Nahum Overview

One hundred years after Jonah's ministry, the Assyrians had turned away from God and become more cruel than ever. Nahum assures the people that God will destroy Nineveh, the capital city of Assyria.

Habakkuk Overview

Habakkuk cries out to the Lord in fear and frustration, asking why is God not acting to right wrongs in Israel and why He will not punish Babylon for oppressing her. The LORD explains that Habakkuk should "Look . . . and see; wonder and be astounded" (Habakkuk 1:5a).

Zephaniah Overview

Zephaniah brings dire warnings to Judah, Jerusalem, and surrounding nations during the reign of Judah's last good king, Josiah.

Haggai Overview

God chastises the Jews who had returned to Judah for rebuilding their own homes while His Temple remained in ruins. Haggai's four sermons spur the Jews to action, leading to the completion of the Temple four years later.

Zechariah Overview

A contemporary of Haggai, Zechariah encourages the people to rebuild both the Temple and their future in preparation for the coming Messiah.

Malachi Overview

In the last book of the Old Testament, Israel is admonished for cheating God out of acceptable sacrifices and for robbing Him of whole tithes and offerings. Despite their backsliding, God promises, "Return to me, and I will return to you" (Malachi 3:7b). The New Testament provides a means by which such a return to God can be realized.

Matthew Overview (Introduction)

This first book of the four Gospels (which means "Good News"), Matthew begins with the genealogy of Jesus, emphasizing that He is the promised Messiah and rightful King.

Things to Look for This Week

As you read, consider:

1. The concept of the coming "day of the Lord," encompassing God's judgment on both His people and their oppressors, the deliverance of His people, and His ultimate restoration of the Kingdom under the reign of the Messiah.

2. God is concerned about people's relationship with Him (vertically) and their relationship with each other (horizontally) which can be summarized as "love God" and "love your neighbor"—the two great commandments of the Law.

3. Following their 70-year exile in Babylon, only a remnant of the Jews return to their homeland where they await the coming of the promised Messiah for another 400+ years.

Supplemental Material

Consider reading the *Intertestamental Period* (events between the Old and New Testaments) found in Appendix 5 on page 330.

Day 64 · **Switching the Rules**

For nearly two millennia, the vast majority of Biblical theologians understood the book of Daniel to have been written sometime in sixth century BC. But a new school of scholarship arose, primarily out of eighteenth century Germany, that changed the rules. Rather than approaching Scriptural analysis with the assumption that the Biblical text is what it claims to be—the Word of God—this school took the text to be mere words of men. Many of these scholars held to a philosophical rationalism that precluded miracles, predictive prophesies, and supernatural events in the Bible; hence, their inclination to develop theories explaining why the supernatural events and prophecies in Daniel should be regarded as "fables and myths." Such theories strip the Bible of its divine authority and render the book of Daniel misleading and deceptive in its claims. As we will see, there is no solid evidence that should motivate us to blindly accept such theories.

Read

You have two reading options: read the full selection of Scripture or a single overview chapter each day.

- Full Reading: Daniel 6 – Hosea 7
- Overview Chapter: Daniel 9

Reflect

Daniel was swept into Babylonian exile with his three friends. The four of them would soon discover what Ezekiel, who would later join them in captivity, would also learn—that the God who was in Jerusalem was also in Babylon. For both Ezekiel and Daniel, ministry would not only continue but would become more pronounced as they served God's people. So astounding are the miracles and so accurate are the prophecies given to Daniel that some modern scholars assume the book to be fictitious. There are sound reasons, however, to accept everything written in the book of Daniel as accurate accounts of God's supernatural work in the world, three of which follow:

1. The Bible itself claims that the stories, miracles, and prophecies in the book can be trusted. Leaders of the faith, from Ezekiel to Jesus, for example, referred to Daniel as a real person whose writings are inspired by God (Ezekiel 14:14, 20; Matthew 24:15). This assumption fits into the great flow of prophecy in Scripture—comprising nearly one-third of the Bible—as proof that it is God's Word (Isaiah 46:9-10; Acts 3:21, 2 Peter 1:19). To dismiss the veracity of Daniel's book and its prophecies is to question the authority of Scripture as a whole and to degrade the faith it inspires. It would be foolish, then, for Christians to simply accept the anti-supernatural bias of critics without first scrutinizing the facts.

Coaching Tip

One of the solid principles of Biblical interpretation is, "Let the Bible interpret itself." This principle can help you to understand difficult texts. The book of Daniel, for example, is best understood by those who concentrate on the practice of Bible reading and Bible study.

2. Liberal scholars attempt to minimize the startling accuracy of the predictions in Daniel in support of their anti-supernatural beliefs by assigning the book a late date—hence the commonly promoted theory that Daniel is a patchwork of writings woven together in the second century BC. The primary argument used to support this late date is the claim that the vocabulary and writing of Daniel, along with certain events mentioned or omitted, reflect the period of the second century. But such linguistic and cultural propositions are easily shown to be, at best, non-conclusive. Furthermore, sections of the book of Daniel, found in the Dead Sea Scrolls, date back to 150 years or more before Christ. The realization that the book of Daniel was a well-established part of the Jewish canon at that time suggests the traditional sixth century dating of the book to be realistic.

3. Those who, despite arguments to the contrary, hold to a second century BC dating of Daniel are left with the additional issue of predictive elements within Daniel that occurred after its writing. The rise of the Roman empire predicted in Daniel 3 and 7, for example, did not take control of Syria and Palestine until 63 BC. Attempts to remove Rome from Daniel's predictions does injustice to the clear and plain reading of the text set against the unfolding drama of history. And the prophecy of the 70 weeks in Daniel 9—which foretells the coming "Anointed One"—fits into the description and timing of the coming of Christ, the long-awaited Messiah.

There is no significant cultural, historical, or Biblical reason that a person should deny the supernatural and miraculous elements in the book of Daniel. Two hundred years of rationalistic scholarship in certain circles need not eclipse the two thousand years of traditional scholarship that has driven the majority opinion through history. There is simply not enough evidence to justify the rationalist's assumptions and their new rules of interpretation. This is not to diminish the importance of sound scholarly efforts to determine the background and sources of Biblical texts through higher criticism; but when human speculation is emphasized to the demise of divine inspiration, it is time for Christians to say, "Enough."

Respond

1. Do you think the date we assign to the book of Daniel is really all that important? Why or why not?

....

....

....

2. What inspires or challenges you about the way Daniel prayed in Daniel 9?

....

....

....

....

✱ 3. Daniel had great impact on the world, even while stranded in exile. Record the qualities of his life that might explain how, against all odds, God used him so greatly. Then pray for the same for your life.

....

....

....

....

Pray

Lord, raise up men and women with faith like Daniel in our day. And begin with me. Amen.

Impact

Daniel was a witness for God in the most difficult situations. Pray today that you can be a witness about God's love, grace, and truth to at least one person.

Close

What do you think is the greatest and most uplifting truth in the entire Bible? How about this: God loves you more than you can know. Once this truth settles into your heart, joy and purpose begin to dominate your life. Get ready to be encouraged through tomorrow's lesson.

Coaching Tip

Like Hosea, we each have a unique life message that's been given to us by God. What is your life message? Keep this question in mind as you read through the Bible and ask God to clarify and confirm it.

Day 65 · Amazing Love

Hosea is the prophet of the broken heart. God told him, "Go, marry a promiscuous woman and have children with her, for like an adulterous wife this land is guilty of unfaithfulness to the LORD" (Hosea 1:2b NIV). Whether Hosea's wife, Gomer, was a prostitute before or after he married her is unclear. But the message Hosea needed to share with the Israelites was very clear: They had violated their marriage covenant with God. By understanding Hosea's message, we open the door to a better understanding of all 12 of the minor prophets. We also come to understand the amazing love of God.

Read

You have two reading options: read the full selection of Scripture or a single overview chapter each day.

- Full Reading: Hosea 8 – Amos 4
- Overview Chapter: Hosea 14

Reflect

Hosea is the first of the 12 minor prophets as they are listed in the Bible. Four of the prophets may have preceded him in the timing of their ministries. These dozen gems of divine inspiration are not called *minor* because they are somehow less important than the major prophets but because they are smaller in size. Each has a unique message, but none more important than Hosea's.

Hosea lived in Israel during a period of rapid change and instability—prior to the nation's destruction by Assyria. Beginning his ministry during the reign of Jeroboam II, he preached to the Northern Kingdom for 25 years, calling the people to get right with God. His message uniquely highlighted God's love through the analogy of marriage. He came to this understanding through his own experience when his wife, Gomer, left him and gave herself to other men. God then commanded the prophet, "Go again, love a woman who is loved by another man and is an adulteress, even as the LORD loves the children of Israel, though they turn to other gods . . ." (Hosea 3:1).

Hosea paid the price required to buy back a slave and put Gomer into exclusion until her heart turned toward him again. God used this painful situation as an illustration to help the Israelites understand why they were about to become exiles in a foreign land. God said, "For the children of Israel shall dwell many days without king or prince, without sacrifice or pillar, without ephod or household gods. Afterward the children of Israel shall return and seek the LORD their God . . ." (Hosea 3:4-5).

How fitting that we begin our study of the 12 minor prophets with an understanding of why Israel would be taken into captivity: God wanted to capture her heart once again with His love. Like an abandoned husband, God knew the pain of unrequited love. Hosea's words likely inspired Jeremiah, Ezekiel, and later prophets and apostles in their common use of the marriage analogy to describe God's love for His people (e.g., Jeremiah 3; Ezekiel 16; Mark 2:19-20; Ephesians 5:25-33; Revelation 19:6-9).

We would do well to ponder the marriage analogy as it relates to God's love today; marriage is meant to be the best example of lifelong, intimate love known to humanity. Although we humans have rarely appreciated and upheld marriage in the manner that God desires, we can grasp from its Biblical context and definition how important it is to God that we receive His love for us. When we fail Him and deny Him, He loves us still. He loves us even when our marriages fail, though He hates to see divorce (Malachi 2:16 NLT). God has remained faithful and forgiving toward His people—His Bride—through the ages, despite the fact that she has violated her covenant with Him again and again (Hosea 2:19; John 15:12-14).

This understanding of God's amazing love kept Hosea preaching the truth even when his heart was bleeding. And it can motivate each of us to hold marriage in high regard as the best picture the world has today of God's love for us. Based on this love, we find motivation to serve God with our whole hearts no matter how difficult our life situations may be. One day our Bridegroom will return to usher us into an eternal celebration; then we will understand as never before what it means to be His glory and His delight!

Respond

✱ 1. If you really believed that the Almighty God loves you with an everlasting love, how would it impact your life?

2. What do the following verses say to you about God's love: 1 John 3:1-3; 4:19; Romans 8:37-39?

3. What practical steps can you take to see more clearly and to believe more fully that God really loves you?

....

....

....

....

Pray

Lord, thank you that, as David wrote, Your love for me is "as high as the heavens are above the earth" (Psalm 103:11a). I really cannot fully understand this truth in my head, but I embrace it with my whole heart. Help me to live in it. Amen.

Impact

Some people may never know God loves them until they experience that love through another person. Ask God to fill you with His divine love to make it evident today to those who need it most.

Close

Day by day we learn vital truths from God's Word. What, however, if there is a day coming that will surpass all others? Tomorrow we will learn about "the day of the Lord," a day that stands alone. Once we learn how to anticipate that day, every day may seem more significant.

Day 66 · **The Day of the LORD**

The minor prophets had some major truths to share. Together they fill in the missing pieces of historic and prophetic insight left by the five major prophets, providing essential finishing touches for our understanding of the plan of God. Consider, for example, the insights they offer about "the day of the LORD." We will study this key topic giving special focus to Joel and Amos.

Read

You have two reading options: read the full selection of Scripture or a single overview chapter each day.

- Full Reading: Amos 5 – Micah 7
- Overview Chapter: Amos 9

Reflect

Rather than attempt to look at each of the minor prophets separately, we will study a key theme that joins them together—much like a golden thread. The phrase, "the day of the LORD," and the concept behind it run repeatedly through these books, especially in Joel, Amos, and Zephaniah. The phrase, "in that day," for example, is found more than 200 times in the Old Testament and is specifically prominent in the minor prophets. Building on such Old Testament references to "the day of the LORD," New Testament writers dust it off like valuable china and display it for the world to see. By combining insights from the minor prophets with those found in the rest of Scripture, they generally define "the day of the LORD" as a future time when God's judgement and our hope will clash like tectonic plates, creating an earthquake of rapid change that will ultimately lead to the collapse of the kingdom of the world and the establishment of the Kingdom of God. Note how the minor prophets give us essential *clarification* and help us make useful *application* about that final day.

Clarification. Hosea speaks in general terms about the coming judgement and hope of God (Hosea 1:10-11), describing it as "that day" (Hosea 2:18-23). Joel, however, uses "the day of the LORD" as a central theme in his writing, using the phrase five times (Joel 1:15; 2:1, 11, 31; 3:14); he was the earliest of the prophets to emphasize "that day." Symbolizing it through the horrid picture of an invasion of locusts, he forecasts God's coming judgement with the vividness of Daniel, the sublimity of Isaiah, the tenderness of Jeremiah, and the bluntness of Ezekiel. Joel's vision involves an invasion of locusts that drives its way into the land with stunning ferocity. The locusts' noisy din, militaristic determination, sheer force, and instinct to destroy their enemy storm the reader's mind and emotions to accentuate the point: God's judgement is near.

Halfway through his exposition, Joel turns from God's certain judgement to our certain hope. If God's people will rend their hearts, God will meet

Coaching Tip

It is easy, when reading through the minor prophets, to want to stop and focus on each one. Remember that our aim in this three-month read is to grasp the panoramic view of the entire Bible. Once you finish reading, you can make your own opportunities to study them in more depth.

them with mercy rather than judgement (Joel 2:12-17). The hope given in Joel brings promise not only for the day the Jews will begin their sixth century return to Jerusalem; not only for the day the New Testament Church is birthed (Joel 2:28-32) but ultimately for the day the Lord of Lords will return to make all things new (Joel 3). Looking back in time, we can say that each generation had their coming "day of the Lord." Two such days have occurred and a third yet is yet to come. Though each "day of the Lord" was separated by centuries, Joel and the prophets likely perceived them all as one single event.

Amos similarly describes "the day of the LORD," but reserves his words about final hope for the last paragraph of his scroll (Amos 5:18-27; 9:13-15). A fig tree farmer and shepherd, Amos received a message from God that required him to travel from his home in Judea to speak to wayward Israel during the days of Jeroboam II. In his writing, the prophet rebukes the nations surrounding Israel (Amos 1:3-2:5), then doubles up his denunciations for Israel as he describes the people's unjust actions, neglect of the poor, idolatry, and spiritual waywardness.

The story of Jonah graphically portrays what that day could look like through an historic account of God's coming judgement against Assyria. Micah also points us to that day, using phrases such as "in the latter days" and "in that day" (Micah 4:1, 6).

Application. Jesus and the Apostles, applying the imagery and theology of the minor prophets, describe the coming "day of the Lord" when God's judgement will reach its apex and usher in a final and eternal hope for those who believe. Using phrases such as the "day of God" (2 Peter 3:12 ; Revelation 16:14), and "the day of our Lord Jesus Christ" (1 Corinthians 1:8 ; cf. 2 Corinthians 1:14; Philippians 1:6, 10; and 2 Peter 3:10), they foresee a time that surpassed all others. The question is, "Are we ready?"

Peter warns that many will begin to live as though that final day will never come. He urges us not to let that day take us by surprise, saying, "But the day of the Lord will come like a thief." We should therefore live in "holiness and godliness" as we await the day when, "the heavens will pass away with a roar, and the heavenly bodies will be burned up and dissolved, and the earth and the works that are done on it will be exposed" (2 Peter 3:10-14). That final day will conclude the kingdoms of the world as we now know them and will usher in an eternal day through which the light of God will never be diminished.

Respond

1. When you hear the phrase, "the day of the Lord," what comes to mind?

✱ 2. To those who think that the Lord's return and final judgment will never come, Peter writes, "But do not overlook this one fact, beloved, that with the Lord one day is as a thousand years, and a thousand years as one day" (2 Peter 3:8). What do you think Peter meant? What do his words mean *to you*?

3. What practical steps can you take to prepare for that final day? (It may be helpful to see 2 Peter 3:10-14.)

Pray

Lord, thank you that a day will come when time will be swallowed by eternity, and darkness will be overwhelmed by the light. Help me to live each day with that day in sight. Teach me to be more patient, loving, bold in my life and witness, and above all, faithful to You. Amen.

Impact

Jesus tells us to live each day as though He may come back tonight (Matthew 24:44). Imagine how your life would change if you lived in such a way. Then do it! Live today as though it could be your last—as though tomorrow you will see God face-to-face.

Close

We all need more hope. And there is no better place to find it than in God's Word. Tomorrow, we will look at a prophet who inspires such hope in our hearts. His name is Habakkuk. And his message will shine the light of God's hope on the pathway of our lives.

Day 67 · **Hope on Display**

Hope is light for the pathway of faith. This is why each of the minor prophets—whether they lived before, during, or after the exile—ended their short books with a message of hope. Some turned up the light of hope more brightly than others, but none shone brighter than the beam of hope displayed in Habakkuk's words:

> *Though the fig tree should not blossom, nor fruit be on the vines, the produce of the olive fail and the fields yield no food, the flock be cut off from the fold and there be no herd in the stalls, yet I will rejoice in the LORD; I will take joy in the God of my salvation. God, the LORD, is my strength; he makes my feet like the deer's; he makes me tread on my high places.* (Habakkuk 3:17-19)

Read

You have two reading options: read the full selection of Scripture or a single overview chapter each day.

- Full Reading: Nahum 1 – Zechariah 3
- Overview Chapter: Habakkuk 3

Reflect

Today we read through the short books of Nahum, Habakkuk, and Zephaniah, noticing how each closes with a brimming sense of hope. Nahum's hope highlights justice and Zephaniah's the coming "day of the LORD." Habakkuk, however, takes us to new heights of hope. Consider that:

1. We may dub Habakkuk "the prophet who asked." He was not afraid to ask God questions in an effort to glean insights. He knew that **strong hope is based on solid understanding**. His entire book is set on the foundation of two key questions. First, he asked why God seemed to be sitting around unconcerned as the people of God misbehaved (Habakkuk 1:2-4). God explained that Judah would be brought into exile by Babylon for her injustices (Habakkuk 1:5-11). This led the prophet to ask God a deeper and more stirring question: how could God allow Babylon, a nation more wicked than Judah, to get away with such a wicked act (Habakkuk 1:12-17)? God consoled the prophet, explaining that eventually Babylon would also be judged for her sins (Habakkuk 2:6-20). Buried in God's answer lies the promise that having been chastened, Judah would learn from her mistakes and turn back to God. Satisfied with this understanding, the prophet surrendered himself to God's will (Habakkuk 3:1-19). From his short book, we learn that when we lack hope, it is because we lack wisdom. And when we lack wisdom, we must humble ourselves and ask, awaiting God's answer.

Coaching Tip

If you seem to have more questions than answers as you read the Bible, remember that questions are the foundation of understanding. It is when you don't have a lot of questions that your knowledge and faith are not as likely to grow.

2. At the close of his book, Habakkuk was so full of hope that he found himself rejoicing even when the economy around him failed (Habakkuk 3:17-19). He knew that **hope in God brings us higher than our circumstances**. So strong was his hope that he likened himself to the stag that pranced along the mountaintops, safe from the arrow and snare of the trapper. This hope kept his faith, guided his life, and gave birth to the famous words, "The righteous shall live by his faith" (Habakkuk 2:4c). These words would be re-quoted in Scripture, framed in history, and preached and taught through the ages (e.g., Romans 1:17; Galatians 3:11; Hebrews 10:38). They remind us that faith becomes empowered by hope when, like Habakkuk, we take time to ask God questions.

Respond

1. Consider this thought: "If a teaching or sermon has no hope, it is not Biblical." Do you agree? Explain.

....

....

....

....

✱ 2. It is not only Habakkuk, nor only each of the minor prophets, but every Biblical writer that brings to us a message of hope. Is your pathway bright with hope? If not, should it be?

....

....

....

....

3. What does it mean to you personally that "the righteous shall live by his faith"?

....

....

....

....

Pray

Lord, teach me to be like Habakkuk, who brought his difficult questions directly to You and waited for Your answers. Forgive my tendency to think I have all the wisdom I need in my little brain. I humble myself and await Your insights, looking to You for hope. Amen.

Impact

Habakkuk lived with great hope. There are many people today, however, who are prisoners to hopelessness. Many hopeless people are also behind bars. For this reason, Scripture Awakening resources are being used to help train prisoners to become believers and followers of Christ while still in prison. You are integral to this ministry. Pray for additional ways that God might use you to bring hope to the hopeless.

Close

Where do you go when you lose motivation and momentum in life? Tomorrow we will find a huge dose of it through the writings of Zechariah and Haggai. Whether you've read their books before or not, you will be inspired by their beliefs.

Day 68 · **Motivation to Get Moving**

The period of writing for each of the minor prophets is generally before the exile. It is clear that Haggai, Zechariah, and Malachi, however, ministered to God's people after the exile. Zechariah and Haggai worked in tandem to exhort the Jewish people to rebuild God's Temple—and with God's help their efforts were successful. Significant insights for spiritual motivation can be drawn from these books.

Read

You have two reading options: read the full selection of Scripture or a single overview chapter each day.

- Full Reading: Zechariah 4 – Malachi 4
- Overview Chapter: Zechariah 4

Reflect

Zechariah—whose name means "God remembers"—was called by God to help those who returned to Jerusalem remember that the Covenant given by Moses was still valid. If the people would simply trust God, it said, He would be their strong support as they rebuilt Jerusalem's Temple (Ezra 5). The Temple's foundation had been laid under the leadership of Sheshbazzar (likely another name for Zerubbabel, Judah's governor) but the work came to a halt for 18 years. The people needed additional motivation to get the job done.

In the first 8 chapters of Zechariah, we find 8 apocalyptic visions; Chapters 9 to 14 contain Zechariah's preaching and prophecies. Drawing from at least 5 prophets who preceded him—and speaking about the suffering Messiah who would follow him—Zechariah used the past and future to motivate God's people in the present. His words can likewise motivate us. Consider, for example, his vision of the golden lampstand in Zechariah 4. Looking at just three lines in that vision, we find three motivations for doing God's work: *power*, *potential*, and *perspective*.

1. **Power.** Zechariah saw a vision of two olive trees feeding oil into a golden lampstand. An angel explained, "This is the word of the Lord to Zerubbabel: Not by might, nor by power, but by my Spirit, says the Lord of hosts" (Zechariah 4:6). The combined effect was a powerful reminder to Zechariah and to each of us that God has an unlimited supply of oil—representing His Holy Spirit—to help us fulfill our calling. The Spirit of God helps us when we pray (Romans 8:26), guides us as we study Scripture (John 16:12-15), uplifts us when we are weary and empowers us for service (Ephesians 3:16-20, Acts 1:8). When we learn to rely on God's Spirit, we find strength and motivation to live for God; then great things can happen.

Coaching Tip

We are about to turn a corner and step into more familiar territory: the New Testament. Take special note of the visions and messages given to Zechariah; you will see references to them scattered throughout the New Testament, from Matthew to Revelation.

2. **Potential.** The Word of the Lord continued: "Who are you, O great mountain? Before Zerubbabel you shall become a plain" (Zechariah 4:7). The Jews were paralyzed by fear because of the opposition of enemies living around them, causing the smallest obstacles to seem mountainous in size. Zerubbabel prophesied that if they would have faith, however, their fears would be flattened before their Great and Powerful God. We are reminded of the Lord's promise that faith in God can move mountains (Matthew 17:20); likewise, we too must trust in God's greatness if we hope to overcome the barriers and fears we face in life.

3. **Perspective.** "For whoever has despised the day of small things shall rejoice . . ." (Zechariah 4:10). You may think the things you find to do for God are small and insignificant. "I'm only teaching third graders," you might say. Or, "I'm too young or too old or too frail to do much for God; just about the only thing I can do is pray. But it is such a small thing." Is anything really small, though, when done in the sight of God and for His glory? Jesus reminded us that even a cup of cold water in His name will not lose its reward (Matthew 10:42).

Our Lord never wrote a book, never earned a degree, never owned a home, and never traveled more than a couple hundred miles outside His place of birth; but He led a small band of seemingly insignificant men to understand that obedience alone creates greatness in the sight of our God. Once we see and understand this truth, we will know that everything we do in God's name and according to His will is truly great. Such a *perspective* can help us to trust God for His *power* as we realize our full *potential* each and every day of our lives.

Respond

✱ 1. Do you tend to think of your service for the Lord as small and almost insignificant? What, according to Zechariah, does God think about such an attitude?

2. Do you doubt that you can really do great things for God? If so, what do Zechariah's words about the mountain tell you about your potential?

3. Describe your number one power source for doing God's will. How might you better draw on the Lord's strength day after day?

Pray

Lord, forgive me for the many times I've tried to do Your work in my own strength. Fill me with Your Holy Spirit; empower me and guide me to be more like Zechariah, a man who was motivated by You and who thus motivated others to know You and to serve You well. Amen.

Impact

Many things can demotivate us as we try to live for God. In this lesson, however, Zechariah gives us three strong reasons to get moving for God regardless of the mountainous obstacles in our way. Take these three—God's *power*, our *potential*, and the *perspective* of God's Word—to get back on track, pushing aside every obstacle as you live for God's glory.

Close

Do you like to study genealogies? Unless a genealogy relates to us directly, it can seem mundane. So it is when we come across genealogies in the Bible—until. Tomorrow, we will look at a genealogy of supreme importance, one linking our lives with the Almighty God.

Coaching Tip

Each of the Gospels has a special emphasis; together the four Gospels give us the fullest word-picture of Christ. As you read through these accounts of Christ's life, try to avoid the tendency to pick a favorite and focus instead on how each account was essential for the whole world to understand and receive the greatest news ever.

Day 69 · Another Genealogy?

A rule of thumb for writing a novel is to begin with a hook to pull the reader into the story. When we read the first words of the first New Testament Gospel—the most important story ever written—we might expect an especially gripping hook or storyline that grabs us. Instead, it opens with a genealogy. As a result, the average modern reader skims through the list of names and hurries to the more exacting accounts of the Lord's birth, ministry, miracles, teachings, death, and resurrection. Why the genealogy? When we ponder the answer, Matthew's Gospel becomes all the more precious to us.

Read

You have two reading options: read the full selection of Scripture or a single overview chapter each day.

- Full Reading: Matthew 1–12
- Overview Chapter: Matthew 1

Reflect

There are several critical reasons for the genealogical list that opens Matthew's Gospel:

1. **Matthew was not merely telling a good story;** he was recounting history. Genealogies were important to the Jews; they had a propensity for collecting records to demonstrate their heritage, as we have seen in the many genealogical lists of the Old Testament. Based on their records, the Jews were able to maintain their identity through times of national upheaval even when dispersed among the nations. The Messiah was born in humble circumstances under the oppressive Roman regime, and the genealogy served as evidence that God's people were not forgotten. God had been with them through every period of their history, and He was with them now, fulfilling each of His long-established promises.

2. **Imagine if there were no genealogy** on which to anchor the account of our Lord's life. *Jesus*, which means "the Lord saves," was a name with Messianic implications. But it was also a common name in His time. Neither His name nor His personal claims to messiahship would be sufficient to cause people to believe in Him. Many people had already appeared on the scene claiming to be the Messiah. Whether they were overcome with grandiose delusions or personally determined to deceive the masses, each lacked one essential quality: a direct link to the promised lineage. From Abraham to David to Christ—just as Matthew spells it out—God's Messiah would be expected to come from the promised line. If this criterion were not met, Jesus of Nazareth would be seen as nothing more than the next impostor.

3. **Matthew wrote especially for the Jews,** and his Gospel served as a bridge between the Testaments. His account of our Lord contains more Old Testament quotes and references than any other New Testament book other than Revelation. Matthew carefully constructed this bridge through prophetic connections, uniting Old Testament predictions with New Testament fulfillments. Jesus' birth, life, and death were laid out ahead of time through hundreds of prophesies about the coming Messiah. The predictive statements about our Lord's birth, however, centered around His promised lineage; hence the necessity of the opening genealogy.

4. **Matthew sought to leave a record** that could be easily remembered by young and old. He stylized his genealogy in a manner that could easily be memorized by the average person. Rather than attempt to put every descendant into his list, he highlighted an even 14 figures representing 3 major epochs of Jewish history: the period from Abraham to David (the founders), from David to the exile (the kings), and from the exile to Christ (the fugitives).

Respond

1. If you were to write an account today of the life of Christ, how would you begin the story?

2. Now imagine if you were writing 2,000 years ago for the Jews. From what you know about their inherent skepticism surrounding Jesus and their long-held expectations about the coming Messiah, how might you begin your account?

✱ 3. In Matthew 4:18-22, Jesus calls the first disciples to follow Him. They immediately drop all that they are doing, leaving behind their livelihood and families. Why do you think they responded so quickly to Jesus' call?

....

....

....

....

Pray

Thank you, Lord, that You came as a human, with real parents and relatives and a family line. This truth reminds me that You care for me, for my family, and for all humanity. You loved us enough to become one of us that we might know You! Amen.

Impact

Many people put time and effort into discovering their personal family histories. In so doing, they come to appreciate all the more how the past helped to shape our lives today. This is also true with our spiritual genealogy through Jesus Christ. Think about the fact that the day you entrusted your life to the Lord, you were adopted into His family, and His family line became your own. Take time today to pray for your living relatives to become part of this greater family of faith.

Close

How can we, who have never lived under a monarchy, actually grasp the Biblical idea of the Kingdom of God? You will be asking yourself this question and many others tomorrow as you learn about God's rule over the world and over your life. The answers will be found in the center of Matthew's Gospel.

Day 70 · **The Kingdom Calls**

The Gospel of Matthew is the hinge book between the Testaments—not simply because of its placement in the Bible but because of its content. It was written to help Jewish people know that Jesus is the Messiah who will usher in the Kingdom of Heaven. The book is framed around five key discourses: the Sermon on the Mount (Matthew 5:1-7:29), the sending of the twelve (Matthew 10:1-42), the Kingdom of Heaven (Matthew 13:1-52), relationships in the Kingdom (Matthew 18:1-35), and the Olivet Discourse (Matthew 24:1-25:46). The centerpiece, Matthew 13, contains eight parables about the Kingdom of Heaven, which is also the primary focus of his entire Gospel.

The Jews languished under the kingdom of Herod and longed for the Kingdom of Heaven. They anticipated its coming through an earthly king who would overwhelm the Romans and give the Jews the freedom they longed for. Breaking with public expectation and fulfilling God's plan, Jesus ushered in an intermediate phase of the Kingdom of Heaven on earth. It was not political so much as it was personal; it came not through the sword but by the Spirit. He promised to die and rise again to secure this kingdom, after which He would return to usher in the final kingdom epoch.

Read

You have two reading options: read the full selection of Scripture or a single overview chapter each day.

- Full Reading: Matthew 13–23
- Overview Chapter: Matthew 13

Reflect

Matthew opens with John the Baptist's Kingdom declaration (Matthew 3:2). We next find Jesus doing the same thing (Matthew 4:17). Crafting his narrative around 29 references to God's Kingdom, Matthew places his reader into the growing tension between God's plan to establish the Kingdom of Heaven and the religious leader's political ambitions for a politically-oriented kingdom on earth. The Lord's Kingdom vision ran counter to that of the religious leaders; hence, the Pharisees and Sadducees' determined effort to persecute Jesus in increasing measure until they pointedly likened Christ to the "prince of demons" (Matthew 12:24). Then comes the turning point in our Lord's ministry. In Matthew 13, He begins teaching in parables to confound His dissenters and to confirm His disciples. By observing the progression of these parables, we find ourselves confronted with a vital choice: accept or reject God's Kingdom.

The word *parable* comes from a Greek compound word: *para*, meaning "alongside of"; and *ballo*, meaning "to throw, lay, or place." A parable lays or places an important truth alongside an illustration to bring it to life. The

Coaching Tip

The stunning complexity and beauty of a book such as Matthew makes us want to stop and study it more in-depth. But like a tourist group that aims to take in a whole country in days rather than years, we find ourselves whisked away for the next stop. And that is okay. Future tours can be arranged during which you return to Matthew, or any book of the Bible, to linger and enjoy.

Kingdom parables in Matthew 13 come in pairs that together promote a progression of thought as shown in the chart below:

Parable	Theme
The Sower (vv. 1-9) & the Weeds (vv. 24-30)	*Surrender to the King*
The Mustard Seed (vv. 31-32) & the Leaven (vv. 33)	*Grow in the Kingdom*
The Hidden Treasure (vv. 44) & the Pearl (vv. 45)	*Commit to the Kingdom*
The Net (vv. 47-50) & the Treasures (vv. 51-52)	*Live for the Kingdom*

By reading and pondering these parables, we are challenged to personally *receive, grow in, commit to,* and *live* for the Kingdom of Heaven. The first step is to *surrender* to God's Word by surrendering to the King, Jesus. He is described in the Bible as King of Kings and Lord of Lords (1 Timothy 6:15, Revelation 19:16). As Creator and Sustainer of all life, there is none greater than He. We should continue learning about God and His Kingdom in order to *grow* spiritually. With each new phase of growth, we must commit to Jesus and His Kingdom. In so doing, we become equipped to *live* for the King, despite all opposition, until the kingdom of the world is finally overtaken by the Kingdom of Heaven (Revelation 11:15).

Respond

✱ 1. Which of the Matthew 13 parables speak to you most personally? Why?

2. Might it be difficult for those who have only experienced a democracy to grasp the full implications of living under a King in the Kingdom of Heaven? Explain.

3. Complete this thought: "I hope to live more fully for the Lord and His Kingdom in the following ways..."

....

....

....

....

Pray

Lord, help me to live on this earth with confidence and expectation, as is fitting for a child of the King. Teach me also to become ever more aware of Your Kingdom, so that my life goals and passions will align with Yours. Amen.

Impact

God's Kingdom permeates all nations. Do you know people of different nationalities or religions? How might God use you to reach them with His love?

Close

Our lives are in a perpetual state of preparation. We plan ahead to get an education, launch a career, build a family, and leave a legacy. But how well do we prepare for the end of time? Tomorrow, we will discover the one thing, above all others, that will get us ready for the end.

Session 11 • Overview

● REVIEW Days 64-70
Minor Prophets: Judgment, Deliverance, Restoration

 Now is the time for your small group meeting to review the week's Scripture readings, cover the discussion questions, and watch the Essential Snapshot video together (or by yourself if reading alone). Point your mobile device's camera on the QR code to access the video entitled "Session 11: The Connection". Or enter this link into your browser: **ScriptureAwakening.com/plus/**

- Discuss the questions marked by an asterisk (✱) from the **Respond** sections in Days 64-70, perhaps adding others if time permits.
- Watch the Session 11 video* (individually or with a small group).
  1. What insights from the video would you like to explore further?
  2. Do you find archaeology to confirm the truth of Scripture in some manner? Explain.
- Summarize the Preview (below) of what is coming next week, encouraging group members to read it on their own.

*Facilitators note: In order to watch the Essential Snapshot video with your group, you will need a large video monitor, if meeting in-person. If hosting a small group remotely, use Zoom (or similar service) to stream the video from your device to share with group participants.

● PREVIEW Days 71-77
Gospels: Incarnation, Crucifixion, Resurrection

Weekly Reading: Matthew 24:1 to Acts 4:37

Summary

The New Testament continues with the four Gospel ("Good News") accounts of the life and ministry of Jesus Christ. The first three authors, Matthew, Mark, and Luke provide *synoptic* accounts ("seeing together") since they employ a significant amount of similar material. The fourth author, John, provides a supplementary account which is mostly new and unique.

The Gospel authors focus on the three years of Jesus' ministry with particular emphasis on His final week in Jerusalem (Passion Week) leading to His death, burial, and resurrection. Written to different audiences with distinct themes, the four accounts provide a compelling case that Jesus was who He claimed to be, the promised Messiah and only Son of God.

The book of Acts continues the narrative with Christs' ascension and the coming of the promised Holy Spirit.

Books You'll Encounter This Week

Matthew Overview (Conclusion)

Matthew's Gospel is organized around five key discourses and is written to emphasize that Jesus is the long-awaited Messiah and rightful King. Throughout the narrative, Matthew carefully documents Christ's fulfillment of numerous Old Testament prophecies, authenticated by His miraculous acts. Tension between Jesus' vision of a heavenly Kingdom and the religious leader's desire to dominate an earthly kingdom ultimately lead to Christ's crucifixion at the hands of the Romans. He rises from the dead, however, bringing the promise that He will come again to establish His Kingdom on earth.

Mark Overview

The shortest of the four Gospels, Mark focuses on the ministry of Christ beginning with His baptism by John the Baptist and ending with His resurrection. In a fast-paced, action-oriented account, Mark reveals Jesus as the servant who came "to give his life as a ransom for many" (Mark 10:45). Appealing to the Roman's action-oriented mindset, Mark emphasizes Jesus' works, particularly His miracles, rather than His words. Drawing his narrative from Peter's first-hand experience, Mark encourages readers to persevere, as Christ did, no matter the difficulties.

Luke Overview

Luke was a Gentile physician who traveled as a missionary with the Apostle Paul. He also wrote the book of Acts. In his Gospel, Luke provides "an orderly account" (Luke 1:3) of the birth, life, death, and resurrection of Jesus, highlighting Jesus' relationship with many different kinds of people and accentuating that Jesus came for all people, not just the Jews. Luke's account emphasizes Jesus as the perfect man in His role as the "Son of Man" who came "to seek and to save the lost" (Luke 19:10). His Gospel is organized around an extended "travelogue" documenting Jesus' final journey to Jerusalem and His teaching in parables.

John Overview

Hearkening back to Genesis, the book of John asserts, "In the beginning was the Word, and the Word was with God, and the Word was God" (John 1:1). John portrays Jesus as the Son of God. Organizing his writing around seven miracles and seven related "I am" statements, John reveals critical aspects of Christ's identity and authenticates His message. In an extended

Upper Room discourse, John highlights Jesus' care and concern for the disciples right before His crucifixion. The book closes with the resurrected Christ reinstating Peter as a reminder that even though the disciples had often failed Him, He would never abandon them.

Acts Overview (Introduction)

Written by Luke, Acts describes the coming of the Holy Spirit, the forming and persecution of the early Church, the conversion and ministry of Paul, and the miraculous spread of the Gospel from Jerusalem, to Judea and Samaria, and ultimately to the ends of the earth.

This week's readings describe the promised outpouring of the Holy Spirit on the Day of Pentecost. The impact is immediate as a group of fearful and timid followers become a courageous band of believers who boldly declare the Gospel throughout Jerusalem, leading to a great ingathering of converts to the faith.

Things to Look for This Week

As you read, consider:

1. The complementary and contrasting roles of Christ as the promised King and suffering servant as presented in the Gospels of Mathew and Mark.

2. The complementary and contrasting identities of Christ as the Son of Man (perfect human) and the Son of God (fully divine) as presented in the Gospels of Luke and John.

3. How Jesus' sinless life and sacrificial death were absolutely necessary for our salvation.

Day 71 · **Ready for the End**

In Matthew 24, Jesus gives us one of the most concise and profound sermons ever delivered about the end of time, commonly called "The Olivet Discourse." He closes His message with three concluding parables for personal application. Through the ages, Christians have often focused on the discourse in Matthew 24 while ignoring its directives in Matthew 25. Let's not make the same mistake. We will study Matthew 25 while asking the question, "Am I ready for the end?"

Read

You have two reading options: read the full selection of Scripture or a single overview chapter each day.

- Full Reading: Matthew 24 – Mark 5
- Overview Chapter: Matthew 25

Reflect

It is natural, when talking about end-time prophecy, to want to know the chronological flow of coming world events. The first concern in Scripture, however, is that we allow prophecy to help us live for God today. Unpacking the truths of Matthew 25 can help us move beyond conflicts surrounding how the end plays out to clarity about how our lives should be lived out. Each parable in Matthew 25 flows into the next to create a progression of thought for personal application.

The Parable of the Ten Virgins (Matthew 25:1-13): Oil throughout the Bible generally represents the Holy Spirit. From the anointing of prophets and kings with oil to the lighting of the oil-filled candelabra in the Tabernacle and Temple, the Old Testament reminds us of our need for the Holy Spirit. Similarly, the New Testament reminds us that we are each like lamps, meant to shine in the dark world (Matthew 5:14-16). Ancient lamps could not function without oil. In the same way, we must learn to depend on the Holy Spirit to accomplish God's purpose in and through us. When the Lord comes back, it is only those who have their lamps filled and trimmed—meaning those who are truly in relationship with the Almighty God through the Holy Spirit—who will be given access to the joyous celebration of God's eternal love (Revelation 19:1-10).

The Parable of the Talents (Matthew 25:14-30): A "talent" in Biblical times was a unit of value equaling a hundred denarii. In this parable, the talent represents our natural abilities and spiritual endowments along with every other resource at our disposal. It was because of this parable that the use of the word *talent* came to mean "gift or skill" in the late thirteenth century. Connecting Christ's words with the previous parable reminds us that once we depend fully on God's Word and His Spirit, we cannot help but invest

Coaching Tip

As we transition from one Gospel to the next, ask yourself questions such as, "To whom might each have been writing?" or "What was the author's main concern?" or "How does this text apply to my life?" It is through such inquisitiveness that we find life-changing answers.

our talents, time, and treasures for God's Kingdom. And the dividends being stored up for us in Heaven will be proportionate to our investments.

The Parable of the Sheep and Goats (Matthew 25:31-46): This third parable is often taken out of context and is, therefore, misconstrued to suggest we can only get to Heaven through our good works. By reading it alone, one might think that Jesus is saying, "You must serve in a soup kitchen or give money to the poor to enter My Kingdom." The first Matthew 25 parable reminds us, however, that we must first surrender to the Lord and His Spirit to enter the Kingdom. As a result, we will naturally invest our lives for God, the point of the second parable. Those who attempt to do good works for God without such surrender will be in for a terrible shock at the end of time.

A key to understanding this parable is found in its closing words, "As you did it to one of the least of these my brothers, you did it to me" (Matthew 25:40). The words "my brothers" implies fellow believers. The Bible calls us to help everyone in need, giving priority to those who are "of the household of faith" (Galatians 6:10). Those who truly love God will naturally desire to help fellow believers. Some unbelievers may find joy in helping the poor and in giving generously to the needy, but their hearts will not be set on God's larger purposes. Jesus gave us three parables in Matthew 25 to help each of us examine our hearts to be sure we have a living and dynamic relationship with Him, from which we will give our best to invest ourselves in serving His people. In so doing, we stand in readiness for His imminent return.

Respond

✱ 1. The Matthew 25 parables were written to help us honestly evaluate our lives. Which of the three is most challenging or encouraging for you? Why?

2. Matthew was a tax collector, an outsider when it came to the Jewish faith. For what reasons might the Lord's Matthew 25 parables have been especially helpful for him?

3. Ask God to give you special sensitivity today about those who are outcasts, as was Matthew. Write down the names of those who come to mind.

Pray

Lord, help me to be ready for the end by making each day a new beginning with You. Show me how to deepen and strengthen my walk with You, that I might live in the strength of Your love, be guided by Your Spirit, and invest myself in Your Kingdom purposes. Amen.

Impact

Matthew was an outsider and Jesus invited him in. He then wrote to help others find their way into the Kingdom of Heaven. You too were an outsider and Jesus has invited you in. Pray for God to help you to invite someone else into the Kingdom of Heaven today.

Close

As we continue to read the Gospels, we naturally ask ourselves, "Why four accounts of Christ's life and ministry? Why not just one or two?" By pondering this question tomorrow, we will come to appreciate more fully each of the timeless records of the life and mission of our Lord Jesus Christ.

Coaching Tip

The whole Bible is the story of God's redemption as offered to us through Jesus Christ. The Old Testament anticipated the Lord's coming; the Gospels revealed it; and the Epistles will explain it. As you continue to read through the Bible, notice how Jesus is central to everything written.

Day 72 · **Why the Four?**

History and tradition attribute the writing of this second Gospel to John Mark. The early Church fathers tell us that Mark captured the preaching and teaching of Peter and organized it into the earliest record of the life of Christ. As we read the Gospel of Mark, we cannot help but note how it differs from Matthew. It opens with no genealogies, no birth narrative, no wise men visiting, and no trip to Egypt. The desert testing of Jesus is cut down to a few lines as Mark carries us forward at a hurried pace, highlighting Jesus' actions over His teachings. Reading his Gospel is like watching a movie. As the producer, Mark clips the scenes together with the word "immediately" (Greek: *amesos*), used 40 times, to create a fast-moving and to-the-point story of Jesus; it served the Romans well.

Read

You have two reading options: read the full selection of Scripture or a single overview chapter each day.

- Full Reading: Mark 6–15:20
- Overview Chapter: Mark 10

Reflect

People sometimes ask, "Why four Gospels? Would it not be simpler to have only one?" Mark, for example, describes Christ as the servant. This second Gospel's central teaching is summarized by the truth that Jesus came ". . . not to be served but to serve, and to give his life as a ransom for many" (Mark 10:45). What could be more important than this fact? Yet each Gospel's emphasis is important; by having all four we capture a more holistic perspective of our Lord and are thus able to bring His truth more fully into the world. Consider that:

1. Having more than one record of an event helps us to remember it. We noted in Deuteronomy, for example, how repetition aids memory and how many important doctrines and events in Scripture are repeated. What could be more important than the coming of God's Son to give us eternal life? That is the focal point of the entire Biblical record. The world's calendars and the Christian message revolve around it; it is good for us to remember it.

2. Imagine if only one person had seen Jesus die and rise again. Who would believe it? In the same way, if we had only one Gospel account, it would not be as credible as having four. And the fact that there are differences, even apparent discrepancies between the Gospels, is further evidence that these accounts are credible. Had a person or group of people fabricated several accounts of Christ, would they or the editors who followed them not collaborate to ensure that each account

fits with the others? Having four Gospels rather than only one provides greater credibility to the Christian message.

3. By having four accounts of the one life, we are better able to capture the whole of that life. And yet each of the four Gospels are unique and important in and of themselves. We can better appreciate this fact by remembering Ezekiel's vision of the Lord on His throne surrounded by four heavenly beings, each with four faces reflecting the person of our Lord (Ezekiel 1). The same faces appear again on the archangels surrounding the throne in Revelation 4:6-7: that of a lion, an ox, a man, and an eagle. Each face represents a king over its respective domain—the forest, domesticated animals, humanity, and the air—showing that the Lord reigns over all.

When we think more specifically about each realm of our Lord's reign, we find a corollary with the four Gospels. Matthew, written for a Jewish audience, focuses on Jesus as the King (the lion, which became the symbol for Judah). Mark, written for the Romans, focuses on Jesus as the servant (the ox, the servant of the animals). Luke, written for the Gentiles, focuses on Christ as the Son of Man (the man's face representing humanity). And John, written for the Greeks, focuses on Christ as the Son of God (the eagle, King of the heavens from which our Lord came).

Respond

✱ 1. Do you wish there were fewer Gospel accounts of Christ's life or are you grateful for all four? Why?

2. Mark focuses on Christ as the servant, a theme the Romans, who had thousands of servants, could easily grasp. What "good news" (the meaning of the word *Gospel*) is found in the idea that Christ came to serve?

3. The word *disciple* means "follower." If we are to follow Christ, we must be like Him. Prayerfully record one or more ways you can better serve God and others today.

....

....

....

....

Pray

Lord, thank you for giving us four accounts of Your life. Thank You also that the Bible has more than a hundred names for You, my God. Thank You that, as David said, Your thoughts are precious, and too many to count. I have reason to worship and praise You all of my days, and forever. Help me to grow in my understanding of how great and wondrous You are. Amen.

Impact

John Mark at first turned away from the difficult call to discipleship (Acts 13:13; 15:36-41). Later, he grew to be a servant and has blessed us with what is likely the first-ever written Gospel of Christ. As you go through the day, prayerfully notice opportunities for service the Lord may be opening before you. Seek to serve the Lord and others with all of your heart.

Close

Have doctors helped you at key times in your life? What if God could step down and become your personal physician? In a profound manner, He not only can, but He is waiting to do so. This is the focus of our next lesson, based on Luke's Gospel.

Day 73 · **The Healer's Heart**

The books of Luke and Acts—originally packaged as one volume of Scripture—have long been assumed to have been written by Luke. And the general understanding from Scripture and tradition is that Luke was a medical doctor (Colossians 4:14). This understanding fits with the focus of the book. Jesus, the Son of Man, is shown by Luke to care for the poor, the outcasts, and those who are sick. He heals hearts, souls, and bodies to demonstrate the Kingdom of God. This emphasis on the Savior's compassion and healing can bring hope to everyone who reads this story; it is everyone's Gospel.

Read

You have two reading options: read the full selection of Scripture or a single overview chapter each day.

- Full Reading: Mark 15:21 – Luke 8
- Overview Chapter: Luke 1

Reflect

Luke has fewer chapters than Matthew; by sheer volume, though, Luke wrote the longest of the four Gospels. When we include Acts, the companion volume, we find that Dr. Luke wrote more than any other New Testament author, including Paul. And he emphasized a topic that every human should find important: the healing heart of God. Healing, of course, is a natural topic for a medical doctor, and Luke presents the Lord's supernatural healing power in a most natural way. Let's take a look at the first several chapters with this theme in mind.

Luke 1-2: Birthed for Healing. As a physician, Luke was well educated; his introduction demonstrates some of the most sophisticated and excellent Greek in the New Testament (Luke 1:1-4). Dr. Luke used his training to capture the great story of Jesus Christ from the coming of the Savior to the birth and growth of the Church. Providing details and background that Matthew, Mark, and John don't cover, Luke offers keen insights about two of the most important births ever—those of John and Jesus. With the care of a skilled physician, Dr. Luke describes these births so that we might better appreciate God's predetermined plan to bring healing to our hearts and homes.

Luke 3-4: Preparation to Heal. Luke introduces John the Baptizer, and then the Lord Jesus who is baptized by John (Luke 3:1-20). A key genealogy follows, tracing the Lord's lineage back to Adam as a way of emphasizing that the Gospel is for everyone (Luke 3:21-38). Jesus is tested in the wilderness and persecuted in His hometown which signifies that through being tried and rejected He might sympathize with our weaknesses and heal our wounds (Luke 4:1-30). He immediately begins to cast out demons and

> **Coaching Tip**
>
> This lesson emphasizes a key aspect of the Gospel of Luke: God's healing power. There are dozens of other key themes that a reader can discern in Luke's writing. So it is with each book in the Bible. A person can read any section of God's divine Word, over and over again, each year of their life, and find new insights and perspectives every time. This depth and detail in Scripture is part of the beauty of God's inspired Word.

heal the sick (Luke 4:31-44). Luke's concern for healing appears throughout Luke and Acts with phraseology fitting for a medical doctor. When he describes Simon's mother-in-law, for example, she is not merely feverish, but high with fever (Luke 4:38). This is a specific terminology in Greek a medical doctor would use. Such attention to details related to the healing power of God is etched into Luke's writing with the care of a medical doctor updating his journals.

Luke 5-8: Launched into Healing Ministry. Luke shows the progression in the Lord's ministry from Galilee (Luke 4:14-9:50) to Judea (Luke 9:51-13:21) to Perea (Luke 13:22-19:27), and finally to Jerusalem (Luke 19:28-24:53). In each phase, we are introduced to the compassion and healing nature of the Lord. In the Galilean ministry of Luke 5-8, for example, the disciples are called to immediately witness the healing of a leper and a paralyzed man (Luke 5:12-26). A tax collector, rejected by the Jews, is invited with his friends into the inner circle to experience the healing compassion of God. When questioned by the Pharisees, Jesus explains, "Those who are well have no need of a physician, but those who are sick" (Luke 5:31). The Lord then appoints His 12 followers and commences to preach a sermon on a plain, emphasizing God's love for the poor, downcast, and mistreated—urging us to love our enemies and to live humbly before God (Luke 6:12-50). In the next chapter a centurion—an outsider—demonstrates unusual faith. A widow's son is raised from the dead, and a sinful woman anoints Jesus with oil and is forgiven her sins. Luke thus shows us, through story after story, God's desire to heal all kinds of people from everything that ails them, even societal ills.

Healing for Our Lives. God chose to communicate His heart to heal through the pen of a medical doctor. Do we really believe the good news found in this third Gospel? Have we entrusted our wounds and pains to the Lord, our Great Physician? A doctor can't heal us if we don't come to him for help.

Respond

1. Do you have a special appreciation for doctors? Why or why not?

2. This lesson emphasized the healing heart of God. Do you believe God desires to heal you, inside and out? Explain.

....

....

....

....

✱ 3. "The greatest desire of God is for the healing of our relationships, first with Him and then with others." Do you agree with this statement? If not, why not? If so, what are the implications for your life? Be specific.

....

....

....

....

Pray

Lord, help me to turn all of my wounds of body, soul, and spirit completely over to You. As You refresh me with Your healing power, also give to me Your heart of compassion for those who need Your healing touch. Amen.

Impact

Almost everyone needs healing on some level, and some people may never turn to God unless they experience God's love directly through you. As the saying goes, *"People don't care how much you know until they know how much you care."* Reach out to someone today, showing them you care.

Close

Who doesn't like a good story? Well, Jesus mastered the art of weaving stories in order to reveal understanding about what the Kingdom of God is like. So tomorrow, Dr. Luke takes us on a brief tour of Jesus' parables, especially those related to godly compassion.

Coaching Tip

Remember as you read that your first goal should not be to complete the entire Bible but rather as you read it all to allow God to complete His work in the entirety of your life.

Day 74 · **Radical Compassion**

One of the world's most common containers of truth is the story. The parable, a common story form in Christ's day, was regularly used in the four Gospels. A parable is a story laid alongside a truth to bring it to life. Matthew, who captures 23 of Christ's parables, uses them primarily to teach about the Kingdom of Heaven. Mark, whose 6 parables are shared by Matthew and Luke, focuses more on the Lord's doings than His teachings. Luke carries the most parables of all: 29 of them. At the heart of Luke's Gospel, we see the heart of Jesus through 24 of His parables as He travels toward Jerusalem to give His life for us (Luke 9:51-19:27). Sixteen of these parables are unique to the book of Luke and are some of the best-remembered and most influential stories in history. As you read them, allow their truths to impact your world.

Read

You have two reading options: read the full selection of Scripture or a single overview chapter each day.

- Full Reading: Luke 9–18
- Overview Chapter: Luke 15

Reflect

If asked, "Which of Jesus' stories best demonstrates God's amazing compassion?" How might you respond? Most people would likely think of the Parable of the Good Samaritan or of the Parable of the Prodigal Son. Both stories, unique to Luke, show our Lord's divine mastery of storytelling. They also reveal the heart of God: a heart of radical compassion.

The Good Samaritan. In Luke 10, an expert in the Law of God tested Jesus, asking what he must do to inherit eternal life. In answer, Jesus asked him what the Law has to say on the matter. To this, the expert repeated the Great Commandment, the call to love God with one's whole being and one's neighbor as oneself. Jesus said, "You have answered correctly; do this, and you will live" (Luke 10:28). Thus was the self-righteous questioner left in a bind. If he was attempting to earn his way to Heaven, how could he ever know he had done enough?

When we think we can get to Heaven by being good enough, the Great Command stands in our way. It is easy to say we love God. But the proof is found in the demonstration of our love for our neighbor, a love that can be seen and measured, and never found to be perfect.

Finding himself stuck, the lawyer asked, "Who is my neighbor?" Hence the Lord's parable of the Good Samaritan. In it, He turned the tables of religious tradition upside-down. Rather than provide a definition of "neighbor" that would allow the lawyer to create a safe haven around which he could limit God's love, Jesus told a parable that would require the lawyer to surrender to God as never before. The only way we can find love for all people, even our enemies, as the Good Samaritan did, is to receive it from God.

The Prodigal Son. A group of Pharisees and Scribes complains about Jesus, saying, "This man receives sinners and eats with them" (Luke 15:2). In response, Jesus tells three back-to-back stories that demonstrate God's compassion. After sharing a parable about a lost sheep and another about a lost coin, Jesus drives His point home through a story about a lost son. At first, this wayward progeny seems to be the focal point of the story; then the amazing love of the father—a picture of God the Father—captures the listener. Finally, the son who never left home and who, like the Pharisees and Scribes, considers himself righteous and more worthy of the Father's love than the other brother, becomes the focal point, leaving us with a piercing question: Do we embrace God's heart of love for all people—even the outcasts of society—or have we hardened our hearts toward those who need God the most?

Dr. Luke clearly chose the latter. He served God through medicine but also through the production of a Gospel that would show the world the compassionate heart of God. After completing his account of the life of Christ, the doctor traveled with Paul to capture the story of the expanding work of Jesus through His Apostles. Luke did anything and everything possible to explain the love and healing power of God to everyone he possibly could. He was touched by the Lord's radical compassion.

Respond

1. As you read the parables of Jesus in Luke, did any one parable most grab your attention? Why?

✱ 2. In a few words or sentences, summarize the radical compassion of our Lord.

3. In what ways might we learn to live by this compassion as did Dr. Luke?

Pray

Lord, thank you for showing compassion and love toward me, even when I sin and fall short of your purpose for my life. Help me to show such compassion for others. Amen.

Impact

Pray for God to give you His heart of compassion for those who need it most. Then ask the Lord to guide you daily as you live by it.

Close

Sun Tzu wrote, *"There are not more than five musical notes, yet the combinations of these five give rise to more melodies than can ever be heard."*[1] Tomorrow we will look at "Unity in Diversity."

---

1 Sun Tzu, *The Art of War*, trans. Lionel Giles (Mineola, New York: Dover Publications, Inc.), 55-56.

Day 75 · **Unity in Diversity**

The first three Gospels are together called synoptic Gospels, suggesting they generally report the same things. When we come to John's Gospel, however, 90% of the content is new and fresh. John brings us intimate and up-close portions of Christ's ministry that the others omit. This doesn't mean the four Gospel writers were somehow lacking unity in their vision and mission. Rather, it reminds us that we can emphasize different parts of the Christian life and faith and still be one in Christ. These truths become obvious to us as we read John's opening prologue.

Read

You have two reading options: read the full selection of Scripture or a single overview chapter each day.

- Full Reading: Luke 19 – John 4
- Overview Chapter: John 1

Reflect

John begins his Gospel with a prologue that sets it apart from the others. The opening words of John 1:1—"In the beginning"—bring us back to Genesis 1:1 and the Creation account. Today's modern reader might hope he is setting himself up to make a scientific statement, but instead, John moves us into theology and philosophy, adding, ". . . was the Word." John here introduces the *logos*, a Greek term used by philosophers; John desires that all people, even the Greek intellectuals, ponder the compelling message of the Gospel.

One God. The Greeks believed in many gods. John introduces them to the One and Only, writing, "And the Word was with God, and the Word was God." The Greek gods each had a beginning. John's depiction of Christ as the "Word" portrays One who was always with God, eternally of the same substance and nature as God, and was thus inseparably part of the Godhead. With but a few strokes of his quill, John confronts the mythology and philosophies that guide Greco-Roman culture. Encouraging his readers to join him on a journey as they read his account of the life of Christ, John writes in language that has long intrigued the most studied scholars of Scripture. At the same time, he writes in a manner that can be grasped by the common person. He deftly describes God's revelation from Heaven in a manner that is relevant to each person on earth.

One Hope. Each Gospel writer builds a unique emphasis around the great central theme of the person of Jesus Christ. Through their diversity—rather than contradicting each other—they complement one another. So it is today for followers of Christ. Christians around the world understand and worship our Lord with a vast and varied array of styles and approaches. This

Coaching Tip

We each come to our readings with tinted glasses. Our age, background, church experience, and life's journey all add color to what we read. The great benefit of discussing our readings with others is that we can enrich our own understanding. If you've not yet done so, seek out conversations with others about what you're learning.

diversity makes the message of the Gospel relevant to the distinct cultures of the world. Carrying the same passion that the Gospel writers etched into their accounts of the life of Christ, Christians today seek to reach all kinds of people with the one eternal hope found in Jesus Christ.

One Church. Efforts made organizationally to unite Christians are generally short-lived, especially if focus is taken away from the eternal Gospel around which followers of Christ are organically unified. When Jesus Christ is lifted up, the divisions the world sees dissolve as the love of God and the vision of God's Kingdom bring a unity through which the diversity in lesser things makes our oneness all the more striking.

Respond

1. Do you think it was wise for God to provide us with four Gospels, each with a unique emphasis, rather than one harmonious whole? Explain.

2. Imagine if every church around the world were exactly the same in format, style, language, and approach. What would be the downside of such unification?

✱ 3. When there is true division among Christians, what do you think is the cause? How can we strengthen our unity despite our differences?

Pray

Lord, forgive me for lacking appreciation for the great variety of Your works around the world. Thank you for the unity we share as believers in the core and essential teachings of the faith, and for the great diversity that helps people to understand and embrace the faith worldwide. Amen.

Impact

Are you being blessed by your reading of God's Word? Pray about inviting friends or family members to join you in a future read through the Bible, that they too might be blessed.

Close

So when you think of the word "hospitality"—what comes to mind? Maya Angelou stated, *"People will forget what you said, people will forget what you did, but people will never forget how you made them feel"* (Maya Angelou 2003). Our next B90+ lesson will explore "Kingdom Hospitality."

Coaching Tip

Ponder how good it has been to take some time out every day to be with the Lord and to receive His guidance and inspiration. Begin thinking about how you can keep the pace when this reading ends. Scripture Awakening will offer you excellent resources to help you get to the next level of intimacy and integrity in your walk with your Lord.

Day 76 · Kingdom Hospitality

When you visit a friend's house, when does that house begin to feel like home to you? Is it when you pull in the driveway? When you walk to the front door? When you are invited in? After you remove your coat and exchange greetings? Once you sit down and begin sharing a hearty meal? Or is it perhaps when conversation begins to roll and laughter and memories fill the room and people begin to share intimately and care for one other personally? Such thoughts remind us of the progression of hospitality leading to a growing intimacy with God that John invites us to experience and enjoy.

Read

You have two reading options: read the full selection of Scripture or a single overview chapter each day.

- Full Reading: John 5–13
- Overview Chapter: John 13

Reflect

The Gospel of John is different from the other three Gospels in many ways. It has more theological discourses than the others, each of them tied to miracles and signs from God. It is guided by a flow of thought from beginning to end that is more thematic than the first three Gospels. Most significantly, its author gives us an inside view of our Lord's life—and invites us to experience it.

The Welcome. This insider perspective is most obvious in the five chapters that contain the Lord's final words to His disciples before He is crucified (John 13-17). Not included by the other writers, these chapters were captured by John as he sat by the Lord's side at the Last Supper. Looking more closely, we ponder John 13—the first of five different scenes in the Gospel of John in which the Apostle is described as the one "whom Jesus loved" (John 13:21-30; 19:26-27; 21:7; 21:20).

John 13 brings us into the Upper Room where the Lord and His disciples will share their final meal. The evening begins with a dilemma. It was customary that, following a long day of travel over dusty Judean roads, sandals would be removed and feet cleaned. But there was no servant available to perform the task. It would have been uncomfortable and humiliating for one of the disciples to do the job; yet, how much more uncomfortable they must have felt when Jesus slipped off His outer garment, grasped a towel and a washbasin, and knelt down to serve them all. This was ultimate hospitality through which Christ called His followers into true intimacy with God.

The Challenge. After washing each of their feet, the Lord told them, "You call me Teacher and Lord, and you are right, for so I am. If I then, your Lord and Teacher, have washed your feet, you also ought to wash one another's feet" (John 13:13-14). If the disciples were to work and live and do ministry together, they would need to adopt a servant-like attitude, caring for one another and those who came their way. Jesus set the standard they would need to follow if they hoped to live as the family of God. Otherwise, Christianity would soon become focused on buildings, budgets, and creeds—but would have no heart.

The disciples left the Upper Room that night with clean feet and humble hearts. They then watched with dismay and astonishment as Jesus continued to serve them by dying on the cross for their sins, rising from the dead, and promising to come back one day to bring them to their eternal home where Kingdom hospitality would be made perfect. On that day they, and we, will learn the true meaning of "welcome." The Lord of perfect love, who has been at His Father's side preparing a home for us will welcome us into His joy to experience His glory forever.

Considering the great hope and the wondrous home that awaits us, our challenge is to allow the Lord to use us to express Kingdom hospitality to others with every opportunity God provides. We have been called by the Lord into His inner circle. Others would like to join us, but they may feel uncomfortable doing so; they may need someone to open the door for them—and maybe even to wash their feet.

Respond

1. What ingredients make a house a real home for you?

2. As you read the John 13:1-17 account of the washing of the disciple's feet, what central truth comes home to you? Why is the servant attitude essential for the Christian life?

✱ 3. Ponder the hospitality that will be shown to you by Jesus when you are welcomed into your eternal home. How does that thought challenge you to be more hospitable to people today?

Pray

Lord, guide me to obey Your call to love and serve others. Help me to humble myself, and to consider others more important than myself, even today. Amen.

Impact

There are millions of people who do not yet know the Lord. Some live in countries where no church exists and where the Word of God is scarce. Take a few moments to pray for those in places where God's Word is not available or it's actively suppressed.

Close

Most of us like surprises, as long as they're good ones. And how about surprise endings, like at the end of a movie that catches you off-guard? Coming up: some surprises as we look at how John closes his Gospel account.

Day 77 · **Surprise Endings**

The end of John's Gospel—Chapter 21—is full of surprises. So unexpected are some occurrences in this final chapter that certain scholars call it an appendage to the Gospel of John; in other words, they assume it was attached after-the-fact. They often add that the close of Chapter 20 would be a fine ending for the entire book.

Nevertheless, the broad consensus is that Chapter 21 was indeed written by John. It carries the same themes, style, and tone as the rest of the book, and its original inclusion in his letter is supported by significant ancient manuscripts. Perhaps rather than question whether Chapter 21 is an appropriate and authentic close to the book, we should ask the more obvious question: "Why the surprise endings?"

Read

You have two reading options: read the full selection of Scripture or a single overview chapter each day.

- Full Reading: John 14 – Acts 4
- Overview Chapter: John 21

Reflect

Consider three of the many surprises in John 21 and think about their implications for our lives:

The Surprise Remembrance (John 21:1-14). In the close to the Gospel of John, the disciples were caught by surprise when their nets were suddenly filled with a record-breaking catch of fish. It would have been difficult for them not to remember how a similar miracle had occurred when Jesus first called them (Luke 5:1-11). The Lord wanted them to know that as surely as He called them into ministry three years prior, He was now reinstating them. As He had been with them before, He would be with them again through the Holy Spirit. If they doubted their call when He left them, they could always look back to this day and remember. In the same way, God wants us to remember His past work in our lives, knowing that what He has done before He can do again.

The Surprise Reinstatement (John 21:15-19). In this closing chapter, Peter, having previously denied Jesus three times, was given the opportunity to confess his love for the Lord three times. By studying the Greek words used in this dialogue, we get the clear sense that Peter was deeply humbled by his previous denials of Christ and that his self-reliance was broken to the core. The rugged fisherman had finally come to the place of knowing that he wasn't capable of becoming a fisher of men. Left to himself, he was prone to failure. Later, when the Holy Spirit was given,

Coaching Tip

We are on day 77 of 90. The end is in sight. But we must keep focused on what God wants to teach us today if we hope to end well.

Peter became alive with a passion that did not quit, even when he was called to give his life for the Lord (John 21:18-19). Like Peter, we also may be surprised when we feel the depth of our failings only to discover that the Lord gives us opportunity to come back to Him for a fresh start. We may be further surprised as we watch God empower us and work in our lives—even through our weaknesses.

The Surprise Remainder (John 21:20-24). Peter, having heard about a difficult ending to his own life, asked how the end of John's life would pan out. To this, Jesus said, "If it is my will that he remain until I come, what is that to you? You follow me!" (John 21:22). Hearing this caused rumors to begin circulating that suggested John would not die (John 21:23). In reality, John would outlive the other disciples, and the Lord would come to him before he died. History tells us that John outlived the other disciples, and tradition suggests he was the only one not to be martyred. But what did the Lord mean by suggesting John would "remain" until the Lord came? One possibility is that Jesus might have simply been telling Peter, "The way John's life ends isn't your business." A second option is to equate the Lord's coming with the fall of Jerusalem in AD 70. A third, most intriguing option, equates the Lord's coming to John late in his life with the visitation of Christ to John as described in Revelation 1. It might be that Jesus implied all three truths by His statement. No matter how we interpret His words, one thing is for sure: the ending of John's life carries an aura of mystery. So it is with each of us. Our lives will always be touched by surprises, right to the end. But the Lord is over it all.

John closes his book with words that serve as a fitting close for our study of the Gospels: "Now there are also many other things that Jesus did. Were every one of them to be written, I suppose that the world itself could not contain the books that would be written" (John 21:25). In the same way, your life is a story still being written by God, and there are more surprises to come.

Respond

1. Why is it important for us to remember how God has worked in our lives through the past?

2. Peter learned the hard way to surrender his life fully to Jesus. Is there an easy way to learn this lesson? Explain, if you can, with examples from your own life.

✱ 3. Jesus gently chided Peter for his undue concern about the way John's life would end, adding, ". . .what is that to you?" (John 21:22). What is the problem with becoming overly concerned about how things will end rather than focusing on giving God our best today?

Pray

Lord, help me to trust You in the present, knowing that each moment I'm resting in Your peace and that the future and every surprise ending will be marked by Your grace. Amen.

Impact

You will soon transition from the Gospels to Acts, a book of history. Notice, as you make this shift, how the same Lord who walked the earth as described in the Gospels continues His work through the disciples in Acts. As you read Acts, reflect on how He is still doing His work today, through you.

Close

If today's lesson held some surprises for you, wait 'til you see how the Holy Spirit drops some surprised amazement upon the Apostle Peter, up on a roof in broad daylight, when God rolls out His welcome mat!

Session 12 • Overview

● REVIEW Days 71-77

Gospels: Incarnation, Crucifixion, Resurrection

 Now is the time for your small group meeting to review the week's Scripture readings, cover the discussion questions, and watch the Essential Snapshot video together (or by yourself if reading alone). Point your mobile device's camera on the QR code to access the video entitled "Session 12: Like No Other". Or enter this link into your browser: **ScriptureAwakening.com/plus/**

- Discuss the questions marked by an asterisk (✷) from the **Respond** sections in Days 71-77, perhaps adding others if time permits.
- Watch the Session 12 video* (individually or with a small group).
    1. What insights from the video would you like to explore further?
    2. How does the life of Christ as demonstrated in the Gospels help you to know and obey God?.
- Summarize the Preview (below) of what is coming next week, encouraging group members to read it on their own.

*Facilitators note: In order to watch the Essential Snapshot video with your group, you will need a large video monitor, if meeting in-person. If hosting a small group remotely, use Zoom (or similar service) to stream the video from your device to share with group participants.

● PREVIEW Days 78-84

History & Pauline Epistles: Expansion, Instruction, Correction

Weekly Reading: Acts 5:1 to Titus 3:15

Summary

The story of the growth of the early Church continues in the book of Acts. The message of the Gospel continues to expand outward from Jerusalem to nearby regions and ultimately to Rome itself.

This week's readings contain 12 of Paul's 13 epistles, titled by addressee (to churches, then individuals) and generally ordered by length. Within our reading there are two major subgroups of epistles: the Prison Epistles (Ephesians, Philippians, Colossians, and Philemon) written during Paul's first imprisonment, and the Pastoral Epistles (1 and 2 Timothy and Titus) written to young pastors.

Books You'll Encounter This Week

Acts Overview (Conclusion)

This week concludes the book of Acts. The early sections of Acts focus on Peter and the ministry of the Apostles in Jerusalem. Then, the stoning of Stephen and growing persecution broaden the focus to Judea and Samaria through which Gentiles are brought into the fold.

The remainder of Acts centers on Paul's ministry, beginning with his miraculous conversion en route to Damascus. The execution of James is followed by a further expansion of the Church as Paul takes the Gospel message into Asia Minor, and then Macedonia and Greece. After his imprisonment, Paul takes a sea voyage and carries the message of life all the way to the gates of Rome.

Romans Overview

Paul's letter to the Church in Rome is his longest epistle and the most complete treatment of the doctrine of salvation in the Bible. Building on the theme of God's righteousness, he explains how people are made right before God (justified), before the world (sanctified) and for eternity (glorified)—all through the power of the Gospel. Paul then discusses implications for Israel, the world, and the Church.

1 Corinthians Overview

Paul appeals to the Church in Corinth to avoid division by elevating Christ above all human leaders. He then describes what it means to be followers of Christ and encourages believers to give themselves always to the work of the Lord.

2 Corinthians Overview

In a second letter to the Church at Corinth, probably written within a year of 1 Corinthians, Paul offers personal advice and defends his apostolic credentials.

Galatians Overview

In this letter to the Churches in Galatia, Paul establishes his authority and then admonishes the Galatians to reject legalism and spurious means of salvation, and to embrace the Gospel of Christ. He earnestly defends the superiority of grace over the Law and justification by faith alone.

Ephesians Overview

Writing to the Church in Ephesus, Paul focuses on the triumphant Church.

Philippians Overview

Paul's message to the Church in Philippi is about the triumphant Christian.

Colossians Overview

Paul writes to the Church in Colossae about the triumphant Christ.

1 Thessalonians Overview

Following a positive report from Timothy about the Church of the Thessalonians, Paul writes to encourage them to continue strong in their faith. He also answers their questions about the return of the Lord and its implications for both the living and the dead.

2 Thessalonians Overview

As a follow-up to his first letter, Paul reiterates that the Thessalonians should stand firm and not be alarmed by false prophecies about the coming "day of the Lord."

1 Timothy Overview

Paul sends a letter to Ephesus to instruct his protégé, Timothy, about church leadership. The Apostle provides counsel on public worship, false teachers, church discipline, and pastoral priorities.

2 Timothy Overview

Paul encourages Timothy to preach the Word, since "all Scripture is breathed out by God," (2 Timothy 3:16a) and prepares Christians to be "complete, equipped for every good work" (2 Timothy 3:17). Aware that his death is rapidly approaching, Paul encourages Timothy to hold fast to the things he has been taught.

Titus Overview

Writing to his coworker Titus, Paul highlights the incarnation of Christ and its practical applications for godliness and church leadership.

Things to Look for This Week

As you read, consider:

1. How severe persecution against the early Church led to its rapid growth and expansion.
2. How Paul typically organizes his letters with guiding truths followed by practical application.
3. Paul's unfailing devotion to the cause of Christ despite the relentless opposition and persecution he faced throughout his ministry.

Day 78 · **God's Welcome Mat**

Peter climbed the stairs to the roof of the home where he was staying, that of Simon the Tanner. While food was being prepared downstairs, he saw a vision from above. A large sheet was being let down to earth by its four corners, filled with all kinds of animals, reptiles, and birds. A voice told Peter, "Get up, Peter. Kill and eat" (Acts 10:13 NIV). Peter objected, for as a Jew this would violate the teachings about clean and unclean foods. The voice responded, "Do not call anything impure that God has made clean" (Acts 10:15 NIV). This happened three times, after which men arrived from Caesarea through whom God would open for Peter an insight about God's desire to welcome everyone into the Church. The truths Peter learned through this Acts 10 encounter need to be remembered again today.

Read

You have two reading options: read the full selection of Scripture or a single overview chapter each day.

- Full Reading: Acts 5–15
- Overview Chapter: Acts 10

Reflect

In Acts 10, Peter was visited by men from Caesarea sent by a Roman centurion named Cornelius. The vision Peter had received just before the visitors arrived prepared the Apostle for what was about to happen. Faith in the Messiah—which until now had almost exclusively included people who followed the Jewish standards such as circumcision—was about to expand across the line of ethnicity and tradition to include the uncircumcised. Until this time, it was considered a violation of God's will for a Jew to even visit a Gentile's home; and now God would call the early Christians to welcome home people from all the nations. This all-inclusive outreach was commanded by Jesus in the Great Commission (Matthew 28:18-20) and enabled through the power of God's Spirit. Jesus told His followers:

> *But you will receive power when the Holy Spirit has come upon you, and you will be my witnesses in Jerusalem and in all Judea and Samaria, and to the end of the earth.* (Acts 1:8)

This verse summarizes the growing reach of the Gospel in the book of Acts from Jerusalem (Acts 1-7) to Judea and Samaria (Acts 8 to 12), then to the ends of the earth (Acts 13 to 28). It corresponds with the commission given to Abraham to become a blessing to all of the nations (Genesis 12:2; 18:18; 22:18). Indeed, Christ died for all the peoples of the earth (Revelation 5:9).

The book of Acts contains the incredible story of God's love and the unfolding of His redemptive plan during a 30-year period following the ascen-

Coaching Tip

Some have suggested that Luke's second volume isn't as much about the acts of the Apostles as it is about the acts of the Holy Spirit. As you read Acts, notice how the Spirit is at work in the lives of the early believers and ask God for insights about how the Spirit can work in your life.

sion of Christ. The early Christians were not alone in this venture. The same Jesus who had walked the earth now empowered them by His Spirit and would carry the Gospel to the nations through them. Luke, who first wrote in his Gospel about what Jesus "began to do and teach" (Luke 1:1), describes in Acts the ongoing work of Jesus Christ and of the Holy Spirit through the people of God. The book has no real ending because the work of the expanding Kingdom of God is now ours and will not be complete until all the peoples of the earth have heard the good news (Matthew 24:14).

Imagine what it was like for Peter when he was commanded to violate thousands of years of Jewish tradition by visiting the home of a Gentile, Cornelius, to create a bridge to the Gentile world. Other followers of the Way were at first upset with Peter's actions and demanded answers. Over time, they came to realize that the Gospel is a big welcome mat for people of all ethnicities and walks of life (Acts 11:1-18). Have you and I come to realize this as well? If so, is it evident in our lives?

Respond

1. Having read through the Old Testament, you have gained a sense of the long and rich tradition of the Jews. After following the Law of God for some 2,000 years, they were now being asked to welcome Gentiles into the fold. Why would this be difficult for them?

....

....

....

....

....

✱ 2. Are there any people you would find difficult to welcome into the Kingdom of God through the open doors of your heart, your home, or your church? If so, explain why.

....

....

....

....

3. God's will is not that we merely *understand* that He loves everyone; He wants us to *show* that love to others—even to people we might normally avoid. What steps might you take to be more welcoming to others?

....

....

....

....

....

Pray

Great and Gracious God, forgive me for the many times I've overlooked opportunities to invite others into Your Kingdom. Help me to grow in the gift of hospitality. Amen.

Impact

The person we think least likely to read the Bible might be the very person who is waiting to be invited to do so. Start thinking and praying now about people you can invite into a group study after this one. You may choose to do Bible in 90 Days again or one of the follow-up Bible studies that will be described on Day 90.

Close

Can you imagine trying to stop even one, huge, crashing wave? Futile. Impossible. What about God's purposes? Men who think (foolishly) that they could stop God's purposes would be just as 'successful' as trying to stop a crashing wave. Tomorrow: "Unstoppable!"

B90+

Day 79 · **Unstoppable**

We may generally divide the book of Acts in half by its focus first on Peter (Acts 1-12) and then on Paul (Acts 13-28). As bookends around Christ's promise in Acts 1:8, Peter's ministry centered in Jerusalem and Paul's on the ends of the earth. Together they and the early followers of Jesus demonstrated the truth of Gamaliel's words about God's advancing Kingdom, "If God is behind it, you cannot stop it anyway, unless you want to fight against God" (Acts 5:39, CEV). God's work is unstoppable still today—and always will be. We will learn more about what this means for our lives after our reading from Acts.

Read

You have two reading options: read the full selection of Scripture or a single overview chapter each day.

- Full Reading: Acts 16–27
- Overview Chapter: Acts 16

Reflect

Jesus gave His disciples the command to preach the Gospel to all the nations—and with it the promise that once this job is complete, the end will come (Mark 16:15; Matthew 24:14). The commission is good still today, and the end might be closer than we think. Three realizations can help us to do our part. We must understand that:

1. **We are part of God's unstoppable purpose.** The story of the expansion of the Church in the book of Acts is given to remind us of this truth. When Paul preached the Gospel, he carried the message of life to as many people as possible. His second missionary journey, for example, took him through Asia Minor—the region of modern-day Turkey—to visit recent converts from his first journey. The Spirit of God then led him to cross the Aegean Sea to bring the Gospel to Macedonia, the region of the Balkans that now includes Greece. Through many hardships, Paul eventually carried the message of life into Rome.

    The unstoppable nature of God's Church is typified by Paul's jail experience in Acts 16, a text that describes a time when it seemed impossible to go forward. God did the impossible, releasing the fetters that threatened to hinder the Gospel. As we continue to follow Paul's journeys in the book of Acts, it becomes clear that God's plan was being fulfilled regardless of the world's obstacles.

    From Paul's day until now, the world population has grown exponentially from approximately 300 million inhabitants to almost 8 billion. Still the task remains the same: "Make disciples of all the nations" (Matthew 28:19a). The word for "nations," *ta ethné*, implies groups defined by re-

Coaching Tip

Have some reacted negatively to you when they learned you are reading through the Bible? Remember the words of Christ, "Blessed are you when others revile you and persecute you and utter all kinds of evil against you falsely on My account. Rejoice and be glad, for your reward is great in Heaven, for so they persecuted the prophets who were before you" (Matthew 5:11-12).

gions, populations, languages, and ethnicity. Because God cares about everyone, He is committed to giving people from all walks of life and in all parts of the world the opportunity to believe. The question is, will you and I be part of this great plan? If so, we can count on two promises from our Lord: "If they persecuted me, they will also persecute you. If they kept my word, they will also keep yours" (John 15:20c).

2. **We will be persecuted.** Jesus promised that many would resist the message of the Gospel. Today, as the population has reached such huge proportions and as God's Kingdom continues to expand, resistance to the Gospel is evident. There are more martyrs for the faith in our generation than ever before in history. And also more converts.

3. **Some will keep God's Word.** As we read through Acts, we see in practically every place Paul was called to minister that at least some people believed. So it is today. We cannot go wrong when we take a stand for God. We are shining the light in the darkness, giving people eternal hope. Not all will believe; yet, if only one person receives God's gift of eternal life and the promise of Heaven, it will all be worth the effort. From Paul's day until now, it has remained true that missionaries, pastors, teachers, elders, deacons, business leaders, common laborers, the unemployed, students, parents, and their children—every member of the family of faith—are part of an unstoppable force.

Respond

1. Which story or stories in your reading of Acts most inspires you? Why?

2. In John 15:20, Jesus promised some would embrace the truth and others would persecute us for proclaiming it. In what ways do you experience one or both of these realities in your life?

✱ 3. Complete this thought: "Since the Kingdom of God is the one unstoppable force that will impact all of eternity, I should . . ."

....

....

....

....

Pray

Lord, help me to get on board with what You are doing today. Let me not focus so much on how others are being used by You as on the specific things You have given me to do for Your Name and for Your glory. And keep me faithful until the end. Amen.

Impact

Paul's boldness for the Lord inspired many, even when he was imprisoned (Philippians 1:14). He wrote, "remember my chains" (Colossians 4:18b). Today, we can remember thousands of others around the world who, like Paul, suffer as prisoners because of their faith. Such thoughts should cause us to say, "I will not complain or be slack in the tasks You have given to me, Lord, whatever the cost. You are worth it."

Close

If God's purposes are unstoppable, then what about His love? What would it take to convince you that nothing can ever separate you from God's love? Next stop on our B90+ journey: the incredible, wonderful, life-giving truths in the book of Romans.

Day 80 · **Inseparable**

Romans is known as the most logical, systematic presentation of the Gospel in the entire Bible. It is also packed with devotional insights that can change our lives. One such insight, a central theme of the Bible, is woven like a golden thread through the book. As you read, ponder what this insight might be.

Read

You have two reading options: read the full selection of Scripture or a single overview chapter each day.

- Full Reading: Acts 28 – Romans 14
- Overview Chapter: Romans 8

Reflect

The Apostle Paul had a grasp on God's righteousness that motivated his life. More accurately, God's righteousness had a grasp on Paul. His systematic treatise in the book of Romans explains why. Beginning with an introduction (Romans 1:1-15) Paul leads us into the book's theme verses (Romans 1:16-17). Following the truths of these verses through the book, we will come to understand how and why we are meant to be inseparable from God.

> *For I am not ashamed of the gospel, for it is the power of God for salvation to everyone who believes, to the Jew first and also to the Greek. For in it the righteousness of God is revealed from faith for faith, as it is written, "The righteous shall live by faith."* (Romans 1:16-17)

Righteousness Lacking (Romans 1:18 to 3:20). Paul begins by showing us our need: there is none righteous. When we compare ourselves with others in the world, we may seek to justify sin in our lives based on degree. But God gave us the Law, such as the Ten Commandments, to show us that no one is truly righteous; no person can earn his or her way to Heaven based on good works.

Righteousness Declared (Romans 3:21 to 5:21). Next, the Apostle tells that on the cross Jesus paid the price for our sins and shortcomings, enabling us to be seen as righteous in God's sight. Our part is to believe. Justification, a gift for our faith, is a legal term which Paul uses to essentially declare that the gavel in Heaven has come down with the pronouncement "not guilty."

Righteousness Instilled (Romans 6-8). Still, we face the daily struggle of attempting to live rightly before God. Paul explains why the Law isn't enough and how the believer must be filled with the Holy Spirit to be changed from within, becoming more like our Savior every day.

Coaching Tip

A traveling tourist can often slow down to spend extra time at favorite sites. In the next few days, however, we will be journeying through the New Testament at a ridiculously fast pace with little opportunity to stop and enjoy the scenery. It is good to remind ourselves that we are aiming to capture the big picture. We will have the rest of our days to return to our favorite spots in the Bible and to take in additional insights.

Righteousness Applied (Romans 9-16). What does God's righteousness look like in the world? Paul explains, telling why Jew and Gentile alike need the Messiah. God's righteousness is a gift; it cannot be earned, obtained, or inherited (Romans 9-11). He then describes the righteous life in a community of faith and in the world (Romans 12:1-15:13), closing with final remarks and commendations (Romans 15:14–16:27).

Inseparable from God (Romans 8:31-39). Romans 8, at the center of this incredible treatise, drives home the reality that because of God's gift of righteousness, we are united with God. It explains how God's Spirit helps us to live for God, bringing Him so close that we can call Him Abba, Daddy (Romans 8:1-17). The Spirit fills us with hope in our suffering, helps us in our prayers, and works all things for good in our lives (Romans 8:18-30). As a result, we are *more than* conquerors in this world, knowing that nothing can come between us and God's love (Romans 8:31-39). We are inseparable from God!

Respond

✱ 1. Do you tend to think of righteousness as something you do for God or a gift God gives to you? Explain.

2. Have you personally received God's righteousness through Jesus Christ? If not, would you like to?

3. God's righteousness is not only positional; it is practical. List ways His righteousness may become more apparent in your life as you continue to grow closer to Him.

Pray

Lord, thank you that You have done everything necessary for me to become inseparable from You. In love, You have given me Your righteousness—now and forever. My part is to believe, receive, and live in that righteousness. Please imprint these truths in my mind and heart until Romans 8 is well illustrated in my life. Amen.

Impact

The majority of people—even many who call themselves Christians—do not understand the righteousness of God. Seek to explain the wondrous truths in Romans to someone you know. See if they agree with them, can add to them, or are confused by them. The discussion is of eternal importance.

Close

God has effectively united us to Himself—we are inseparable. Yet that also means, as His children, we must remain separate from worldly influences. We continue our B90+ journey as Paul instructs immature Corinthians about how to keep from sinking in the cultural waters of the world.

Coaching Tip

The process of spiritual growth, if it is real, takes time. Like a tree, we must remain exposed to water (the Word) and light (the truth and love of God) as we continue to grow. That is what these daily times in the Word for reflection and prayer are all about. Ask the Lord to give you the mindset to keep this practice of daily devotion for the rest of your life.

Day 81 · **The Sinking Ship**

Corinth was a city with every conceivable commercial and material advantage. Strategically located with two harbors at the crossroads for travel and trade, Corinth received its business from all directions. It was also famous for its Greek temples, houses for the worship of Greek gods. One such temple, that of Aphrodite, was home to 1,000 priestess prostitutes. Immorality was so rampant in Corinth that the Greek term, "to corinthianize," came to mean "to engage in sexual immorality." Paul wrote to Christians in Corinth, urging them to follow Christ's will rather than the culture's ways. We can learn much from Paul's words to help right the Church today.

Read

You have two reading options: read the full selection of Scripture or a single overview chapter each day.

- Full Reading: Romans 15 – 1 Corinthians 14
- Overview Chapter: 1 Corinthians 1

Reflect

Paul sought to bring correction to Christians driven by worldly values rather than God's commands. From his writings to the Corinthians, we note five steps we can take to help others remain true to God and to His Word:

1. **Despite their problems, Paul was thankful for the Corinthians.** 1 Corinthians opens not with admonitions but with thanksgiving. Paul knew that if you don't love people, you cannot help them. Despite the fact that the Corinthians abused God's grace, Paul thanked God for offering grace to them (1 Corinthians 1:4). Despite the fact that the Corinthians abused their spiritual gifts, he gave thanks that they had spiritual gifts (1 Corinthians 1:5-7). We should find the good in a person and point it out before we find the bad and attempt to rout it out.

2. **Paul made sure his own life was right before confronting others.** With the tenacity and determination of an Olympiad training for the races, Paul strove to make sure his life was right with God (1 Corinthians 9:24-27). In love, he then reached out to others to help them along the same path. He urges us to follow his example, not judging or condemning others but seeking to encourage their spiritual growth (1 Corinthians 10:33-11:1).

3. **Paul was direct and honest about the Corinthian's spiritual compromise.** He wrote specifically to confront the Corinthians' disunity (Chapters 1-4), immorality, and strife (Chapters 5-6). Like Paul, we should learn to diagnose problems if we hope to offer solutions, helping others perceive how culture has crept into their hearts and how they can get back on track with God.

4. **With the heart of a shepherd, Paul carefully used Scripture and wisdom to answer their questions** about marriage (Chapter 7), food sacrificed to idols (Chapter 8), self-discipline (Chapter 9), idolatry (Chapter 10), worship (Chapter 11), and spiritual gifts (Chapters 12-14). When people know we care, they will open up about their struggles and through their honest questions allow us to wrestle with them to find Biblical answers.

5. **When the time and place was right, Paul was able to instruct them with solid teaching.** Despite the serious nature of the problems in the Corinthian Church, Paul wrote them one of the best poetic treatises ever crafted about love (Chapter 13) and the fullest Biblical exposition on the resurrection (Chapter 15).

If we want to help the ship of the Church sail safely in the sea of the culture, we should follow Paul's pattern. We must love people and be thankful for them before we attempt to approach them. We can then be straightforward about their areas of weakness and compromise. And they may open up to us with their questions and concerns. Built on the platform of such honest dialogue, we are positioned to begin bailing the sea out of the ship.

Respond

✱ 1. Christ warned us to get our lives right before judging another person (Matthew 7:1-3). Do you perceive ways in which the culture around you has infected your life and dampened your desire and ability obey this command? Explain.

2. What steps will you take to come clean with the Lord and to live fully as His son or daughter in the world?

3. As you consider the previous list of five steps to help someone else get right and strong in their faith, in what ways might you use these steps to help another?

....

....

....

....

Pray

Lord, You call us to be light in the darkness. Forgive me for allowing the dark influences of the world to creep into my heart. Change me, Lord, and help me to grow strong and solid in my walk with You so that together, we might help others to change. Amen.

Impact

Do you know any Christians who are living much like the Corinthians? If so, pray and ask God to lead you to be a positive force in such lives.

Close

A well-known idiom used to mean "authentic" or "the genuine article" is the phrase "he's the real McCoy." Paul's credentials as a true apostle were challenged by those spreading "fake news" about him in Corinth. Tomorrow: was Paul "the real McCoy?"

Day 82 · **True Credentials**

In 2 Corinthians, Paul finds the need to defend himself against those who claim to be apostles and who are unsettling the Church in Corinth. Demonstrating his right to wield apostolic authority, he pulls out his credentials. As we read and consider what Paul describes as the marks of a true apostle and follower of Christ, he calls us to examine our own lives as well.

Read

You have two reading options: read the full selection of Scripture or a single overview chapter each day.

- Full Reading: 1 Corinthians 15 – Galatians 3
- Overview Chapter: 2 Corinthians 11

Reflect

In 2 Corinthians, Paul bears his soul as he seeks to convince the Corinthians that he is their true spiritual father and a real apostle of the Lord Jesus Christ. He closes his words with this stunning challenge: "Examine yourselves, to see whether you are in the faith. Test yourselves. Or do you not realize this about yourselves, that Jesus Christ is in you?—unless indeed you fail to meet the test" (2 Corinthians 13:5)! He then says, "I hope you will find out that we have not failed the test" (2 Corinthians 13:6). Here are his two primary testing points:

The Credential of Changed Lives. Jesus said one can discern the true believer "by their fruits" (Matthew 7:15-20). We can then examine our lives for the fruit of the Spirit (Galatians 5:22), resulting in the fruit of other lives being touched and changed by ours. In his first letter to the Corinthians, Paul applies this test to his own life, defending his apostleship by pointing to the fruit of lives that have been changed because of God's work through him. He writes, "If to others I am not an apostle, at least I am to you, for you are the seal of my apostleship in the Lord" (1 Corinthians 9:2). Likewise, in 2 Corinthians, he makes the point even clearer as in chapter after chapter he pours out his heart to the Corinthians, pleading with them as his own children to get right with God.

The Credential of Challenged Lives. In Romans 8:17, Paul reminds us that we are ". . . heirs of God and fellow heirs with Christ, provided we suffer with him in order that we may also be glorified with him." There is a vast difference between suffering for our sins and suffering for the Lord. Paul suffered as he loved Christ, followed Christ, and served Christ. Such regular challenges were a by-product of his deep and abiding relationship of trust and love with God. And he certainly suffered.

B90+

Coaching Tip

As you read about the suffering that early Christians experienced, remember also the many Christians around the world who suffer still today—whether in distant lands or right down the street. Such thoughts can make your reading all the more impactful.

Reminding the Corinthians of his sufferings for the Lord in 2 Corinthians 11, Paul writes, "Five times I received at the hands of the Jews the forty lashes less one. Three times I was beaten with rods. Once I was stoned. Three times I was shipwrecked; a night and a day I was adrift at sea . . . in toil and hardship, through many a sleepless night, in hunger and thirst, often without food, in cold and exposure" (2 Corinthians 11:23-28).

Our Credentials. We may not be the facilitators of a great movement for God as was Paul, and we may not suffer to the degree that Paul did, but the evidences of true faith that marked his life should also mark ours. As a result of an abiding relationship with the Lord, do we sincerely long to see others grow in their faith, and are we investing our gifts to help them do so? Are we willing, in this worthy pursuit, to pay a price; to obey the Lord even when it is difficult? If so, our lives provide genuine evidence that we are in the faith. For we are not merely talking about it but are living it.

Respond

1. As you ponder those around you, do you think the average person who claims to be a Christian has the credentials of true faith? Explain.

✱ 2. One of the credentials of a true believer is spiritual fruit. What kinds of fruit should we look for in our lives as we examine ourselves?

3. Another credential mentioned by Paul is a willingness to suffer for the Lord. Is your life marked by such willingness? Explain.

Pray

Lord, fill me with Your presence and purpose that true fruit might become more evident in my life. Grant me the resolve and strength I need each day to live for You, even when the going is difficult. Amen.

Impact

Paul wrote, "Be imitators of me, as I am of Christ," and "Remember my chains" (1 Corinthians 11:1, Colossians 4:18b). The author of Hebrews also said, "Remember those who are in prison, as though in prison with them, and those who are mistreated, since you also are in the body" (Hebrews 13:3). Remember to pray for those who suffer for their faith and thankfully use the freedoms God has given to you for His glory.

Close

Gems. Jewels. Our next B90+ lesson is set to display four small books, yet each one sparkles resplendent with the glory of God's purpose, wisdom, and love. Tomorrow we will mine treasure to uncover the triumphant works of God revealed in these four precious epistles.

Coaching Tip

Reading God's Word does not—in itself—change us. When we listen to the Lord, ponder what we are learning, and allow God's truth to renew our minds and hearts, life-change begins to occur. As you read, ask God for at least one spiritual insight each day.

Day 83 · The Jeweled Necklace

There are four precious gems, four small books that are packed with spiritual riches in the heart of the New Testament: Galatians, Ephesians, Philippians, and Colossians. Galatians, one of Paul's earliest letters, was probably written around AD 52. The other three are believed to have been composed during Paul's imprisonment in Rome a decade later. Each of these short epistles captures an essential element of the victorious Christian life; when taken together, they show the triumph of God's work in the world.

Read

You have two reading options: read the full selection of Scripture or a single overview chapter each day.

- Full Reading: Galatians 4 – Colossians 4
- Overview Chapter: Colossians 1

Reflect

Even as it took four Gospels to give a complete picture of Christ's life on earth, four epistles fill out our understanding of His continued life through us. Galatians showcases the triumphant Gospel; Ephesians displays the triumphant Church; Philippians describes the triumphant Christian; and Colossians presents the triumphant Christ.

Galatians • The Triumphant Gospel. Galatians is Romans in miniature: a concise blueprint of the Gospel of liberty. In this short letter, we find the Gospel defended (Chapters 1-2), the Gospel explained (Chapters 3-4), and the Gospel applied (Chapters 5-6). Paul wrote to the Church in Galatia either after his first missionary journey or after his second visit to Galatia. Either way, his concern was to confront the legalism that threatened the early Church. The idea that we must work our way into God's good favor was a carryover from centuries of Jewish religious tradition, and the Gospel triumphed over it.

Ephesians • The Triumphant Church. Ephesians was written by Paul from prison, along with Philippians, Colossians, and Philemon. Containing Paul's most profound statements about the meaning and mystery of the Church, Ephesians reminds us that God's work cannot be imprisoned or held back. Beginning with doctrine (Chapter 1-3) and closing with application (Chapters 4-6), this book has inspired Christians through the ages with the confidence that not even the gates of Hell can hinder the advance of God's work on earth through God's triumphant people, the Church.

Philippians • The Triumphant Christian. In Philippians, Paul expresses his deep appreciation for the believers in Philippi, the very place where opposition to his message had been so pronounced. It was in Philippi that he had been beaten with rods, put in stocks, and imprisoned (Acts 16). Intervening, God sent an earthquake to bust the prison doors wide open and to establish a strategic beachhead for the Gospel in Macedonia. Each page and paragraph of Philippians resounds with joy as Paul celebrates the work of Christ in the lives of the Philippians and shares insights to help us experience such spiritual victories and triumphs for ourselves.

Colossians • The Triumphant Christ. Colossians reminds us that the Church, the Christian, and the Gospel all win in the end because of our triumphant Christ. This book displays the deity and supremacy of Christ with stunning clarity. Confronting the extremes of legalism and Gnosticism, Colossians puts the Lord on center display as supreme over all (Chapters 1-2). As we become aware of Christ's triumph over vain philosophies, He will become triumphant also in our lives (Chapters 3-4) until He fulfills the promise that we will reign victoriously with Him forever!

Conclusion • Our Triumphant Choice. I recall the day when my father bought an expensive pearl necklace and placed it proudly around my mother's neck. But neither that necklace nor the crown jewels in the Tower of London compare in worth to the spiritual truths contained in these four books, displayed in the showcase of God's Holy Word. As you read them, enjoy their riches. Plan to return to them after you complete your reading of the Bible, to meditate and draw insights for your life again and again. The choice to read, reflect and respond to these books can make the difference between a mediocre life with God and one of supreme triumph!

Respond

1. What part of this week's reading most impacted, challenged, or encouraged you most? Why?

....

....

....

....

2. Recalling that three of these books were written while Paul was in prison, can you think of times in your life when you were forced to slow down and found special grace and spiritual growth as a result? Explain.

....

....

✱ 3. Do you tend to think of the Gospel, the Church, the Christian, and Christ all as triumphant? If not, should they be? How can we help it to be so? (Or does it not depend on us?)

Pray

Lord, open my eyes to see that I am already a victor when I follow and obey You. Help me to see beyond the veil of this world and to perceive the eternal Kingdom You are building. And lead me to do my part faithfully. Amen.

Impact

Bible in 90 Days Plus is designed to help people become triumphant in their spiritual lives. If it has been a help to you, then email us at: info@scriptureawakening.com or write to: Scripture Awakening, 512 N. Grove St, Suite 202, Hendersonville, NC 28792, telling us how. And when you write, please also include your permission that we can share your testimony to encourage others.

Close

You may have heard the common expression, "Your life may be the only Bible some people will ever read." Never forget the importance of remaining faithful to the Lord as was Paul when he wrote his letters from prison.

Day 84 · **What Matters in the End**

1 & 2 Thessalonians were, like Galatians, among the first letters Paul wrote. 2 Timothy and Titus were the very last of his writings. The early letters—1 & 2 Thessalonians—give special attention to the unfolding of end-time events. One would think that the last letters Paul ever wrote, closer to the end of time, would provide even more focus on concerns related to the Lord's Second Coming than the early letters. What we find is just the opposite. The progression of Paul's thought is both helpful and informative for our lives today.

Read

You have two reading options: read the full selection of Scripture or a single overview chapter each day.

- Full Reading: 1 Thessalonians 1 – Titus 3
- Overview Chapter: 2 Timothy 4

Reflect

Paul's letters to Titus and Timothy were his last-recorded writings in the Bible. 2 Timothy, the latest of all, was like Paul's last will and testament to Timothy. We might expect such writings to give special focus on the end of time; but they focus instead on right now, today. Consider the implications for our lives.

Why the First Letters Focus on the Future. The Thessalonians were young in their faith and confused about basic doctrines. They wanted to be reassured that their loved ones who had died already would be resurrected on the last day (1 Thessalonians 4:13-18). Paul helped them to see the whole scenario of the latter days, explaining that the world will grow dark at the end and that a world ruler—the Antichrist—will arise; he will persecute God's people and deceive the world (2 Thessalonians 2:1-12). Paul also reminded them that the Lord may return to bring us home at any time, so we should always stand in readiness (1 Thessalonians 5:1-11; 2 Thessalonians 2:13-17). He chastened the Thessalonians for quitting their jobs and waiting around for the Lord's Second Coming, urging them to work hard until the end (2 Thessalonians 3:6-15). In other words, a right understanding of the future should lead us to live faithfully for the Lord today. The Thessalonians needed such an understanding.

Why the Final Letters Focus on the Present. As we grow in our understanding of God and His Word, it becomes clear to us that nothing matters more than faithfulness to the Lord today. It should be no surprise to us then to see that faithfulness is the primary focus of Paul's letters to Timothy and Titus. Because these two men were pastors, Paul's letters to them are often called "pastoral epistles." These final letters focus on topics that pastors and mature believers can grasp and teach to the flock of God, such

B90+

Coaching Tip

Some of Paul's writings can be easily misunderstood. When, for example, Paul tells women to wear a veil in church, he was writing within a culture that might easily assume an unveiled woman to be a prostitute. In context, Paul was compassionate and fair toward women; he engaged them in ministry and honored them as coheirs of eternal life. Nevertheless, he did not provide absolute clarity about how Christians should deal with questions about women in church leadership; debates on this topic have continued from his day until now. Paul was clear in his thinking and writing, however, about the top priority Biblical concerns that all Christians must live godly lives and that we are here to help unbelievers to know God. Such should be our number one concerns as well, as we prepare for the day of our Lord's return.

as: correction of false teachings (1 Timothy 1:2-11; 4:1-16; 2 Timothy 2:14-4:8; Titus 3:9-11), criteria for leadership (1 Timothy 3:1-13; 5:17-25; Titus 1:5-16), care for widows (1 Timothy 5:1-16), the stewardship of resources (1 Timothy 6:6-19), and godly living (Titus 2:1-3:8).

The churches under Paul's care must have understood the basic doctrines about the end of time, such as those written early on to the believers in Thessalonica. As a result, they knew that faithfulness today makes for a better tomorrow; their first concern was obedience, growth, and fruitfulness. How about you and me? Do we have a clear sense of what will matter most in the end?

Respond

1. Do you consider yourself well-versed on the end times prophecies? Why or why not?

✱ 2. On a scale of 1-10, how well do you follow core Biblical commands, such as loving God and your neighbor and living faithfully today? Explain.

3. Why should an understanding about the Lord's imminent return motivate us to give God our best today?

Pray

Lord, thank you that You are in control. No matter how crazy or evil things may seem in the world, You are working for good. And in the right time, You will return to create a new Heaven and a new earth. Help me to live in holiness and godliness, focusing on ministry and the things that matter most until that final day. Amen.

Impact

The more we read and understand the Word, the better hope we have of living it. The world in general is devoid of such knowledge. Scripture Awakening leverages giving and impact in the Word through its social media outreach. Consider ways you might use social media to impact more lives with the power of God's Word.

Close

We all must face and deal with difficulties and troubles in life. It's a normal part of our earthly existence. Yet the Bible provides perspective on trials . . . that they are part of a refining process in our lives, faith, and character. Tomorrow's lesson: "Refined by Reality."

Session 13 • Overview

● REVIEW Days 78-84

History & Pauline Epistles: Expansion, Instruction, Correction

 Now is the time for your small group meeting to review the week's Scripture readings, cover the discussion questions, and watch the Essential Snapshot video together (or by yourself if reading alone). Point your mobile device's camera on the QR code to access the video entitled "Session 13: Knowing God". Or enter this link into your browser: **ScriptureAwakening.com/plus/**

- Discuss the questions marked by an asterisk (✱) from the **Respond** sections in Days 78-84, perhaps adding others if time permits.
- Watch the Session 13 video* (individually or with a small group).
  1. What insights from the video would you like to explore further?
  2. Do you think the study of God (theology) is an important aspect of the Christian life? Why or why not?
- Summarize the Preview (below) of what is coming next week, encouraging group members to read it on their own.

*Facilitators note: In order to watch the Essential Snapshot video with your group, you will need a large video monitor, if meeting in-person. If hosting a small group remotely, use Zoom (or similar service) to stream the video from your device to share with group participants.

● PREVIEW Days 85-90

General Epistles & Prophecy: Persecution, False Teachers, and the Apocalypse

Weekly Reading: Philemon 1:1 to Revelation 22:21

Summary

This week's readings bring us to the close of the New Testament and the entire Bible. They begin with Paul's final epistle, followed by the eight General Epistles, and conclude with the single prophetic book of the New Testament: Revelation.

The General, or Non-Pauline, Epistles were written by five different authors. Each offers a unique perspective on practical Christian living. Unlike their Pauline counterparts, the General Epistles are titled by their authors rather than their addressees (with the exception of Hebrews). They share a number of common themes: coping with persecution, dealing with false teachers, engaging in hospitality, and the dynamic between works and faith.

The Bible appropriately culminates with a final prophetic vision unveiled in the book of Revelation. This book anticipates a coming period of tribulation, followed by Christ's return and His millennial reign on earth, leading ultimately to a new Heaven and new earth.

Books You'll Encounter This Week

Philemon Overview

In this brief and masterfully crafted letter to his friend, Paul asks Philemon to free Onesimus, a slave, and charge anything Onesimus owes to Paul's account.

Hebrews Overview

In this letter of unknown authorship to the Hebrews, Jewish believers in the Messiah are exhorted to press on in their faith and not be tempted to fall back into old religious practices (particularly Judaism) in the face of increasing persecution.

James Overview

James, a half-brother of Jesus, encourages his readers to submit to God in humility. This book is a call to action with James asserting, "a person is justified by works and not by faith alone" (James 2:24).

1 Peter Overview

In his first letter, the Apostle Peter calls believers to live in holiness, to submit to one another, and to be faithful when persecuted.

2 Peter Overview

In his second letter, Peter reminds Christians that they must stand firm in their knowledge of the faith and resist the seductive heresies of false teachers who claim to be believers.

1 John Overview

Like Peter, the Apostle John writes as one who witnessed Christ's life firsthand. He encourages readers to walk in the light, love one another, and fear not because "perfect love casts out fear" (1 John 4:18).

2 John Overview

The Apostle tells his readers to love one another and to be wary of those who do not teach sound Biblical truth.

3 John Overview

John encourages his friend Gaius to walk in truth and protect himself from evil while offering hospitality to other true believers.

Jude Overview

A half-brother of Jesus, Jude calls on believers to build themselves up and persevere in the faith, particularly against false teachers whose character and conduct mark them for future judgment.

Revelation Overview

The Apostle John's apocalyptic vision is a fantastic end to an extraordinary journey through the Bible. John opens his letter by conveying messages of admonition and encouragement from Christ to seven churches in Asia Minor. Next, the Apostle brings the reader into the heavenly throne-room from which God's wrath is poured out on unrepentant humanity and His protection given to true believers. At the end of a worldwide tribulation, Christ returns to rescue His people and establish His millennial reign on earth. The vision culminates with the final judgment and the establishment of a new Heaven and earth.

Fine points of interpretation for the book of Revelation have long been debated; nevertheless, the message of hope it brings has encouraged God's people through the ages. We can strengthen our faith through the promises found in this grand finalé of Scripture by taking time to read and meditate on its truths.

Things to Look for This Week

As you read, consider:

1. How Christ's promise, "If they persecuted me, they will also persecute you" (John 15:20b), is a promise we can count on until the end of the ages.

2. How God will protect His people, even in difficult times. False teachers, however, will be judged by God for their deceptive ways.

3. That Christ is coming again as King of Kings and Lord of Lords, fulfilling prophecy and His promise that we will be eternally rewarded for obedience and faithfulness.

Day 85 · **Refined by Reality**

The books of Philemon, Hebrews, and James each highlight an essential aspect of God's refining work in our lives. Together, these books show us that God can use people and things that oppose us to refine us. Philemon shows us how *hostile world forces* are used to refine our *lives*; Hebrews reminds us how *contrary beliefs* refine our *faith*; and James explains how *adverse circumstances* refine our *character*. In God's refining process—from *life* to *faith* to *character*—reality becomes our instructor. God will use whatever is needed to get the job done.

Read

You have two reading options: read the full selection of Scripture or a single overview chapter each day.

- Full Reading: Philemon – James 2
- Overview Chapter: Hebrews 12

Reflect

The greatest gift we will ever receive in life next to salvation is sanctification. Through salvation, we are given promise of an eternity with God; then through sanctification, we learn to live by that promise each day. Sanctification is the refining work of God that makes us more like Jesus. Notice the progression of life-change and refinement as described in Philemon, Hebrews, and James.

Philemon • Refined Life. This short book provides deep insight into the struggles Paul and the early believers faced in a society built on the backs of slaves. Onesimus, a run-away slave, came to Rome where he met Paul and was captivated by the Gospel. Paul knew that by running away Onesimus had broken the law. He also knew Onesimus' master, Philemon. A plan was made for Onesimus' return. Paul sent him with a personal letter, appealing to Philemon's faith in Christ. With grace, tact, and a touch of humor, Paul urged Philemon to receive Onesimus back, not only as a household servant but also as a brother. Paul exhorted Philemon to treat Onesimus with all fairness and kindness. If there was any indemnity to pay, Paul promised to cover it himself.

This endearing story shows how early Christians remained true to God even when governments and legal jurisdictions opposed them. Christianity, which has been the driving force behind the abolition of slavery worldwide, has long shown the world that love can prevail, even over injustice. When in any country the laws of the land require Christians to deny their faith, they must obey God first and accept the legal ramifications. In this way, God is honored, the saints are refined, and God's eternal Kingdom is advanced.

Coaching Tip

As we read about a runaway slave and about the intense persecutions faced by Christians in the early Church, we may tend to think our readings don't relate to us personally. As we read, however, let us remember that such trials and challenges have been the norm for believers through the ages and are commonplace around the world today. We too might encounter such difficulties; we are wise to learn from these texts so that we will be ready for whatever may come our way.

Hebrews • Refined Faith. We don't know for sure who wrote Hebrews: Paul, Barnabas, Apollos, or another of the many candidates. But we do know it has passed the test of time as one of the books included in the canon of Scripture. Linking the Old Testament to the New, it provides keen understanding about Christ as the fulfillment of the symbols and types upon which the Jewish faith was built. This understanding is essential not only to the Jews but to followers of Christ from every nation.

In Hebrews 12, we are encouraged to picture ourselves in an Olympic race with Jesus running before us as the pacesetter, "the founder and perfecter of our faith" (Hebrews 12:2a). With the faith of those mentioned in Hebrews 11 spurring us on, the writer urges us to remain faithful to God to the end, even as God is faithful to us. And one day we will cross the goal line as victors in Christ with our faith refined!

James • Refined Character. James grew up as a brother of the Lord and initially rejected Jesus' claim to be the Messiah; after the Lord's resurrection, however, James learned to follow Jesus with a resolve that did not quit. God refined his character, and James wrote to explain how God is doing the same with us. Character is that quality of the soul that has been tried and tested and made complete (James 1:2-12). Our Lord Jesus, the only man without sin, was tried and tested that He might lead us successfully through this process of character development (Hebrews 4:15). Focusing on our works (James 1-2), our words (James 3:1-12), our wisdom (James 3:13-4:17), and our wealth (James 5), James urges us to follow Christ even as we face the reality of our weaknesses—that we too might be refined.

Respond

1. What thought from your reading or from today's commentary would you like to explore more deeply? Why?

✱ 2. Philemon reminds us how God uses opposing forces in the world to refine our lives. Are you trusting God to work through opposition in your life? Why or why not?

3. Hebrews and James show us how this process of refinement works its way down to our faith and even to our character. Describe an area in which you are being challenged today. Write or say a short prayer of surrender, trusting God to help you become more like Jesus through it.

Pray

Lord, thank you for refining us from inside out. Help me to let go of every encumbrance and to run the race You have set before me with the endurance that You inspire by Your life and by Your presence. Amen.

Impact

We have only three days of readings left, after which we will celebrate a great accomplishment! In the final lessons, we will invite you to continue your journey of growth in the faith and offer some specific suggestions to assist you. If you have set a good pace over the past three months, the ongoing journey can be as natural as is a walk in the park, and at the same time, as challenging and life-changing as an Olympic marathon. You are following Jesus. Nothing could be more important.

Close

The phrase "True blue" was derived from the blue cloth made in Coventry, England in the late Middle Ages. The town's dyers had a reputation for producing material that didn't fade with washing, that is, it remained 'fast' or 'true.' Tomorrow: encouragement and exhortations from Peter and John for believers to remain true to God.

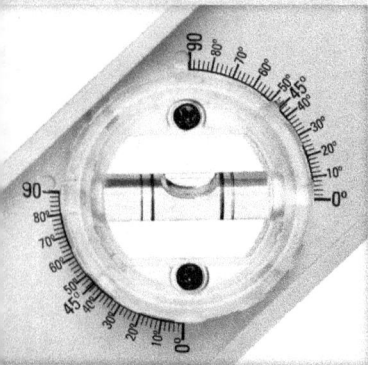

Coaching Tip

The Bible is a library with sections designed for each stage and situation in our lives. By reading the whole, we are more likely to know the parts of the library for quick access in times of need.

Day 86 · Stay True

In our reading today, we focus on the letters written by Peter and John. Each of their letters dealt with the unique challenges facing the Church as it expanded into Asia Minor (modern day Turkey). The difficulties encountered by these early Christians are remarkably similar to challenges we face today, and the advice they give can help us stay true to God.

Read

You have two reading options: read the full selection of Scripture or a single overview chapter each day.

- Full Reading: James 3 – 3 John
- Overview Chapter: 2 Peter 2

Reflect

1 & 2 Peter and 1-3 John were circular letters, along with James, Jude and possibly Hebrews; they were not written to specific churches but for circulation among the churches. Peter wrote from "Babylon," which may be a reference to Rome (1 Peter 5:13). John wrote from Ephesus. Peter faced pressures arising from without and John dealt with problems from within. Both urged believers to stay true to the faith. As we read their letters together, it seems they were written also for us, as they address problems Christians can expect to face at the end of time, and we are closer to the end than any prior generation.

Stay True When Confronted from Without. Peter wrote to encourage Christians under attack, "To those who are elect exiles of the Dispersion in Pontus, Galatia, Cappadocia, Asia, and Bithynia . . ." (1 Peter 1:1). After persecution came down hard on the saints in Jerusalem, followers of Jesus were scattered throughout Asia Minor, which covered in whole or in part the modern-day countries of Italy, Greece, Egypt, Turkey, Libya, Israel, Lebanon, Albania, Bulgaria, and Macedonia (Acts 2:9-11, 8:1-3). These early believers accepted persecution as their lot and embraced the call to live in holiness though the whole world be against them (1 Peter 1-5). Peter exhorted them to remain faithful to the end; for the Lord's coming is imminent (2 Peter 1-3).

Today, as Christians worldwide experience persecution and martyrdom in greater numbers than ever before, Peter's words could not be more relevant. He teaches that when we face opposition we should look up for our true home and eternal hope is in Heaven. We must remember that God's timetable is measured not by our watches but by His eternal plan. God is patiently waiting for every last possible person to believe that they might be saved from Hell and granted eternal life (2 Peter 3:9). We too must be patient, for the day is soon coming when the universe will be consumed by fire (2 Peter 3:10-12) and then made new (2 Peter 3:13). Our duty is to live in holiness, remaining steadfast in our faith, and growing in the knowledge and grace of God (2 Peter 3:14-18).

Stay True When Confused from Within. Pressures from outside the Church purifies it; confusion from within the Church divides and weakens it. Writing with the care of a spiritual father, John warns all believers about the false teachers who will arise from within the Church as the end draws near. He also provides an antidote. Weaving the themes of God's light, God's love, and God's truth into his letters, John reminds us to remain true to the Word and to keep the main thing the main thing.

Years before John wrote his letters, Paul warned the elders over the Church at Ephesus that false teachers would arise in their midst (Acts 20:25-31). John lived to see and confront such teachers as he shepherded the believers in Ephesus. From his day until now, the situation has only gotten worse; false teachers are everywhere. We do well to heed John's advice by holding fast to the core teachings in the Bible about God's light, love, and truth. If we have fallen short, God will forgive our failures and will help us remain true (1 John 1:1-10) for Christ is our advocate (1 John 2:1-2). As we follow Him, we are to keep His commands (1 John 2:3-9). His greatest command is for us to love Him and to love each other (1 John 2:10-17). We must therefore avoid false teaching (1 John 2:18-24) and live by the Spirit's anointing (1 John 2:25-29). In other words, we don't need advanced degrees to stay true; we must simply remain close to God and His Word.

Respond

1. Based on your reading of today's Scriptures or the commentary, what did you find most challenging or encouraging this week? Explain.

....

....

....

2. Do the swirling agendas of the world tend to distract you from core teachings about God's love, light, and truth? If so, what practical things can you do to keep your focus on the Lord and His Word?

....

....

✱ 3. Peter and John were, along with James the Apostle, part of our Lord's inner circle (Mark 5:37; Matthew 17:1; Luke 8:51). Like Jesus, they had no advanced degrees, wrote no books, and had no wealth to boast of. What does this say to you about things most important for those who wish to remain true to the Lord?

Pray

Lord, help me to stay true to You. Guide me to know You and Your Word better each day and to walk in obedience, with my head lifted high and my eyes set on Your promised Second Coming. Amen.

Impact

Do you know one or more persons who are struggling with their faith? Pray for them today and, as God leads you, seek to encourage them. Remember Paul's admonition, "We who are strong have an obligation to bear with the failings of the weak, and not to please ourselves" (Romans 15:1).

Close

Do you realize that you're just a couple of days away from completing B90+? The last days of our journey will take us through John's Revelation, the only book in the Bible that promises blessings to those who read it. Challenge: choose the full readings instead of the overview chapters these next two days!

Day 87 · **Treasures Unveiled**

It has long been pointed out that Revelation is the only book in the Bible that promises blessings to those who read it. There have been so many varied approaches to preaching and teaching Revelation that the average person has little confidence she or he can confidently read and glean riches from the book on a personal level. In this opening lesson, we offer a few simple insights that can help you to understand this book more holistically in order to embrace its blessings for your life.

Read

You have two reading options: read the full selection of Scripture or a single overview chapter each day.

- Full Reading: Jude – Revelation 17
- Overview Chapter: Revelation 1

Reflect

Revelation, one of the most important books in the Bible, can easily be misunderstood and misrepresented, causing us to shy away from reading it altogether. Yet, by avoiding the book, we miss its blessings. Here are five interpretive insights that help us begin to unlock truths about Revelation to reap its riches in our spiritual lives:

1. **Riches for Everyone.** Revelation is packed with simple and profound truths that jump off the surface of its pages to any open-hearted reader. I recall as a young man reading through Revelation and making the note that "this book is filled with golden insights that any average reader can readily discover for themselves." Those truths include strong confirmation of the sovereignty of God over the affairs of humans, the ultimate victory of God over the forces of evil, and words of promise, challenge, hope, and comfort for your life today.

2. **Riches for Those Who Suffer.** Revelation is written in a specialized literary genre called *apocalyptic*. The word *apocalypsis*, translated "revelation," means an *unveiling*. The book of Revelation uses this literary style to unveil the person of Christ and the plan of His Father. Common in the days of the early Church, apocalyptic literature features visions, vivid imagery, and stark symbolism, all woven together to bring hope and insight for those who suffer.

3. **Extra Riches for Those Who Know the Bible Well.** The imagery in Revelation is best unlocked by understanding the rest of the Bible. From the very first chapter of Revelation, which contains a vision of the Lord, we discover images and symbols that can be understood by their use in other portions of Scripture. Every chapter of Revelation contains

Coaching Tip

Tomorrow's reading will be shorter than normal and will culminate our read through the Bible. The following day, we will encourage you to make a commitment to continue your daily journey of spiritual growth. Take a minute to praise God for bringing you this far and pray for God to begin speaking to you about what is next.

such embedded imagery; ours is to unpack and enjoy it by making key Biblical connections. Those who know Scripture as a whole will find it easier to connect the dots and experience firsthand the truth behind the axiom: "A picture is worth a thousand words."

4. **Riches for Every Generation.** Revelation, like most Biblical prophecy, is relevant for each generation. Some have suggested its teachings and predictions were written for and fulfilled in the first century AD. Others have demonstrated how Revelation describes the ongoing conflict between good and evil through history. Still others say Revelation is primarily about the future, about what is yet to occur. Might all three viewpoints be true? Indeed, those who take time to study the book and the history of its interpretation may realize that this prophetic scroll has been relevant for each generation, bringing encouragement to followers of Christ from the past, for the present, and for each generation to come.

5. **Riches for the Reader.** Revelation is the only book in the Bible that promises blessing to those who read it and heed it (Revelation 1:3). Ultimately, the entire book blesses those who read it by encouraging them with the knowledge that God will be victorious over the unseen battle that rages in the heavens and its open expressions on earth. He is in control. No matter how evil forces of darkness may come against us, the Lord's plans are being accomplished and we will reign with Him forever! So keep Revelation on your reading list to continue receiving God's rich blessings!

Respond

1. In a sentence, complete this thought: "I especially like (or dislike) the book of Revelation because . . ."

....

....

....

....

2. In what ways do you believe you are being blessed by reading Revelation?

....

....

....

✱ 3. Do you sometimes have a hard time believing God is in control of world affairs, even using evil for His ultimate glory? How can Revelation help you trust God more?

Pray

Lord, reveal Yourself to me through the book of Revelation and every other means; I want to know You. As I learn to follow in Your steps, empower me to be Your witness that others might know You as well. Amen.

Impact

As you come near the end of this read through the Bible, pray for the Lord to show you ways that you might use what you have learned and continue learning. Ask God to help you press deeper into His process of spiritual growth, potentially bringing others on the journey with you.

Close

Last lap? Perhaps. Or a stepping stone toward something new? That choice is yours. As we turn the corner to finish Bible in 90 Days Plus, we hope there's been a Scripture awakening in you. And if so, all we can say is: "There's more to come. . . because His WORD is boundless!"

Coaching Tip

Any worthwhile and successful accomplishment requires both commitment (a conscious decision) and execution (proper follow-through). Think back about what allowed you to successfully complete reading through the Bible in 90 days. How will you apply what you have learned to continue your journey of spiritual growth?

Day 88 · The Best Ending

As your read through the entire Bible comes to an end, you have great reason to celebrate—not only because you have completed the journey but because of what will occur when Christ returns to make all things new. The last few chapters of Revelation give promise of the best possible ending for the world and for our lives. But we have choices to make if we wish to make this ending our own.

Read

You have two reading options: read the full selection of Scripture or a single overview chapter each day.

- Full Reading: Revelation 18–22
- Overview Chapter: Revelation 22

Reflect

The final pages of Scripture tell of a future time when God will make "all things new" (Revelation 21:5). The word "new" refers not to a remake of what has been, but to a complete start-over—newness of a type and quality we have never known. This newness, however, will be forged with a familiarity of the old to bring us great joy and comfort. Let us consider, then, the things that will remain the same and those that will be radically changed:

What Will Remain the Same

The Same God. God never changes, but our perceptions of Him do (Hebrews 13:8). Even during our best moments, we are able to capture only veiled glimpses of the glory and greatness and grace of our God. He is more powerful and loving than any mortal can fully comprehend (Ephesians 3:20-21). When all things are made new, however, there will be no more darkness, distractions, or doubt to veil Him. As we see His face, He will "wipe every tear" from our eyes (Revelation 21:4), and we will be made whole and complete as He renews us in His love.

The Same Believers. A question people commonly ask about the next life is, "Will I be able to recognize the people I now know and love?" Scripture and common sense suggest to us that it must be so. The disciples somehow recognized Moses and Elijah when both men appeared in spiritual bodies on the Mount of Transfiguration; how much more easily, then, will we be able to recognize and know others when we are given our new, improved, glorified bodies (Matthew 17:3-4)? If on earth we experience special intimacy with other believers, how much more must it be so in Heaven!? In our glorified state we will be unified, satisfied, and glorified in our relationships in ways we cannot now begin to appreciate or comprehend (1 Thessalonians 2:19-20; Genesis 35:29, 49:29; Revelation 7:9-10).

What Will Be Radically Changed

Our New Bodies. Our new bodies will be much like the resurrected body of Christ. The disciples were able to recognize the Lord in His new immortal body, but He was not restricted by temporal things. He was able to appear and disappear like an angel. He could eat food; yet He wasn't dependent on food (Luke 22:17-18; 24:42-43). The things that limit us in our mortal flesh will not limit us in our immortal bodies.

God promises that in Heaven, "death shall be no more, neither shall there be mourning, nor crying, nor pain anymore, for the former things have passed away." (Revelation 21:4b).

Our New Home. When God makes all things new, we will find ourselves living in the home we have always longed for. There will be no more worry about break-ins, no more dangers, no rent to pay; our new homes will be perfect for God will be sharing His home with us (Revelation 21:3). We will experience joy and happiness forever in a measure that we can only dream of in our present condition.

A New Ending. With all of this in mind, some people say the only thing that could make the end of all things better than that described in Revelation would be if everyone we know personally would be there—not merely those who believe. God understands this concern and carries it on His heart as well. In His love, God will not force anyone into His presence. He has entrusted us with the responsibility to do something about it.

Understandably, none of us wants to be separated from people we love. If, however, God were to welcome into His new Heaven and earth those who do not believe, those who refused His gift of eternal life, and those who hate Him and His children, would not the darkness of the world cloud the bright perfections God has promised? Furthermore, it is impossible for people who strive to please God in their own righteousness and good works to enter God's unshielded presence (Exodus 33:20; Romans 3:23; 6:23). This is why Christ died—to grant all who believe access into the eternal celebration. Those who refuse to believe have no basis for such access (John 3:36, Hebrews 10:26). Let us remember, then, that our purpose for being on earth today, and each day, is to tell others the Good News!

Respond

1. What is most encouraging to you about the things in the next life that will remain the same?

2. What is most exciting to you about the things in the next life that will be new? Why?

✸ 3. Now that you've completed a read through the entire Bible, does the warning in Revelation 22:18-19 about adding to or taking away from God's Word carry a special meaning for you? Why or why not?

Pray

Lord, thank you for giving us enough information about what awaits us in the next life to provide us hope and strength for this life. It grieves us, however, to think that many people do not believe in You and may miss the eternal celebration. Help us to recognize our opportunities and responsibilities to be Your witnesses on earth, helping others to know and to trust in You. Amen.

Impact

The wondrous ending of all things will also be the best possible beginning for a new life for those who believe. This future hope should stir within us a fresh resolve to know God better. We hope to see you tomorrow for thoughts about how you can continue the journey of spiritual growth through Scripture.

Close

Do you realize that when you finish today's reading you will have completed Bible in 90 Days Plus? Stay with us for the next two days as we consider what's ahead on your journey of faith.

Day 89 · **Continue the Journey**

Congratulations! You've made it all of the way through Bible in 90 Days Plus. We are grateful that you have completed this journey with us. Together, we can impact more and more lives through the power of God's Word! Rather than thinking of completing your readings as a "check the block" or "bucket list" accomplishment, we encourage you to view this as a major milestone on a continuing journey of faith. We'll talk about that more in a moment.

Read

If you have not already done so, complete all previous readings. If by chance you have a significant amount left to read, create a schedule to complete the task.

Reflect

You've probably heard the expression, "Life is a journey." This is certainly true for the Christian. Our journey is led by Christ, and as we follow Him, we are changed into His likeness. The question is, how are we doing?

There was a time before satellite technology made possible the Global Positioning System (GPS) when planning a long road trip often meant unfolding a paper map or getting a AAA "trip-tik." Today, the Internet makes traveling feel seamless, from start to finish. And while we enjoy the ease of digital maps to direct our every turn, we can often miss things along the way.

As a child, I remember riding in the back of our station wagon when our family took trips around the country. We would pull out our AAA booklets and read with great anticipation about the landmarks we were passing . . . and those we would see next. It was an exciting journey . . . not just going from point A to point B. Likewise, that is how it's meant to be in our journey of spiritual growth. Unfortunately, we seem to be missing something.

In our Internet age, we have a wealth of resources to enhance Bible study. It's easy to search and download a host of online Bibles and study apps.

But what good are they if we don't use them?

Surveys reveal that most Christians don't grasp the basic principles, premises, and promises in Scripture—and are growing weaker not stronger. As a result, Christian influence in the West has declined rapidly, and cultures have become increasingly secularized.

After three decades of serving as a pastor, I've come to believe that the primary reason our spiritual growth is stunted is that we have replaced true knowledge of God with mere head knowledge about God. As a result, we expect to mature overnight rather than through time and testing. It

Coaching Tip

As you come to the end of this three-month journey, you may logically ask, "What's next?" Aware that those who read through the Bible are hungry for next steps in their spiritual growth, we offer "BNEXT" — a whole library of excellent study resources that we will describe in tomorrow's lesson. Don't miss Day 90, the ending to this series and an invitation to begin the next stage of your journey of spiritual growth.

takes time, wisdom, and consistent obedience to develop healthy spiritual growth. Many believers resemble sprouting weeds, rather than being solid oak trees.

Scripture Awakening is here to encourage, guide, and support sustained, substantial spiritual growth in your life. How? Through a long-term and balanced practice of reading, studying, and living out God's Word. Our *Bible in 90 Days Plus* reading program is only the start. Tomorrow we will look at some of the resources available to assist you in your ongoing journey of faith.

Respond

1. What is the most significant thing that you have learned about God through reading His Word these last 90 days?

....

....

....

....

2. What is the most significant thing you have learned about yourself and your relationship with Him?

....

....

....

....

✱ 3. Why is it often so difficult to find time to spend alone with God each day? What can you do to ensure that quality time with Him remains a priority in your life?

....

....

....

....

Pray

Lord, thank you for what You have revealed to me about Yourself through Your Word during these last 90 days. Help me be committed to spending quality time with You in Your Word each day. And help me to allow Your Holy Spirit to continue molding me to the image of Your Son. Amen.

Impact

A recent study showed that, on average, it takes over two months before a new behavior becomes a normal part of one's daily routine. Commit or recommit to making it a vital part of your daily activities. Pick a duration (20 to 30 minutes) and a time of day (early morning, mid-day, after dinner) when you will give God your focused attention. You'll be surprised at how easy it will be now that you have three months of practice.

Close

Congratulations! We rejoice with you for completing Bible in 90 Days Plus! And to help you to celebrate that achievement, we created a "Certificate of Completion" for you to download, print, sign, and frame, if you like. Go to: ScriptureAwakening.com/b90pcert.

Session 14 • Review

● REVIEW Days 85-89

General Epistles & Prophecy: Persecution, False Teachers, and the Apocalypse

 Now is the time for your small group meeting to review the week's Scripture readings, cover the discussion questions, and watch the Essential Snapshot video together (or by yourself if reading alone). Point your mobile device's camera on the QR code to access the video entitled "Session 14: One Last Thing". Or enter this link into your browser: **ScriptureAwakening.com/plus/**

- Discuss the questions marked by an asterisk (✱) from the **Respond** sections in Days 85-89, perhaps adding others if time permits.
- Watch the Session 14 video* (individually or with a small group).
    1. Do you agree with the notion that it's not so much one truth that motivates us to believe in God and His Word but the combination of all 12 truths we studied in this series? Why or why not?
    2. The video talked about "one last thing"—the challenge to make a personal relationship with God our number one priority. How did you, or do you, embrace this challenge?

*Facilitators note: In order to watch the Essential Snapshot video with your group, you will need a large video monitor, if meeting in-person. If hosting a small group remotely, use Zoom (or similar service) to stream the video from your device to share with group participants.

Day 90 · **What's Next?**

Renewal Journey

 For your next step, we encourage you to experience *Renewal Journey*. This study follows the same basic format of Bible in 90 Days Plus. *Renewal Journey* is a devotional tour of some of the greatest revivals in Scripture and in history. You will encounter personal understanding and application of God's Word in new ways. *Renewal Journey* is a 40-day walk through nine topics of spiritual focus: Nurture, Scripture, Repentance, Hope, Prayer, Guidance, Surrender, Empowerment, and Faithfulness. Each topic will be explored consecutively from an Old Testament example of revival, to accounts of revival in church history, and then from insights given to us in the New Testament. To learn more go to: ScriptureAwakening.com/RJ/ or point your phone's camera at the QR code.

BNEXT

BNEXT Bible studies cover a wide array of Biblical books and topics. They're available for your mobile device or can be downloaded and printed for a very reasonable price. BNEXT is designed to be used personally or in small groups or even for an entire congregation or ministry. They are a perfect supplement to your devotional life, providing consistency and direction to support your spiritual growth. BNEXT studies feature well-crafted tools to facilitate excellent small group discussions, whether in homes, businesses, Christian education programs, or in church-wide discipleship efforts. These time-tested studies are ideal for integrating the pastor's Sunday morning sermon with each church member's personal devotions and small group interaction. You can learn more about BNEXT and see a complete catalogue of studies at ScriptureAwakening.com/BNEXT.

The Amazing Journey

The BNEXT course selection is continually expanding. We have most recently completed a comprehensive study of Scripture called, *The Amazing Journey*. This series covers the entire Bible in just over a year, highlighting major themes with guidelines for personal application. These studies include weekly videos and parallels the format of Bible in 90 Days Plus. *The Amazing Journey* is divided into various sections of the Old and New Testament, and each section can be used as a stand-alone study, if desired. Whether you enjoy it as a whole series or in its parts, *The Amazing Journey* can enhance your faith and accelerate your spiritual growth.

Bible in 90 Days—Again

When you decide to read through the Bible in 90 Days again, plan ahead for maximum blessing and impact in your life and others. If you took the single Overview Chapter track over the past three months but did not read every chapter, consider taking the "B90 Challenge" next time by reading every word of Scripture. Consider also inviting others to experience the power of God's Word with you. If you are a pastor, take the "Whole Church Challenge" and encourage all of your members to join you as you read and preach through the Word.

Additional Resources

Scripture Awakening also offers radio programming and hundreds of free, informative, and inspirational podcasts. To learn more and listen, go to BeyondWordsRadio.org. Also, consider subscribing to Scripture Awakening emails (ScriptureAwakening.com/subscribe/) for news updates, resources, encouragement, and insights that will strengthen your faith and walk in Christ.

Finally, please take just a few short minutes to fill out the B90+ Survey to help us to better assist you and others in the journey of spiritual growth. https://www.surveymonkey.com/r/b90plus1

Thank you! Let's keep in touch.

W.P. Campbell
Founder & President · Scripture Awakening

Appendix 1
Facilitator's Guide

Almost anyone can facilitate a Bible in 90 Days Plus small group. Special training or vast knowledge of Scripture isn't required; a heart to serve and a basic understanding of group dynamics will suffice. Sometimes great teachers can engage themselves too much and actually diminish group discussion and growth. Below are some pointers and suggestions to help you serve in the facilitator's role.

Note: A complete B90+ Guidebook for facilitating small groups is available at ScriptureAwakening.com/b90guidebook. This free electronic publication can significantly enhance your approach as small group facilitator.

General Guidelines

- You may use any Bible version. Groups run smoother, however, if everyone is using the same version. Verses quoted in this B90+ series are taken from the ESV Bible.

- Encourage small group members to consider purchasing the NIV Bible in 90 Days Bible, which is specially formatted for 12 pages a day reading with no commentary or notes to distract you. Years of testing has shown those who use this Bible have a higher completion success rate.

- Some people prefer to listen to the daily Scripture readings online. Studies demonstrate a higher rate of retention comes through reading from a physical page, or from reading as you listen.

- You and your group members can sign up for the email version of B90+ at ScriptureAwakening.com/b90plus, providing the option of reading lessons on a phone or mobile device. If you choose this option, then also record your answers to the daily questions in your Bible in 90 Days Plus book in preparation for the weekly small group meeting.

- Encourage group members not to get behind in their readings; but, if they do, they should set aside time to catch up. The aim is to read every word thoughtfully.

- If a person falls more than a few days behind, they may consider switching to the one-chapter overview each week. They could choose to return to do a full cover-to-cover reading of the Bible in the future.

Small Group Meetings

- Small group meetings will enhance your reading as you share with others what you've learned, helping to cement God's Word in your heart.

- Keep your groups small, maybe 12 or fewer.

- If you have more than one group (such as in a church setting), make sure you have a facilitator for each group and a back-up facilitator.
- Meet once a week for 14 weeks for 60-90 minutes, depending on how you want to structure your meetings. You can meet only to discuss the reading and questions; or, you may follow up weekly discussions with the videos. If you need to keep the group time shorter, then ask participants to watch the video on their own.

Role as Facilitator

- Pray for those in your group.
- Lead discussion (*don't teach*); keep everyone on track. Notice there are recommended questions for discussion marked with this **asterisk (✶) symbol** each week (a complete list of asterisk questions can be found in Appendix 2 on page 320). You may also wish to incorporate some of the other questions.
- Remind the group that Scripture interprets itself and that if some questions seem too difficult to answer, that's okay.

Small Group Participant Rules of Engagement

- It is of utmost importance to treat one another in Christian love.
- Begin each reading/review session with prayer.
- Come prepared: complete the reading and study questions.
- Respect the facilitator's leadership and one another.
- Do not expect the facilitator to be a Bible expert. They are there to guide the discussion and keep everyone on track.
- Everyone is welcome to join the discussion, but it is not mandatory.
- Because time is limited, don't dominate any discussion so that everyone has a chance to participate.
- Respect everyone's answers and views on Scripture. This is not about right or wrong answers.
- Allow the Holy Spirit to speak/teach through God's written Word.

Session Structure Ideas

- The first session (weekly meeting) is unique as there is no reading for this session. During this session, have an opening prayer and introductions (10 minutes). Then describe the B90+ book structure (5 minutes). Go over the rules of engagement (5 minutes). Finally, guide group discussion around some of the following questions (20 minutes):

    a. Have you ever tried to read the entire Bible before? Why or why not?

    b. In trying to read the entire Bible, what challenges did you face?

-
  - c. Why did you decide to commit to Bible in 90 Days?
  - d. What are your expectations in reading the Bible cover-to-cover, especially in 90 days?
- If you are using the videos as part of your weekly gatherings, watch the first video together (20 minutes) and as time allows, discuss the following questions (15 minutes):
  - a. What insights or truths did you glean from this video?
  - b. The video identifies 12 areas that individuals often struggle with in terms of trusting the Bible: Cosmology, Typology, Morality, Glory, Chronology, Philosophy, Psychology, Prophecy, Probability, Archaeology, Biography, and Theology. Based on your initial thoughts or impressions, which of these areas might especially interest you? Why?
- Look at the Scripture passages you will cover the next week, and as time allows, guide the group through the Preview section.
- Close in prayer.

Subsequent Session Structure Ideas

- Open in prayer, welcome and introduce new members. Ask the group how their experience of reading 12 pages a day went over the past week. Seek to encourage them to keep up, and if they fell behind to take time to catch up (10 minutes).
- If it seems needed, have group members encourage each other with any insights they received during the week about ways they keep up with the readings.
- If your group has 15 or more participants, then break into smaller groups, assigning a facilitator to each group. Designate a time they should break from their group discussion (depending on your situation, between 25 and 40 minutes) to assemble again for the video if you are using the video in your weekly gathering.
- Following the video, close out with the final questions related to the video and then look at the next week's Preview, as time allows.

Appendix 2
Small Group Discussion Questions

For ease of use, the suggested questions for discussion from each week's session, one per day, are highlighted by an asterisk in the daily commentaries and are listed in a combined document below. For the average small group discussion time, the seven discussion questions provided for each weekly gathering should suffice. Based on the time you have allotted for your small group discussion, however, you may find there are more questions here than needed. Or you may find it helpful to add a few additional questions from the daily readings.

Session 1

This is the only Session that does not have recommended questions for discussion (as marked by an asterisk) in the Respond section of the B90+ commentary.

1. Have you ever tried to read the entire Bible before? Why or why not?
2. In trying to read the entire Bible, what challenges did you face?
3. Why did you decide to commit to Bible in 90 Days?
4. What are your expectations in reading the Bible cover-to-cover, especially in 90 days?

Session 2 [Key: D1=Day 1 · Q3=Question 3]

D1 Q3 There are numerous stories and symbols in Genesis showing the sinful nature of humanity and God's gracious plan of redemption. Describe one that especially impacts you and explain why.

D2 Q1 What insights can you draw from 1 Timothy 2:1-6 about our responsibility to pray for those who influence our lives as leaders?

D3 Q3 Ponder the lives of Jacob and Joseph alongside the words in Romans 8:28. Can you see how God is also working all things for good in your life as well? Explain.

D4 Q3 How does the belief that God knows the future give you greater confidence to live for the Lord today?

D5 Q2 Does the Bible encourage us to expect immediate solutions and quick fixes when we are dealing with difficulties? Support your answer with Scripture if you can.

D6 Q3 What distortions may occur in our perspective of God if we read only the Old Testament? What if we read only the New Testament? Why are both parts of the Bible important?

D7 Q3 From your daily reading and the commentary, what were the benefits the people of God experienced when they put aside their idols and made God first in their lives?

Session 3

D8 Q2 Why do you think holiness is important?

D9 Q3   Do you sometimes find it difficult to believe that God will guide you in ALL of your ways and will give you wisdom whenever you ask? Why or why not? Read Proverbs 3:5-6 and James 1:7. Claim God's promises.

D10 Q2 Romans 12:3-8, reminds us that we each have specific spiritual gifts given to us by God. What do you perceive your spiritual gifts to be? Are you content with your gifts, or do you find yourself trying to be like someone else?

D11 Q2 How does Paul link these Old Testament stories with ours (see 1 Corinthians 10:1-11)? How does he tell us to deal with any rebellion or complaining thoughts that have filled our hearts (1 Corinthians 10:12-33)?

D12 Q3 The Israelites also ate food sacrificed to idols. A modern parallel would be the pursuit of enjoyments at the expense of God's declared will. Give examples of the ways we do this in our society today or ways in which you struggle with this personally. Pray for God's help and strength to remain faithful.

D13 Q3 What is one core truth from your reading in Deuteronomy that you hope never to forget?

D14 Q1 How should we respond to the grace and mercy of God shown to us through the sacrifice of Christ (Hebrews 10:19-23)?

Session 4

D15 Q2 According to Joshua 1:8-9, what is the key to being courageous, even in the face of change?

D16 Q2 What are the upsides of being courageous? When you are courageous for the Lord, are there any downsides?

D17 Q3 Have you experienced a time when you really knew you were weak, cried out to God, and saw God move in a powerful manner? If so, describe it.

D18 Q1 What is the primary message we should draw from Samson's life? Why?

D19 Q2 Have some of your heart's desires remained unfulfilled? Should you then give up (see Luke 18:1-8)? Explain.

D20 Q3 What do you think Samuel meant by, "... to obey is better than sacrifice" (1 Samuel 15:22)? How might you apply that to your life today?

D21 Q2 Read Hebrews 5:8. Why do you think that Christ, the sinless God-man, needed difficulties for His personal growth to maturity?

Session 5

D22 Q1 Do you think God was too harsh on David for his sin with Bathsheba and against Uriah? See 2 Samuel 12:10-12. Explain.

D23 Q2 Make a short list of several things that you most want to be remembered for. What will matter in the end—when you meet God face-to-face?

D24 Q1 How do you measure success?

D25 Q2 What steps could Solomon have taken to guard his heart and stay right with God?

D26 Q2 What sins did Gehazi commit in 2 Kings 5? What can we learn from his mistakes?

D27 Q2 As you read the story of Hezekiah, what encourages or challenges your faith?

D28 Q2 Do you think God judges nations today as He did Judah and Israel? Why or why not?

Session 6

D29 Q3 If someone told you, "Every genealogical list should be removed from the Bible," how would you answer them?

D30 Q1 Why is it important to understand the context of the books of the Bible?

D31 Q1 What is the most helpful learning point for you as you consider King Asa's life?

D32 Q2 Why is it essential that we humble ourselves before God?

D33 Q2 How should an awareness of God's plan for us to be with Him forever impact our focus on His presence today?

D34 Q1 What are your favorite parts of your reading from Ezra and Nehemiah? Why?

D35 Q3 The book of Esther supports the Biblical promise that no matter how bad things seem on the world scene, God is working out His eternal purpose. Do you believe this? Explain.

Session 7

D36 Q3 How might you rekindle the childlike curiosity that is fitting for children of the Most High God (Matthew 19:14)?

D37 Q3 Do you know anyone who has rejected God because of evil in the world? If so, do you think that person's perspectives are justified? Explain.

D38 Q3 Psalm 1 promises fruitfulness in season for those who remain connected with God through His Word. Record one or more reasons why that might be true.

D39 Q3 How does the reading and hearing of Scripture help our faith and the faith of others to grow (Romans 10:14-17)?

D40 Q3 What can we learn from Psalm 42 about receiving God's strength and help in times of doubt, depression, or even despair?

D41 Q1 Do you think the level of praise in our hearts is a reflection of what we believe about God? Explain.

D42 Q1 Psalm 100 gives us seven essential imperatives for a life of worship. Which of the seven do you connect with most readily? Why?

Session 8

D43 Q2 Some Christians claim to love God but do not believe or follow Scripture. Is it possible to love God without loving God's Word? Why or why not?

D44 Q3 If you really believed the words of Psalm 139, in what ways might your life be changed?

D45 Q1 If you could have more knowledge or more wisdom which would you choose? Why?

D46 Q3 Complete this thought, "I need God's wisdom because without it . . ."

D47 Q2 Read the conclusion of the book: Ecclesiastes 12:13-14. Do you agree with the Teacher's assessment? Explain.

D48 Q2 In what ways do you think our modern culture has lost the true meaning of love?

D49 Q3 As we see God more clearly and tell others about Him, should we expect the world to gladly receive our message all of the time (John 12:37-43)? Why or why not?

Session 9

D50 Q2 Do you find it hard to speak the truth in love to others? Explain.

D51 Q2 List all of the promises you see in Isaiah 40:28-31.

D52 Q2 Do you have any favorite verses or passages that contain prophetic elements? If so, which?

D53 Q1 Which verses or ideas from Isaiah 53 are most challenging or encouraging for you? Why?

D54 Q3 Do you think we need more people who will proclaim God's will amid great opposition, like Jeremiah, for our day? Why or why not? If you believe we do need such people, ask the Lord to raise them up in our day.

D55 Q1 Do you think that in some ways the Church of today faces challenges similar to those faced by believers in the Old Testament before the exile? Explain.

D56 Q2 Do you generally assume things are out of control around you, or do you believe God is in control even when you cannot understand why or how? Explain.

Session 10

D57 Q1   If you were put behind bars for your faith and were prohibited from having any books or any portions of Scripture, do you think you would come to appreciate God's Word in a new way? Explain.

D58 Q2   Can you envision a world government forming on the global scene in this generation? If so, do you think it will be sympathetic toward Christians and Jews? Explain.

D59 Q2   Read Psalm 46:1-3 and Hebrews 4:14-16. Do you believe that God is with you in your times of sorrow? Why or why not?

D60 Q1   As you read from the book of Ezekiel, does the prophet seem a bit off to you? Or might it be that the world around him was spiritually off, and his seemingly extreme measures were necessary to get their attention? Explain.

D61 Q2   The Proverbs tell us that, "Pride goes before destruction, and a haughty spirit before a fall" (Proverbs 16:18). How might this truth be applied to your life? Be specific.

D62 Q3   What do you think might cause God to manifest His presence yet more fully in your life or in the world? It may help to think of stories in the Bible, such as those in the book of Acts.

D63 Q3   Which story in the first half of Daniel encourages or challenges you most? Why?

Session 11

D64 Q3   Daniel had great impact on the world, even while stranded in exile. Record the qualities of his life that might explain how, against all odds, God used him so greatly. Then pray for the same for your lives.

D65 Q1   If you really believed that the Almighty God loves you with an everlasting love, how would it impact your life?

D66 Q2   To those who think that the Lord's return and final judgment will never come, Peter writes, "But do not overlook this one fact, beloved, that with the Lord one day is as a thousand years, and a thousand years as one day" (2 Peter 3:8). What do you think Peter meant? What do his words mean to you?

D67 Q2   It is not only Habakkuk, nor only each of the minor prophets, but every Biblical writer that brings to us a message of hope. Is your pathway bright with hope? If not, should it be?

D68 Q1   Do you tend to think of your service for the Lord as small and almost insignificant? What, according to Zechariah, does God think about such an attitude?

D69 Q3   In Matthew 4:18-22, Jesus calls the first disciples to follow Him. They immediately drop all that they are doing, leaving behind their livelihood and families. Why do you think they responded so quickly to Jesus' call?

D70 Q1   Which of the Matthew 13 parables speak to you most personally? Why?

Session 12

D71 Q1   The Matthew 25 parables were written to help us honestly evaluate our lives. Which of the three is most challenging or encouraging for you? Why?

D72 Q1   Do you wish there were fewer Gospel accounts of Christ's life, or are you grateful for all four? Why?

D73 Q3   "The greatest desire of God is for the healing of our relationships, first with Him and then with others." Do you agree with this statement? If not, why not? If so, what are the implications for your life? Be specific.

D74 Q2   In a few words or sentences, summarize the radical compassion of our Lord.

D75 Q3   When there is true division among Christians, what do you think is the cause? How can we strengthen our unity despite our differences?

D76 Q3   Ponder the hospitality that will be shown to you by Jesus when you are welcomed into your eternal home. How does that thought challenge you to be more hospitable to people today?

D77 Q3   Jesus gently chided Peter for his undue concern about the way John's life would end, adding, ". . . what is that to you?" (John 21:22). What is the problem with becoming overly concerned about how things will end rather than focusing on giving God our best today?

Session 13

D78 Q2   Are there any people you would find difficult to welcome into the Kingdom of God through the open doors of your heart, your home, or your church? If so, explain why.

D79 Q3   Complete this thought: "Since the Kingdom of God is the one unstoppable force that will impact all of eternity, I should . . ."

D80 Q1   Do you tend to think of righteousness as something you do for God or a gift God gives to you? Explain.

D81 Q1   Christ warned us to get our lives right before judging another person (Matthew 7:1-3). Do you perceive ways in which the culture around you has infected your life and dampened your desire and ability obey this command? Explain.

D82 Q2   One of the credentials of a true believer is spiritual fruit. What kinds of fruit should we look for in our lives as we examine ourselves?

D83 Q3 Do you tend to think of the Gospel, the Church, the Christian, and Christ all as triumphant? If not, should they be? How can we help it to be so? (Or does it not depend on us?)

D84 Q2 On a scale of 1-10, how well do you follow core Biblical commands, such as loving God and your neighbor and living faithfully today? Explain.

Session 14

D85 Q2 Philemon reminds us how God uses opposing forces in the world to refine our lives. Are you trusting God to work through opposition in your life? Why or why not?

D86 Q3 Peter and John were, along with James the Apostle, part of our Lord's inner circle (Mark 5:37; Matthew 17:1; Luke 8:51). Like Jesus, they had no advanced degrees, wrote no books, and had no wealth to boast of. What does this say to you about things most important for those who wish to remain true to the Lord?

D87 Q3 Do you sometimes have a hard time believing God is in control of world affairs, even using evil for His ultimate glory? How can Revelation help you trust God more?

D88 Q3 Now that you've completed a read through the entire Bible, does the warning in Revelation 22:18-19 about adding to or taking away from God's Word carry a special meaning for you? Why or why not?

D89 Q3 Why is it often so difficult to find time to spend alone with God each day? What can you do to ensure that quality time with Him remains a priority in your life?

Appendix 3
Patterns in 1 & 2 Kings

Instructions: As you read 1 Kings and 2 Kings, mark the diagram below with a check (✔) next to the names of the kings who "do right in the eyes of the LORD" and an (X) next to the names of the kings who don't.

Northern King (Israel)	Does or does not do right in the eyes of the LORD	Southern King (Judah)	Does or does not do right in the eyes of the LORD
Jeroboam I		Rehoboam	
Nadab		Abijah	
Baasha		Asa	
Elah		Jehoshaphat	
Zimri		Jehoram	
Tibni		Ahaziah	
Omri		Athaliah (Queen)	
Ahab		Joash	
Ahaziah		Amaziah	
Joram		Azariah (Uzziah)	
Jehu		Jotham	
Jehoahaz		Ahaz	
Joash/Jehoash		Hezekiah	
Jeroboam II		Manasseh	
Zechariah		Amon	
Shallum		Josiah	
Menahem		Jehoahaz	
Pekahiah		Jehoiakim	
Peka		Jehoiachin	
Hoshea		Zedekiah	

Appendix 4
Putting the Prophets in Their Place

Book	Era	Audience	Theme(s)
Isaiah (chs. 1–39)	Pre-Exile c. 700 BC?	Judah	Judgment against Judah and Israel; prophecies of promise and blessing; judgments against nations
Isaiah (chs. 40–55)	Exile c. 680 BC?	Judah	Deliverance and restoration of Israel; the servant's ministry; God's call to salvation
Isaiah (chs. 56–66)	Uncertain	Judah	Condemnation of wicked; worship; restoration; everlasting deliverance, everlasting judgment
Jeremiah	Pre-Exile 7th/6th century BC	Judah	Warnings and exhortations; his suffering; fall of Jerusalem; judgment against nations
Lamentations (Jeremiah)	Pre-Exile/Exile c. 580 BC	Judah	Laments over destruction of Jerusalem
Ezekiel	Exile 6th century BC	Jews in Babylon	God's sovereignty over creation, people, nations, and history; God's holiness; judgment against Judah and pagan nations; God's future work in history
Daniel	Exile c. 530 BC?	Jews in Babylon	Prayer; spiritual warfare; living by God's standards in a hostile environment; God's sovereignty
Hosea	Pre-Exile 8th century BC	Israel	Just as Hosea is betrayed by his beloved, God is betrayed by His beloved Israel; loving commitment can overcome betrayal
Joel	Pre-Exile Uncertain	Judah	God's people have a choice: keep doing wrong and be judged, or repent and receive God's forgiveness and salvation

Amos	Pre-Exile 8th century BC	Israel	Israel ignores what matters to God—justice, compassion, and worship from the heart—and God's impending judgment
Obadiah	Pre-Exile c. 587 BC	Edom	Edomites, who treated Israel unjustly, now face God's anger
Jonah	Pre-Exile 8th century BC	Assyria	God's forgiveness of us; our need to forgive others
Micah	Pre-Exile 8th century BC	Judah	God's judgment for idolatry and oppression; His mercy for the obedient; our need to show mercy; the coming Messiah
Nahum	Pre-Exile 7th century BC	Assyria	The judgment of Assyria and its capital, Nineveh
Habakkuk	Pre-Exile 7th century BC	Judah	Is God ignoring evil or will He settle the score?
Zephaniah	Pre-Exile 7th century BC	Judah	Judgment day is coming; closing promise
Haggai	Post-Exile 6th century BC	Jews in Jerusalem	God's blessings and what the Jews did to hinder them; Jews rebuild the Temple
Zechariah	Post-Exile 6th/5th (?) century BC	Jews in Jerusalem	God's encouragement to exiles who return from Babylon; prophecies about the coming Messiah; salvation
Malachi	Post-Exile 5th/4th (?) century BC	Jews in Jerusalem	God's readiness to replace the Old Covenant with the new; prophecies about the Messiah who will usher in the New Covenant

Appendix 5

The Intertestamental Period

Summary

The period between the Old and New Testament is variously called the "Intertestamental Period," the "Time Between the Testaments," or the "Silent Years." Most Protestants declare these years silent regarding revelations from God. Catholic and Orthodox Christians, however, generally accept a list of 14 apocryphal books describing this gap between the Testaments as God's inspired Word. Protestants acknowledge these 14 books, often called The Apocrypha, as beneficial for historic content but do not place them on par with the rest of Scripture. Regardless of one's view of The Apocrypha, an understanding of the period between Malachi and John the Baptist can provide insight about the historical and cultural setting of the New Testament and how God used the Intertestamental Period to prepare the way for the promised Messiah.

The Intertestamental Time Periods

The four centuries between the Testaments can be separated into four distinct time periods based on governmental influences over Jerusalem.

Persian Period (425 to 333 BC)

The Old Testament closes during the period of the Persian Empire. Unlike the Assyrians and the Babylonians who preceded them, the Persians were generally tolerant toward the Jews and allowed them to remain in their homeland. Over time, Persian kings even granted increased political power and religious authority to the Jewish High Priest.

Greek Period (333 to 164 BC)

Alexander the Great and his Macedonian army conquered Persia and marked out an empire from Greece to Northwestern India in a relatively few short years. After his untimely death, his generals divided the kingdom among themselves, fighting over some of the contested areas, including Judea. In an effort to retain control of the empire, they imposed Greek language and culture throughout the region (Hellenism). As a result, trade increased and standards of living improved, but the language, religion, and cultural practices of the Jews were threatened. Initially, two ruling dynasties competed for control over Judea: the Seleucids in Syria, Asia Minor, and Mesopotamia, and the Ptolemies in Egypt. These kingdoms fought for over 100 years until the Seleucids prevailed. As predicted in the latter chapters of Daniel, the Seleucid ruler, Antiochus IV Epiphanes, desecrated the Temple in 168 BC and forced the priests to offer sacrifices to Greek gods.

Hasmonaean Period (164 to 63 BC)

The priestly family of the Maccabees refused to participate in the demanded sacrifices and began an armed uprising against the Seleucids. They ultimately triumphed and gained a degree of political independence. Their successors established the Hasmonaean dynasty over Judea.

Roman Period (63 BC and beyond)

Pompey the Great conquered Jerusalem in 63 BC and about 20 years later, the Roman Senate appointed Herod the Great as King of the Jews. Herod was an Idumean—a descendant of Esau. To gain favor with the Jews, Herod rebuilt and expanded the Jewish Temple. He also constructed a palace at Caesarea Maritima and built fortifications at numerous sites, such as Masada and Herodium. Despite his bodyguard of 2,000 solders, Herod was haunted by an irrational paranoia about threats to his reign. He murdered anyone he suspected might oppose him, including many of his own family members and staff.

Religious and Political Sects

During this 400-year period a number of religious and political sects arose.

Jewish Sects

Pharisees: "The pious or separated" ones. They rejected all forms of Hellenization and steadfastly adhered to even the smallest provisions of the Jewish law.

Sadducees: An "elite" priestly aristocracy. They focused on Temple administration and ritual while enjoying positions of wealth and influence within the existing political order.

Essenes: Withdrawing from society, this sect sought to escape the corrupting influences of the Graeco-Roman world through a monastic lifestyle devoted to the study of Scripture and manual labor.

Political Sects

Herodians: Secular opportunists who supported Herod. They gained positions of influence and material wealth by cooperating with the Romans. Their fellow Jews hated them.

Zealots: Fanatics opposed to Roman rule. These Jewish nationalists were determined to resist Rome at all costs and actively sought opportunities for armed insurrection.

Other Groups

Sanhedrin: The Jewish ruling council. Lead by the High Priest, this 71-member group of priests, elders, and scribes was the final court of appeal for religious offenses.

Publicans: Tax collectors for the Romans. Seen as "tools of the oppressors" by the other Jews, the Publicans were resisted, ridiculed, and even excommunicated from Jewish society.

About the Author

Dr. William P. Campbell, son of the founders of Community Bible Study, knows from personal experience that people grow in spiritual depth and Biblical knowledge when they use carefully constructed Bible studies illuminated with well researched commentary background. Bill saw Community Bible Study develop from his parents' living room to an international ministry serving many thousands of people which is still going strong today. Having written commentaries for Community Bible Study, he began writing material for the churches he pastored so he could connect Sunday sermons to weekly devotional reading and small group Bible studies. He researched, tested and improved Scripture Awakening materials in congregations over a period of 20 years and through his Doctor of Ministry studies at Fuller Theological Seminary. He also holds a Master of Divinity degree from Princeton Seminary and a Bachelor of Biology from Westmont College. Bill has written a variety of articles, publications, and books. He serves as executive director and president of the board for Scripture Awakening.

Acknowledgments

I am grateful for the tireless efforts of those who kindly contributed and carefully edited this work: David Smith and Susie Shields; and for Scripture Awakening's Marketing Team who guided this book to publication: Frank Felsburg, Susie Shields, and Diana Kostigen; and to Mark Lucas for the book's layout, closing sections, and graphics. Above all, I give thanks to our God for giving us His Word, a manual to help us live as a renewed people.

Proceeds

All proceeds from sales of Scripture Awakening publications and donations to the ministry go to support:

- The creation of digital materials to assist those who cannot afford to pay for print versions.
- Translating Scripture Awakening resources into other languages.
- Supplying Bible study materials to select audiences including prison ministries, military personnel, and English-speaking Bible Colleges and Seminaries in Africa and other locations.
- Development of new study materials to engage more people with God's Word.
- Beyond Words Radio broadcasts worldwide to help people apply Scripture to their lives.
- The development, marketing, and administrative costs necessary to make these outreach efforts and expanding ministry programs possible.

To make a donation to Scripture Awakening please go to ScriptureAwakening.com/donate/ or mail to: Scripture Awakening, 512 N. Grove St, Ste 202, Hendersonville, NC 28792. Many thanks for your support of this ministry!

www.ingramcontent.com/pod-product-compliance
Lightning Source LLC
Chambersburg PA
CBHW081353070526
44583CB00020B/2538